The Women's Movement
in Latin America

Thematic Studies in Latin America

Gilbert W. Merkx

Series Editor

*The Women's Movement in Latin America: Participation
and Democracy*, Second Edition, edited by
Jane S. Jaquette

*The United States, Honduras, and the Crisis
in Central America*, Donald E. Schulz
and Deborah Sundloff Schulz

*Divine Violence: Spectacle, Psychosexuality,
and Radical Christianity in the Argentine "Dirty War,"*
Frank Graziano

*Land, Power, and Poverty: Agrarian Transformation
and Political Conflict in Central America,*
Charles D. Brockett

SECOND EDITION

THE WOMEN'S MOVEMENT IN LATIN AMERICA

Participation and Democracy

edited by
Jane S. Jaquette
Occidental College

Westview Press
Boulder • San Francisco • Oxford

Thematic Studies in Latin America

Copyright © 1994 by Westview Press, Inc.

Published in 1994 in the United States of America by Westview Press, Inc., 5500 Central Avenue, Boulder, Colorado 80301-2877, and in the United Kingdom by Westview Press, 36 Lonsdale Road, Summertown, Oxford OX2 7EW

Library of Congress Cataloging-in-Publication Data
The Women's movement in Latin America : participation and democracy /
[edited by] Jane S. Jaquette.—2nd ed.
    p.   cm.—(Thematic studies in Latin America)
  Includes bibliographical references and index.
  ISBN 0-8133-8486-9.—ISBN 0-8133-8488-5 (pbk.)
    1. Women in politics—South America—Case studies.   2. Feminism—
South America—Case studies.   3. Democracy.   4. South America—
Politics and government.   I. Jaquette, Jane S., 1942– .
II. Series.
HQ1236.5.S63W66   1994
305.42'098—dc20   94-17202
                                                                                                                CIP

Printed and bound in the United States of America

The paper used in this publication meets the requirements
of the American National Standard for Permanence of Paper
for Printed Library Materials Z39.48-1984.

10   9   8   7   6   5   4   3   2

Contents

Acknowledgments

I have enjoyed preparing this volume. Discussions of the women's movement in Latin America almost always provoked a strong response and brought out new ideas from the many women and men whom I interviewed. I would like to acknowledge personally many of the researchers I have come to know as a result of this study and without whose materials, ideas, and active encouragement this book would never have been written.

I want to thank the authors of the chapters included here, who suffered through my insistence that they write, rewrite, and then rewrite again. The American Political Science Association gave me a travel grant in 1986, and Occidental College gave travel support in 1986 and 1988. I would like to express my gratitude and appreciation to those who assisted my research on two field trips to South America: Cecilia Blondet, Virginia Vargas, Amelia Fort, Ana María Portugal, and Jeanine Anderson Velasco in Peru; Ximena Bunster, María Eugenia Bitar, María Elena Valenzuela, Natacha Molina, Adriana Muñoz, Soledad de Larraín, and Antoineta Saa in Chile; Elizabeth Jelín, Liliana De Riz, Patricia Pittman, Beatriz Schmukler, and Marta Roldán in Argentina; Fanny Tabak, Carmen Barroso, Eva Alterman Blay, Cheywa Spindel, Neuma Aguiar, and Ruth Correa Leite Cardoso in Brazil; and Nea Filgueira and Suzana Prates in Uruguay. Suzana's death in 1988 left a void in the women's movement that cannot be filled.

I owe a special debt to Elsa Chancy for her pioneering work on women in Latin American politics and for her continuing encouragement. I also thank Julio Cotler, Manuel Antonio Garreton, Guillermo O'Donnell, Marcello Cavarrozi, the late Charles Gillespie, and Juan Rial for helping me to understand the political context of the transition in their countries. I am grateful to Enrique Hermosillo and Celeste Elig, who located documents and provided research assistance; Santiago O'Donnell, who helped with the translation; and Linda Lowenthal, who assisted me with editing.

The second edition would not have been possible without the very able assistance of Bernarda Duarte, who was my Ford Anderson summer intern at Occidental in 1992. Jennifer Moulton helped me take care of all the last-minute details.

My family's patience, encouragement, and cooperation—so essential to all of my projects—are greatly appreciated.

Jane S. Jaquette
Santa Monica, California

Acronyms

AHC	Academia de Humanismo Cristiano (Academy of Christian Humanism)
AID	Agency for International Development
ALIMUPER	Acción para la Liberación de la Mujer Peruana (Action for the Liberation of Peruvian Women)
AMA	Asociación de Mujeres Argentinas (Association of Argentine Women)
AMAS	Asociación de Mujeres Alfonsina Storni (Alfonsina Storni Women's Association)
AMNLAE	Asociación de Mujeres Louisa Amanda Espinosa (Louisa Amanda Espinosa Women's Association)
AMPRONAC	Asociación de Mujeres Confrontando la Problematica Nacional (Nicaraguan Association of Women Confronting the National Problem)
ANDEN	Asociación de Educadores (Association of Educators)
APDH	Asamblea Permanente para los Derechos Humanos (Permanent Assembly for Human Rights)
APRA	Alianza Popular Revolucionaria Americana (The Popular Revolutionary Alliance of the Americas)
ARENA	Aliança de Renovaçao Nacional (National Renovating Alliance)
ATC	Asociación de Trabajadores del Campo (Agricultural Workers' Union)
ATEM	Asociación para el Trabajo y el Estudio de la Mujer (November 25 Association for the Work and Study of Women)
CDM	Comisión de Derechos Humanos-Mujeres (Women's Committee of the Chilean Human Rights Commission)
CDMB	Centro de Desenvolvimento da Mulher Brasileira (Center for the Development of Brazilian Women)
CEBs	Comunidades Eclesiais de Base (Christian Base Communities)
CEDAW	UN Convention on the Elimination of All Forms of Discrimination Against Women
CEDEM	Centro de Estudios para el Desarrollo de la Mujer (Center for Studies for the Development of Women)
CEM	Centro de Estudios de la Mujer (Women's Studies Center)

CEMAs	Centros de Madres (Mothers Centers)
CEPIA	Cidadania, Estudos, Pesquisa, Informação, e Acão (Citizenship, Study, Research, Information, and Action)
CESMA	Centro de Estudios de la Mujer Argentina (Center for the Social Study of Argentine Women)
CFEMEA	Centro Feminista de Estudos e Assessoria (Feminist Center for Research and Consulting)
CIERA	Centro de Investigación y Estudios sobre Reforma Agraria (Center for Research and Study of the Agrarian Reform)
CMB	Centro da Mulher Brasileira—Seter São Paulo (Center of the Brazilian Women—São Paulo)
CNDM	Conselho Nacional dos Direitos da Mulher (National Council on Women's Rights)
CNI	Central Nacional de Inteligencia (National Central Intelligence)
CNS	Coordinadora Nacional Sindical (National Trade Union Coordinator)
CODEM	Comité de Defensa de los Derechos de la Mujer (Committee for the Defense of Women's Rights)
CONADEP	Comité Nacional para los Desaparecidos (National Committee on Disappeared Persons)
CONAMUP	Coordinadora Nacional del Movimiento Urbano Popular (National Coordinating Committee of Urban Popular Movements)
CONAPRO	Confederación Nacional de Organizaciones de Profesionales (Confederation of Professional Organizations)
CRM	Consejo Regional de Mujeres (Woman's Regional Council)
CST	Central Sandinista de Trabajadores (Sandinista Workers' Central)
CTM	Confederación de Trabajadores Mexicanos (Confederation of Mexican Workers)
CUT	Central Unida dos Trabalhadores (United Worker's Central)
DDMs	*delegacias da mulher* (women's police precincts)
DF	Departamento Femenino (Women's Department)
EPF	El Poder Femenino (Woman Power)
FES	Federación de Estudiantes Secundarios (Federation of Secondary School Students)
FETSALUD	Federación Nacional de Trabajadores de la Salud (Health Workers' Federation)
FIP	Frente de Izquierda Popular (Popular Leftist Front)

FM   Movimiento Feminista (Feminist Movement)
FMC   Federación de Mujeres Cubanas (Cuban Women's Federation)
FMS   Federación de Mujeres Socialistas (Federation of Socialist Women)
FSLN   Frente Sandinista de Liberación Nacional (Sandinista Front for National Liberation)

GALF   Grupo Ação Lésbica-Feminista (Lesbian-Feminist Action Group)

HP   *Hora do Povo* (a Brazilian newspaper)

IACW   Inter-American Commission of Women
IMF   International Monetary Fund
IWD   International Women's Day

LBA   Legião Brasileira de Assistência (Brazilian Legion of Charity)

MAS   Mujeres en Acción Solidaria (Women for Solidarity Action)
MDB   Movimento Democrático Brasileiro (Brazilian Democratic Movement)
MEDH   Movimento Ecuménico para los Derechos Humanos (Ecumenical Movement for Human Rights)
MF   Movimento Feminista (Feminist Movement)
MLC   Movimento de Luta por Creches (Struggle for Day Care Movement)
MLF   Movimento para Liberación Feminina (Women's Rights Movement)
MMS   Movimento de Mujeres por el Socialismo (Movement of Women for Socialism)
MOMUPO   Movimiento de Mujeres Pobladoras (Movement of Shantytown Women)
MUDECHI   Mujeres de Chile (Women of Chile)

NGOs   nongovernmental organizations

OEPs   *organizaciones económicas populares* (popular economic organizations)
OFA   Organización Feminista Argentina (Argentine Feminist Organization)
OLM   Oficina Legal de la Mujer (Women's Legal Office)

PAN   Partido Acción Nacional (National Action Party)

PC	Partido Communista (Communist Party)
PDC	Partido Democracia Cristiana (Christian Democratic Party)
PDS	Partido Democrático Social (Democratic Social Party)
PDT	Partido Democrático Trabalhista (Democratic Labor Party)
PEM	Programa de Empleo Mínimo (Program of Minimum Employment)
PES	Programa de Emergencia Social (Program of Social Emergency)
PHV	Partido Humanista-Verde (Humanist-Green Party)
PIE	Partido de la Izquierda Erotica (Party of the Erotic Left)
PMDB	Partido do Movimento Democrático Brasileiro (Party of the Brazilian Democratic Movement)
PN	Partido Nacional (National Party)
PNR	Partido Nacional Revolucionario (National Revolutionary Party)
POJH	Programa de Jefes de Hogar (Program for Heads of Households)
PP	Partido Popular (Popular Party)
PPD	Partido por la Democracia (Party for Democracy)
PRD	Partido de la Revolución Democrática (Democratic Revolution Party)
PRI	Partido Revolucionario Institucional (Party of the Institutionalized Revolution)
PRN	Partido Renovación Nacional (National Renovation Party)
PRONASOL	Programa Nacional de Solidaridad (National Solidarity Program)
PS	Partido Socialista (Socialist Party)
PT	Partido dos Trabalhadores (Workers' Party)
SERNAC	Servicio Nacional del Consumidor (National Consumer Service)
SERNAM	Servicio Nacional de la Mujer (National Women's Service)
SNM	Secretaría Nacional de la Mujer (National Secretariat of Women)
UNAG	Unión Nacional de Agricultores (National Farmers' and Ranchers' Union)
UNE	Unión Nacional de Empleados (State Employees Union)
UNO	Unidad Nacional Opositora (United Opposition Coalition)
VR	Vanguardia Revolucionaria (Revolutionary Vanguard)

ONE

———

Introduction: From Transition to Participation — Women's Movements and Democratic Politics

JANE S. JAQUETTE

The authors of the first edition of *The Women's Movement in Latin America* documented and analyzed the role of women's organizations and women's politics in the transitions to democracy in Brazil, Argentina, Uruguay, Peru, and Chile. Since 1988, several changes have occurred that require a new analysis. In these five countries, history has moved on: The transitions are over; with the exception of Peru, democratic institutions have been maintained, and the issue has become how to build democratic societies that can sustain democratic political institutions and provide some measure of social justice.

During this period, the term "transition" has also evolved, taking on a new, global meaning and a wider application in Latin America. The authors of the earlier volume compared five countries as they emerged from very similar experiences of military rule; with the exception of Peru, these were all bureaucratic authoritarian regimes, notable for the intensity with which the military took to its self-assigned task of restructuring society and for the terrorist tactics used in pursuing its opponents, real and imagined, on the Left. The term "transition" now covers a broader range of political evolutions in Latin America, thus making it appropriate to expand the case studies of women's mobilization to include two countries that have experienced very different kinds of transitions: Nicaragua and Mexico.

In 1989, the most striking facts about women's movements in Latin America were the extent and variety of women's mobilization and the success of the feminist movements in bringing their perspectives to bear on the core issues of

1

delegitimizing military rule and reconstructing civil society. Yet it seemed then that women's successes might be ephemeral, a product of crisis mobilization. It was not clear whether the feminist movements would be able to evolve from being part of the opposition to competing in a political arena controlled by male-dominated political parties. It seemed likely that the return to democratic politics as usual would require the new social movements to become more like interest groups.[1] With democratic politics understood as the art of the possible, many felt that the movements would have to relinquish their utopian visions and aim for more realistic goals.[2]

This volume moves from women's visions to women's political practices. We are more cautious about women's ability to capture parts of the state, but more confident about the extent and persistence of women's mobilization and its transformative effects on women themselves. We are more sober about the difficulties of negotiating and implementing a women's agenda, yet encouraged by the ability of women's movements to adapt to new circumstances and to evolve appropriate agendas and strategies.

Women's Activism in Historical Perspective

Women's political participation is not new in Latin America. From the time of the conquest, when La Malinche's role in aiding Cortez's conquest of Mexico was matched by women's resistance, to Sor Juana "voicing her protest against the injustice of women's place in her hypocritical society"[3] to the heroism of women in the wars of independence in the early nineteenth century, women of all classes took active roles in politics, which are now being seriously studied and documented for the first time.[4]

In the twentieth century, women have organized campaigns to change women's legal status and to demand women's suffrage, and women have been active participants in the movements that have challenged the maldistribution of wealth and power from the Mexican to the Nicaraguan Revolutions.[5] Women have organized demonstrations and taken part in miners' strikes and peasant movements. They joined political parties even before they had the right to vote. Since World War II, when women swelled the ranks of those migrating to the cities, women have participated in land invasions and in neighborhood organizations to protect their homes and gain water, electricity, and other urban services; they have organized with other women to protest consumer price increases, create health care and day care programs, and build and maintain schools.[6]

Like women's work,[7] women's politics has been invisible. The leadership roles taken by Latin American women in international politics, from the Latin American scientific congresses beginning in 1898 and the First International Women's Congress (Congreso Feminino Internacional) held in Buenos Aires in 1910 to the Inter-American Commission of Women (IACW), which began meeting in 1930, are now forgotten. Few remember, if they ever knew, that the reference to "the equal rights of men and women" in the first paragraph of the UN Charter was included because the IACW representatives from Brazil, the Dominican Republic, and Mexico insisted that it be there.[8]

The standard interpretation of Latin American feminist thought, shared by Latin Americans and North Americans alike, is that it is "derivative."[9] The notion that there are women's movements and feminist movements in Latin America that need to be recognized and respected on their own terms or that others might learn from the theory and practice of Latin American women's movements remains foreign to most feminists in the advanced industrialized countries. If studied at all, Latin American women are included to respond to the demand for diversity in university curricula. This has the perverse effect of making their experiences seem exotic[10] and leaves the impression that the feminisms of the West are more advanced or mature. The feminist and women's movements in Latin America discussed and analyzed in this volume profoundly challenge these assumptions.

Women and the Transitions to Democracy

In 1989, *The Women's Movement in Latin America* documented a new phase of women's political activism. The authors argued that in the mid- to late 1970s, several factors had come together to give women's movements the motive and opportunity to become vocal and visible political actors. The first was the economic crisis that began in Latin America when the OPEC cartel raised oil prices fourfold in 1973 and that accelerated sharply during the debt crisis of the 1980s.[11] The economic crisis brought cuts in government spending on social services, reductions in investment (thus reduced incomes and growth), and high levels of inflation.

The crisis—and the structural adjustment policies that governments adopted to deal with it—hit the urban poor, especially women, very hard. The mass base of women's movements from the mid-1970s to the present has been lower-class urban women *(mujeres populares)* who organized to demand relief from the state, supply the basic services that the state could no longer provide, or feed their families collectively when it was no longer possible to do so individually.[12] In the 1970s and early 1980s, the mass protests of the *mujeres populares* made it difficult for the military governments to claim that their economic policies had succeeded.

Women's mobilization took a different form in the emergence of human rights movements. Provoked by the terrorist tactics of the state, which "disappeared" their children without admitting responsibility, the women who formed and often led these groups were willing to risk their lives to demand that their children be returned to them. The Argentine Madres of the Plaza de Mayo (Mothers of the Plaza de Mayo), to take the best known and most illustrative case, were women who had not been active in politics before and who developed new forms of protest that were extraordinary both in the way that they politicized women's identities as mothers[13] and in their effectiveness against the military's claims to power.

The reemergence of a self-conscious and activist feminist movement was a third element in this new wave of women's mobilization. In many countries, the meetings held to prepare for the 1975 International Women's Year Conference in Mexico City established new networks, revitalized dormant organizations, and made gender a political issue. Middle-class professional women formed "grupos de reflexión" in which they "could develop a new identity, delve into the past, read feminist texts, create new forms of interaction, and dream of a utopian future."[14] The feminist groups held conferences, organized national and regional *encuentros* (meetings), and formed study and action groups to establish connections with the *mujeres populares* and with women in peasant and industrial unions. Women political activists in leftist parties became increasingly impatient with the Left's failure to take women's issues seriously.

A fourth factor was the transition itself. Ironically, military authoritarian rule, which depoliticized men, had the unintended consequence of mobilizing women. Shared opposition to military rule unified the various women's movements and provided an opportunity to make women's issues an integral part of national debates. At the same time, women developed new modes of political action. Although women's human rights groups did not identify themselves as feminist, both human rights and women's rights organizations expanded the new Latin American discourse of rights and citizenship.

Some in the human rights and feminist movements made a connection between the recurring pattern of military dictatorships in Latin America and the prevalence of authoritarian relations in society as a whole and in the family in particular.[15] The treatment of women political prisoners, who were raped and even tortured in front of their own children,[16] the invasion of homes by the police, and the parceling out of infants born to women prisoners to couples with close ties to the military elite revealed the hypocrisy behind the military's attempt to glorify motherhood and to manipulate the traditional symbols of women's self-sacrifice.[17]

In the early stages of the political transitions, meetings organized by feminist groups attracted large audiences who were able to use the political spaces organized by women to debate political alternatives and begin to construct a public opposition. Not knowing exactly how to respond, the military governments at first allowed these meetings while still banning those organized by men. Feminist groups, along with other social movements, organized themselves under the protective umbrella of the Church, although many later found it necessary to break away in order to keep their independence or to raise issues opposed by the Church, including divorce and reproductive rights.

As the military regimes moved toward genuine democratic openings and as the political parties and other groups began to reconstruct themselves, the close ties between women's groups and their allies in the civilian opposition weakened. Yet by making it possible to imagine that the return to democracy could bring about a more humane society and represent a much larger citizenry, women's groups helped rebuild the promise of democratic government, which had been devalued by repeated attacks from the Marxist Left and the oligarchic Right throughout much of the twentieth century.

The Latin American Feminist Encounters

Feminism is undergoing a worldwide process of dynamic change. Even the U.S. women's movement has evolved in ways unanticipated by its founders. Earlier debates between liberal and socialist feminists have been superseded by the rise of "maternal" and "difference" feminisms; all of these have come under attack for failing to incorporate race and class in their analyses. Some have argued that feminism is dead, and others that we are in a postfeminist era, although egalitarian issues are still a priority for women in traditional male strongholds such as the Catholic Church and the armed forces.[18]

Debates over feminist theories and practices have also characterized the evolution of women's movements in Latin America. In their insightful analysis of the biannual feminist *encuentros* held since 1981, Nancy Sternbach, Marysa Navarro, Pat Chuchryk, and Sonia Alvarez trace how the issues changed during the 1980s as the participation in the *encuentros* expanded from 200 to nearly 3,000, including women from the urban movements, from Central America and the Caribbean, and from South America.[19]

In Bogota in 1981, autonomy and its implications for feminist practice was the issue. The feminists *(feministas)* challenged political party militants *(militantes)*, arguing that feminism itself was a "legitimate and comprehensive political practice" that had to be separated from the debates that divided the parties and fragmented the Marxist Left. The *militantes* countered that feminist objectives could not be separated from "the struggle to end class oppression."[20]

In 1983 in Lima, the theme was patriarchy, despite opposition from those on the Left who associated this term with "'bad' imperialist feminism."[21] The debates between the *militantes* and the *feministas* were expanded by the participation of women from the popular women's movements themselves. (The length and severity of the economic crisis in Peru had already made the *movimientos de mujeres* a political force.) For some, such as Virginia Vargas, Lima opened up the possibility that women could define and act on their *own* interests: "It was the first step away from the awareness of permanent guilt (for being middle class, for not thinking about hunger, for thinking about ourselves, for not being sufficiently political) toward a consciousness that all of these attitudes were in fact legitimate and necessary."[22]

In 1985, at the *encuentro* held outside São Paulo, Brazil, race and sexual preference were explicitly part of the agenda for the first time. Class remained the central issue, heightened by the refusal of the organizers to allow women bused in from Rio's shantytowns to be admitted without paying the entry fee. The ensuing debates among different groups at the conference deepened the divisions between the feminists and the militants, and between them and the women of the *movimientos de mujeres.*

The 1987 meeting at Taxco (Mexico) had 1,500 participants, many from Central America (including 50 from Nicaragua) and the Spanish Caribbean. Women represented new sectors as well: government programs and ministries, the new nongovernmental organizations (NGOs), and Catholic feminist activists. But Taxco revealed generational and regional as well as class divisions among feminists. The mostly South American feminists who had organized and attended the early *encuentros* responded to the growing participation of women from the *movimientos de mujeres* and from Central America by asking whether the latter were really feminists. They asked whether problems of urban services, health programs, and the communal kitchens (*practical* gender interests) should not be left to the *movimientos de mujeres* while the feminists focused on strategic gender issues such as "abortion, domestic violence and sexual and reproductive freedom."[23]

The reply, which would increasingly become the dominant view, was that the *movimientos de mujeres* were developing a new kind of feminist practice, that by organizing themselves and making demands as women and as mothers, they were effectively confronting both political and economic repression, empowering women of all classes, and politicizing the issues of survival, of everyday life. At the next *encuentro,* in Argentina, the shift in the balance of power was made clear when the group decided to hold the following *encuentro* in Cuba (later changed to Costa Rica) rather than in Chile to mark its return to democracy.

The rapidly changing internal dynamics of the women's movements in the region, combined with the unprecedented restructuring of the international environment that has been occurring since 1989, strongly suggest that concepts developed to describe that impact of feminism in Latin America in the 1980s will need to be rethought for the 1990s. For example, today, despite the similarity of issues for the movements of the region and the importance of women's mobilization in each country, one would not speak of a women's movement but of women's movements and feminisms. And although most of the movements have the experiences of economic and political liberalization in common, the transitions framework diverts attention away from some of the key issues.

The chapters on Nicaragua and Mexico illustrate some of this framework's limitations. In the Nicaraguan case, Norma Stoltz Chinchilla asks whether the transition *from* a socialist regime explicitly committed to women's equality can be a transition *to* a new feminist consciousness or new political spaces for women, as occurred in the transitions from bureaucratic authoritarianism. And whatever transition is occurring in Mexico, it is not a reaction against military rule or against a rightist ideology. Although the hegemonic PRI (Partido Revolucionario

Institucional, or Party of the Institutionalized Revolution) was not explicitly Marxist and therefore did not emphasize "the woman question," its ideology has traditionally been leftist in its commitment to redistribution and in its secularism—at the opposite end of the spectrum from the ideology of property, family, and Catholicism, which provided the social rationale for bureaucratic authoritarianism.

Some argue that the transitions framework has been too narrowly confined to studying elite behavior, to using "rational actor" models, and to analyzing the social pacts by which key elites agreed to return to democracy. Social pacts may keep divisive issues and groups out of the political bargaining process.[24] Those who study women's movements recognize not only that there are new political actors but that these groups are demanding new forms of democracy and attention to a new set of issues.

But those who have gained a broadened perspective of the women's movement may have lost sight of the issues that were foremost in the Marxist and dependency analyses. Class has disappeared as a category of analysis even as class differences are widening,[25] and dependency has become passé despite the fact that the position of the Latin American economies in the world trading system has worsened.

In Brazil, Chile, Argentina, Uruguay, and Peru, the return to democracy was the result of domestic political forces. That is not the case in Nicaragua. Mexico's liberalization has been conditioned by its international economic strategy. In all of these cases, it is clear that elections alone cannot resolve the underlying problems of the region or create a political consensus sufficient to ensure that democratic institutions can be maintained.

What is needed is a political analysis that goes beyond elites to the participation of groups and the formation of public opinion, that explores the development of political demands and the emergence of political leadership, and that studies how social movements interact with other groups, with parties, and with the state.

*   *   *

In 1989 a central issue was whether women's movements would survive the transition from opposition politics to democratic politics. Democratic governments seemed to edge out social movements, leaving in place the political parties, institutional actors such as the military and the bureaucracy, and elite associations. The boundaries of political debate seemed to be narrowing, making less space for feminist demands. For their part, women's movements were resistant to recasting themselves as interest groups. Would women "go home" once the crisis was over? Would social movements adapt to the patterns of clientelism and corporatism that have characterized relations between the state and civil society throughout Latin American history, or would they challenge these patterns?

Although the solidarity and utopianism of the transition stage has worn thin, the chapters in this book show that women's mobilization continues that political discourse and has expanded to include the politics of gender. The authors document women's roles in the transitions, giving special attention to the organization of feminist groups. They also assess the implication of women's mobilization for the consolidation of democracy and for the future of feminist politics in each country.

In Chapter 2, Sonia Alvarez analyzes the successes of women's movements in Brazil, using case studies of health care and day care movements in São Paulo. She examines the feminist strategy of establishing the innovative Conselhos (Councils on the Condition of Women) and *delegacias,* police stations with personnel trained to respond to rape and domestic abuse; both these mechanisms have been widely imitated elsewhere in Latin America and beyond. Alvarez documents the problems encountered when feminists could no longer rely on their initial political allies or on the support of the president. She makes a compelling case for independent women's organizations that can pressure the government from the outside to maintain their spaces in the state, regardless of which party is in power.

Chile's late transition allowed feminists to learn from the experiences in other countries. In Chapter 3, Patricia Chuchryk documents the emergence of feminist organizations and the role of women in the opposition to the dictatorship. The fact that women played a role in the fall of the socialist government of Salvador Allende in 1973 has continued to complicate relationships between feminists and leftist parties, but feminists gained influence in the new democratic government by helping to win votes against Augusto Pinochet in the plebiscite of 1988 and for the opposition candidate, Patricio Aylwin, in 1989.

In Chapter 4, María del Carmen Feijoó looks at the role of Argentine women's participation in the transition under the two democratic presidents elected since 1983: Raúl Alfonsín of the moderate Radical Party and Peronist Carlos Menem. She discusses the effect of the persistent economic crisis and the continuing attempts of the Madres of the Plaza de Mayo to bring to justice those responsible for the disappearances. Feijoó analyzes the strategy and the rhetoric of the Madres and probes the linkage of state and gender by asking how the state will recognize and nurture women's mobilization.

Carina Perelli, in Chapter 5, begins with the observation that many young women of her generation in Uruguay admired the women fighters who joined the Tupamaros, an urban guerrilla organization active in the 1960s and early 1970s. She finds that women's resistance to the military dictatorship was effective precisely because it was not political in the ordinary sense but argues that it had conservative implications for both politics and women. In her concluding section, Perelli questions the feminist article of faith that blurring the line between the private and the political is always positive, showing instead that it can be used to make unlimited private claims and deny the common good.

Maruja Barrig's analysis in Chapter 6 of the popular women's movements in Peru shares a theme with the chapters on Brazil and Mexico, although the threat from the Maoist Sendero Luminoso (Shining Path) makes Peru unique. Barrig is particularly interested in the issue of autonomy: Did the feminists' autonomy distance them from their mass base in the 1980s? Can the *movimientos de mujeres* maintain their autonomy in the face of state and party efforts to coopt them? Dismayed and disheartened by the Senderista assassinations of women leaders and by the breakdown of relationships of trust within women's organizations, Barrig asks whether the urban women's movements may have centralized too rapidly, leaving their leaders and their local organizations vulnerable.

In Chapter 7, Norma Stoltz Chinchilla reconstructs the evolving debates within the FSLN (or Sandinista Front for National Liberation) over its strategy toward women. Her account shows the evolution of feminist thinking within the party and in relation to independent groups. She suggests that the rigidity of the leadership and the reliance on traditional images of women during the campaign gave mixed messages to women and may have contributed to the FSLN's electoral defeat in 1990, but that women's efforts to organize and have an impact on policy-making have continued.

Carmen Ramos Escandón, in Chapter 8, puts the mobilization of Mexican women in historical perspective, beginning with the first transition to a new political order following the Constitution of 1917. The case of Mexico is particularly ironic: Despite the stature and political influence of feminist leaders, especially during the 1930s, Mexico was among the last countries in the hemisphere to give women the vote. Ramos analyses two contemporary case studies of women's groups, arguing that women have become important political actors in Mexican politics and illustrating the similarities in women's modes of political organizing throughout the region.

Taken together, these chapters show the vitality and the complexity of women's and feminist movements in Latin America. By looking at women's roles in democratic transitions, and their goals and strategies in democracies that are far from consolidated, the authors show how far women's movements have come and how much more work remains to be done.

Notes

1. Alain Touraine distinguishes the new social movements from those of the past, which were directed toward the "transformation of the State," arguing that today's movements attempt to "control cultural patterns (knowledge, investment, ethics) in a given societal type." From "An Introduction to the Study of Social Movements," *Social Research* 52, 4 (1985): 776–777. See also Alessandro Pizzorno, "On the Individualistic Theory of Social Order," in Pierre Bourdieu and James Coleman, eds., *Social Theory for a Changing Society* (Boulder, Colo.: Westview Press, 1991).

2. See Norbert Lechner, *Los patios interios de la democracia: Subjectividad y politica* (Santiago: Fondo de Cultura Economica, 1988), chap. 3.

3. Emilie L. Bergman, "Sor Juana Ines de la Cruz: Dreaming in a Double Voice," in Seminar on Feminism and Culture in Latin America, ed., *Women, Culture and Politics in Latin America* (Berkeley: University of California Press, 1990), 153.

4. See Francesca Miller, *Latin American Women: The Search for Social Justice* (Hanover, N.H.: University Press of New England, 1981).

5. See Linda Labao, "Women in Revolutionary Movements: Changing Patterns of Latin American Guerrilla Struggle," in Guida West and Rhoda Lois Blumberg, eds., *Women and Social Protest* (Oxford: Oxford University Press, 1990); Jane S. Jaquette, "Women in Revolutionary Movements in Latin America," *Journal of Marriage and the Family* 35 (May 1973): 344–354.

6. On education, see essays in Nelly P. Stromquist, ed., *Women and Education in Latin America: Knowledge, Power and Change* (Boulder, Colo.: Lynne Rienner, 1992), especially Beatriz Schmukler, "Women and the Microsocial Democratization of Everyday Life."

7. For a review, see Lourdes Beneria, "Accounting for Women's Work: The Progress of Two Decades," *World Development* 20, 11 (1992): 1547–1560.

8. Miller, *Latin American Women*, 12, 21.

9. Ibid., 11.

10. This argument is made very effectively by Rey Chow, who argues that feminist social scientists "use Chinese women—and the more remote they are from Western urban civilization, the better—for the production of the types of explanations that are intelligible *(valuable)* to feminism in the West, including, in particular, those types that extend pluralism to "woman" through "race" and "class." In "Violence in the Other Country: China as Crisis, Spectacle, and Woman," in Chanra Talpade Mohanty, Ann Russo, and Lourdes Torres, eds., *Third World Women and the Politics of Feminism* (Bloomington: Indiana University Press, 1991), 93. For a postcolonial approach to Latin American women's mobilization, see Sallie Westwood and Sarah A. Radcliffe, "Gender, Racism and the Politics of Identities in Latin America," in Radcliffe and Westwood, eds., *Viva: Women and Popular Protest in Latin America* (London: Routledge, 1993).

11. See Helen Icken Safa, "Women's Social Movements in Latin America," *Gender and Society* 4, 3 (1990): 354–369; Neuma Aguiar, coordinator, *Mujer y crisis: Respuestas ante la recesion* (Rio de Janeiro: DAWN/MUDAR, 1990); Caroline O. Moser, "Adjustment from Below: Low Income Women, Time and the Triple Role in Guayaquil, Ecuador," in Radcliffe and Westwood, *Viva*.

12. This book focuses on urban women; there are several important studies of rural women's mobilization. See, for example, the chapter on Paraguay in Jo Fisher's *Out of the Shadows: Women, Resistance and Politics in Latin America* (London: Latin America Bureau, 1993); Carmen Diana Deere and Magdalena Leon, *Rural Women and State Policy* (Boulder, Colo.: Westview Press, 1987); Sarah A Radcliffe, "'People Have to Rise Up—Like the Great Women Fighters': The State and Peasant Women in Peru," in Radcliffe and Westwood, *Viva*.

13. See Jean Bethke Elshtain, "The Power and Powerlessness of Women," in *Power Trips and Other Journeys* (Madison: University of Wisconsin Press, 1990).

14. Marysa Navarro-Aranguren, "The Construction of a Latin American Feminist Identity," in Alfred Stepan, ed., *Americas: New Interpretive Essays* (New York: Oxford University Press, 1992), 144.

15. For example, Julieta Kirkwood, *Ser politica in Chile: Las feministas y los partidos* (Santiago: FLACSO, 1986).

16. Ximena Bunster-Burotto, "Surviving Beyond Fear: Women and Torture in Latin America," in June Nash and Helen I. Safa, eds., *Women and Change in Latin America* (South Hadley, Mass.: Bergin and Garvey, 1985).

17. For example, see María Elena Valenzuela, *Todas ibamos a ser reinas: La mujer en el Chile militar* (Santiago: CESOC, 1987).

18. Mary Fainsod Katzenstein, "Feminism Within American Institutions: Unobtrusive Mobilization in the 1980s," *Signs* 16, 1 (Autumn 1990): 27–54.

19. Nancy Saporta Sternbach, Marysa Navarro-Aranguren, Patricia Chuchryk, and Sonia E. Alvarez, "Feminisms in Latin America: From Bogota to San Bernadino," *Signs* 17, 2 (Winter 1992): 393–434.

20. Ibid., 409.

21. Ibid., 410.

22. Virginia Vargas, Las mujeres en movimiento (o de como somos políticas las mujeres), paper presented at Centro Flora Tristan, Lima, 1985; cited in Maruja Barrig, this volume.

23. See Sternbach et al., "Feminisms in Latin America," 414–416; the distinction between strategic and practical gender interests is from Maxine Molyneux, "Mobilization Without Emancipation? Women's Interests, the State and Revolution in Nicaragua," *Feminist Studies* 11, 2 (1985): 232.

24. For a general critique, see Daniel H. Levine, "Paradigm Lost: Dependence to Democracy," *World Politics* 40 (April 1988): 377–394.

25. Ronald H. Chilcote, "Post-Marxism: The Retreat from Class in Latin America," *Latin American Perspectives* 17, 2 (Spring 1990): 3–24.

TWO

The (Trans)formation of Feminism(s) and Gender Politics in Democratizing Brazil[1]

SONIA E. ALVAREZ

Transition politics temporarily brought down some of the patriarchal barriers that customarily bar women from political life. Hundreds of thousands of Brazilian women of all social classes and racial and ethnic groups took to the ramparts in opposition to military rule. And, I will argue, it was the political contradictions experienced by women active in a wide variety of opposition organizations—both in civil and in political society—that prompted some to organize as feminists in the mid-1970s and to formulate new claims grounded in gendered needs and identities.

Feminists, in Brazil as in the other cases discussed in this volume, have always been a subset of a larger women's movement that encompasses a broad spectrum of organizations, strategies, tactics, and ideologies. The "mosaic of diversity"[2] evidenced in women's organizing experiences during Brazil's transition from authoritarian rule was indeed striking: Women spearheaded protests against the regime's human rights violations; poor and working-class women crafted creative solutions to meet community needs in response to gross government neglect of basic urban and social services; women workers swelled the ranks of Brazil's new trade union movement; rural women struggled for their rights to land that were increasingly being usurped by export-agribusiness; Afro-Brazilian women joined the United Black Movement and helped forge other organized expressions of a growing antiracist, Black-consciousness movement; Brazilian lesbians joined gay males to launch a struggle against homophobia; young women and university students enlisted in militant student movements; some took up arms against the military regime, and still others worked in legally sanctioned parties of the opposition. By the 1980s, thousands of women involved in these and other collective struggles had come to identify themselves as feminists.

It is, of course, impossible to do full justice to all of these forms of collective resistance in the space allotted here. In the first part of this chapter, I instead seek to explain how a *distinctive feminist political identity emerged* and developed over the course of the 1970s and early 1980s amid this intricate mosaic of women's collective action. Brazilian feminist politics during that decade is situated within the context of transition politics more generally. I argued that a collective feminist identity and a gendered political agenda were also fruits of the multiple tensions that characterized the intimate but always tortuous relationship of Brazilian feminism to the political party opposition, especially the Left, and to the progressive sectors of the Church and other collective actors who began to carve out new rights in society and demand those rights from the state. Because significant regional differences demarcate Brazil's vast national territory, I should specify that most of the ensuing discussion traces the trajectory of feminism(s) in metropolitan São Paulo, signaling other regional or national developments where possible.

The second section of this chapter turns to an analysis of feminism's changing relationship to political society and the State. Over the course of Brazil's singularly protracted transition from authoritarian rule,[3] feminist activists were compelled to constantly rethink their relationship to male-dominant political parties and to a masculinist, capitalist, and racialist State whose institutional parameters and policy agendas underwent rapid, and sometimes dramatic, transformations over the course of the transition period. In the context of military rule, the authoritarian State was, of course, viewed as the chief enemy of feminism and of all other progressive social movements that emerged during the 1960s and 1970s. In the early 1980s, when the opposition gained control of several state governments and augmented its presence in the federal, state, and local legislative arenas, feminists and other progressive activists suddenly encountered a more permeable political arena. And in the first few years of Brazil's "New Republic," they were able to advance a relatively successful and fairly radical policy agenda.

From the mid- to late 1980s, feminists who worked from within political parties and the State were legitimized and supported by their constituencies in civil society—independent feminist groups and other women's movement organizations. They secured notable gains for women in the policy realm and promoted significant public debate about the status of women in Brazilian society. But since the turn of the decade, as conservative hegemony over national and state politics was consolidated, feminists have had to struggle to secure further gains and to prevent setbacks in some of the advances made during the transition period. The implications of this (partial) closing of the "gendered political opening" of the mid- to late 1980s is the subject of the final section.

The Formation of a Distinct Feminist Political Identity Within the Brazilian Women's Movement

Engendering Opposition to Military Rule

The evolution of Brazilian feminism during the 1970s was inextricably linked to the unfolding dynamics of the larger opposition to military authoritarian rule. Opposition discourses concerning human rights, social justice, equality, and liberation, coupled with the rise of feminist discourses on an international plane, implanted ideological seeds that would later be cultivated by Brazilian women to disseminate discourses about women's rights, gendered justice, equality between women and men, and, ultimately, women's liberation. Because both secular and Church-linked opposition groups were male-dominated, the discriminations suffered by women in such groups triggered an incipient gender consciousness among many active in the opposition. Still, the political networks forged in opposition to the military regime furnished critical resources for women's mobilization *as women*. And after 1974, political liberalization enabled women to articulate publicly their new gendered political claims.

The political and institutional transformation of the Brazilian Catholic Church proved a critical factor in the genesis of contemporary feminism. As in other Latin American nations during the 1960s and 1970s, sectors of the Brazilian Church gradually turned toward the poor and against the military regime.[4] Actively promoting the organization of the lower classes, creating new "communities of equals" among the "people of God," the progressive Church provided a vital organizational umbrella for the opposition and cloaked its activities with a veil of moral legitimacy. The Church's shielding of the opposition drew middle-class secular activists and intellectuals, many of them women, into Brazil's peripheral urban neighborhoods and rural areas. Many of these women militants began working with thousands of poor and working-class women's groups, such as the mother's clubs and housewives' associations, which sprang up throughout Brazil in the 1970s and 1980s. Often linked to the Catholic Church or to secular, neighborhood-based organizations, these groups composed what Brazilians commonly refer to as the "feminine movement."[5]

As Moema Viezzar notes, "Many of these [mothers'] clubs and [women's] centers were created within the scheme of North-South aid, through large assistance or development programs whose target populations were 'low income' groups."[6] Others were created as women's auxiliaries to the Church's Christian Base Communities or as vehicles for channeling the charitable activities of the Legião Brasileira de Assistência (Brazilian Legion of Charity) during the late 1960s and early 1970s.[7] Nonetheless, women's community organizations soon took on a political dynamic of their own. Poor and working-class women began organizing around their immediate survival needs. In keeping with their socially ascribed roles as the wives, mothers, and nurturers of family and community, women of the lower classes were among the first to protest the authoritarian regime's regressive social and economic policies. They organized against the rising cost of living; demanded adequate schools, day care centers, running water, sewers, electrification, and other urban infrastructural necessities; and clamored for their right to adequately feed their families, school their children, and provide them with a decent life. Community mothers' clubs served as the organizational base for several political movements that expanded into citywide, and even nationwide, political campaigns. What I have called "militant motherhood" provided the mobilization referent for the Feminine Amnesty Movement, the Cost of Living Movement, and the Day Care Movement in the 1970s and 1980s.[8] Through mothers' club–like organizations, hundreds of thousands of working-class women participated in community politics for the first time. That participation in itself empowered many women activists, sometimes leading them to question gender power imbalances within their marriages, their families, their communities, and even their parishes.[9]

Much of the Church hierarchy, and some of the progressive clergy, remained doctrinally opposed, if not overtly hostile, to feminist demands for sexual autonomy, changes in the family, and reproductive freedom.[10] Nonetheless, the politicization of gender within Church-linked community women's groups provided nascent Brazilian feminism with an extensive mass base not found in any of the other countries under consideration in this volume, with the partial exception of Peru and Chile. The intransigence of otherwise progressive sectors of the Catholic Church to what would become core issues of the feminist political agenda—divorce, contraception, abortion, sexuality, and the like—eventually prompted feminists to radicalize their discourses on precisely those issues that were held sacred by their erstwhile allies in the Church. Feminists were further emboldened by the fact that issues such as contraception and sexuality found substantial resonance among poor and working-class activists in neighborhood women's associations linked to the Church.

The rearticulation of the militant Left in the wake of the severe government repression of the late 1960s and early 1970s was a second factor that helped galvanize nascent Brazilian feminism in the mid-1970s. Many of the women who would become the cadre of organizers of the contemporary Brazilian feminist movements were active in militant Left organizations and student groups. And many of the feminists I interviewed discussed their experience within those organizations as having implanted the seeds of feminist consciousness within them.

The revolutionary Left made only passing reference to the "woman question," as the class struggle and the armed struggle against the regime were deemed paramount after military hard-liners closed off all peaceful channels of protest in 1968–1969. Moreover, the advent of socialism would bring about the liberation of women, so leftist groups and militant student movement organizations enjoined women to enlist in the revolutionary struggle that would eventually bring about their emancipation.

But for many women militants, the revolutionary opposition's formulation of the woman question and its sexist organizational practices left much to be desired. Though Guevarist theory argued that the presence of "women and old men" among combatants could hamper guerrilla effectiveness,[11] the model Brazilian revolutionary cadre was ostensibly genderless. As one former *guerrilheira* put it, "I was a militant, a soldier of the revolution, and a soldier has no sex." Yet in practice, she noted, the relations between the sexes were "very different."[12] Gender "sameness" in revolutionary theory led revolutionaries to ignore or deny the very real differences between men and women, with profound implications for the women in the resistance movement. Revolutionaries were to leave their families and their pasts behind them and devote themselves entirely to the revolutionary struggle. Female revolutionaries, however, were often encumbered by their childbearing and childrearing responsibilities, responsibilities that, many women complained, were neither acknowledged nor shared by their male comrades in struggle. One woman told me, for example, that when a female leader in her political organization became pregnant, the central committee called an emergency meeting to vote on whether she should have the child. Others actually had their children and raised them in the underground, receiving little or no support (either material or moral) from their male colleagues for doing so.

Former *guerrilheiras* and student activists I talked to also complained about the fact that women were rarely given positions of authority within the militant Left. As in traditional political parties, female militants were instead entrusted with much of the "infrastructural" work of the Brazilian New Left—women ran safe houses, worked as messengers, cooked meals, cared for the sick and the wounded, and were sometimes called upon to use their "feminine charms" to extract information from the enemy. Many of these women resented their relegation to subordinate positions within the internal power structure of militant groups. But as one woman suggested, they lacked a language, an analysis, that would enable them to understand their resentment in political terms:

> For a long time, I was not conscious of the existence of women's oppression within the political groups. Today, I understand that the oppression existed and that it was very much marked by the type of power structure which existed within the political organizations in general. When these organizations assumed Leninist principles of democratic centralism, this in practice translated into highly pronounced hierarchies, where there were different scales and structures of power, where there had to be a boss. What happened was that women almost always wound up in an inferior position within that structure.[13]

The economistic orthodoxy of many political organizations made it difficult to question existing gender power relations, and the tendency toward rigid hierarchy also prevented women from setting the course of revolutionary theory and practice. But when the Left turned toward organizing a mass base for the revolution in Brazil's urban periphery in the mid-1970s, many former *guerrilheiras* and student movement activists directed their efforts at women of the popular classes.

Some of the women I interviewed suggested that, almost unconsciously, their experience as women in the Left led them to begin working as *assessoras,* or consultants, to Church-linked mothers' clubs or youth groups. They helped poor and working-class women learn the ropes of local political institutions so that they could better articulate their demands for improved urban infrastructure, schools, health care, and so on.

The experience of young middle-class women in the Left also had direct implications for the emergence of feminist movement organizations in contemporary Brazil. Former clandestine networks and networks established among student movement activists were remobilized around feminist issues in the mid- to late 1970s. Former female comrades in the would-be Brazilian revolution became comrades in a new kind of revolutionary struggle—one that encompassed the transformation of both class and gender relations of power in Brazilian society.

Many of the women involved in the militant opposition also formed networks while in political exile in Europe in the early to mid-1970s. And many became involved in the feminist movements, which by then were at their peak in the West. To the extent that feminism was imported to Brazil in the 1970s, it was through the lived experience of these exiled women, themselves active in opposition organizations in the host countries. In Chile until 1973 and in France and Italy until the late 1970s, for example, Brazilian women associated with the Left formed their own autonomous women's groups, often joining former Montoneras, Tupamaras, and other Spanish American *guerrilleras* also in exile. Though many of these women's groups began as fronts for the political organizations in exile, some, such as the Círculo de Mulheres Brasileiras in Paris, developed an autonomous feminist theory and practice that they brought back to Brazil after political amnesty was conceded in the late 1970s.[14]

The rearticulation of the Brazilian Left was strategically feasible owing to the regime's top-down policy of political liberalization—a third factor contributing to the reemergence of feminist activism.

By the time General Ernesto Geisel came to power in 1974, the claims that had sustained the legitimacy of the authoritarian regime throughout the 1960s and early 1970s were no longer viable. The elimination of the guerrilla movements and much of the radical opposition by the State security apparatus had dispelled middle-class fears of an imminent communist threat, which had been the central rationale of the State's "defensive project" during previous administrations. The "economic miracle" of the 1960s and early 1970s seemed less miraculous after it was severely shaken by the 1973 oil crisis and the excessive expansion of the money supply under Minister of Planning Delfim Neto, and the growing statism of the regime's offensive economic project led many of its bourgeois allies in civil society to join forces with popular sectors of the opposition.[15]

Political liberalization represented what Doug McAdam calls a change in the "structure of political opportunities" available to sectors of civil and political society excluded from power. According to McAdam, "Movements do not emerge in a vacuum. Rather, they are profoundly shaped by a wide range of environmental factors that condition both the objective possibilities for successful protests as well as the popular perception of insurgent prospects."[16] The "objective possibilities" for political protest and claims-making were altered under Geisel as the repressive apparatus of the State was curbed of its excesses and as avenues for a would-be dialogue between State and civil society were reopened for the first time since 1968–1969. Popular perception of the possibilities for successful protest also changed drastically with Geisel's *distensão* (decompression), as the authoritarian regime at least brandished a new "democratic" discourse.

Thus, though *distensão* did not generate political mobilization, it unquestionably fueled it. Without the more flexible political climate of decompression, the climate of fear that reigned under Emilio Garrastazú Medici (1970–1974) might have prevailed and dissipated many of the mobilizational initiatives of nascent social movements.

A further consideration helps explain the emergence of feminist groups and neighborhood-based women's organizations. The ingrained belief that women are indifferent to politics may have led the military rulers of Brazil to believe that anything women do is intrinsically apolitical.[17] Thus, even when women began organizing campaigns against the rising cost of living or for human rights in Brazil, the military seems to have allowed women's associations greater political leeway than was granted to the militant Left and to student and labor organizations, which were seen as more threatening to national security.[18] The 1975 celebrations of International Women's Day were thus among the first public assemblies permitted since the mass mobilizations of 1967–1968. The Feminine Amnesty Movement was allowed to organize in the mid-1970s when a conventional movement of that sort might have been actively repressed. In short, the institutionalized separation between the public and the private may, in an ironic historical twist, have helped propel women to the forefront of the opposition in Brazil.

Finally, in the mid-1970s, due in part to political pressures brought to bear by international feminist networks and feminist policy advocates in the Third World, the international aid and development establishments began to insist that governments integrate women into development, pointing to women's inequality and traditional values as obstacles to successful capitalist growth and development. These new international pressures fueled the growth of incipient women's movements because they provided women in Brazil and elsewhere in the Third World with two key resources: new funds poured into women's projects (including the mothers' clubs mentioned earlier); and new development discourses on gender that legitimated some emergent feminist claims even in Brazil's authoritarian political context.

The Beginnings of the Contemporary Women's Movements, 1964–1978

During the 1960s and early 1970s, mothers' clubs were created throughout São Paulo's urban periphery as a direct outgrowth of generalized community self-help efforts promoted by the Catholic Church. Signs of an incipient feminist consciousness were evident among some middle-class women in São Paulo.[19] Female participants of student movement organizations and militant organizations of the Left began meeting in small groups, usually to discuss Marxist-feminist texts from the United States and Europe in translation,[20] and a debate about the specificity of women's oppression unfolded in the alternative press.

From the start, however, some Brazilians distinguished between a legitimate Brazilian feminism, which dealt with sex discrimination in the context of a larger class struggle, and a second type, which was dismissed as one more instance of ideological imperialism. When noted North American feminist Betty Friedan visited Brazil in 1971, she was ridiculed by both the mainstream and the alternative press as an "ugly, bourgeois, manhater." In a paper delivered in 1972, journalist Rose Marie Muraro denounced Friedan's brand of feminism, arguing that there are

> two types of feminism: an older one, [which is] within the system and favors the system and which pits woman against man, is a neurotic expression of resentment by the dominated—that one merely increases the existing antagonism [against feminism]. More schizophrenia! But there is another which sees women's oppression within a more global social struggle and dialectically synthesizes that struggle for justice. And it is in that sense that I position myself [as a feminist].[21]

Similarly, prominent economist Paul Singer, in an article published in the alternative press in 1973, argued that

> it is necessary that ... we not merely transplant the feminist problematic developed in industrialized countries to our context. ... The great majority of Brazilian women do not have the conditions with which to free themselves from economic subjection to their husbands. ... Until those conditions are radically altered (and in this men and women are equally interested), the feminist movement in Brazil will have to present itself with the vital problem of women's work, if it does not want to speak in the name of a limited group who, under current circumstances, enjoys a privileged situation.[22]

When President Geisel's political decompression allowed for public commemorations of International Women's Year in São Paulo, Rio de Janeiro, and Belo Horizonte in 1975, this more politically acceptable feminism (from the point of view of the progressive political opposition) took full organizational form and came to predominate within the nascent Brazilian feminist movement until the late 1970s. The UN's proclamation of International Women's Year in 1975 and the regime's decision to endorse its three basic goals of equality, development, and peace enabled women who had been concerned with issues of gender inequality in Brazilian society to organize publicly for the first time. The proclamation also provided the still politically repressed left-wing opposition with a new forum for political action.

Under the sponsorship of the United Nations and the Metropolitan Episcopal Tribunal of São Paulo, the Encontro para o Diagnóstico da Mulher Paulista (Meeting for the Diagnosis of the Situation of Women in São Paulo) was held in October 1975. Attended by only 30 or 40 people, among them members of neighborhood associations, unions, Church-linked associations, political parties, and research and academic institutions, the *encontro* nevertheless represented the first step in the articulation of women's political claims on a citywide level.[23]

The final document resulting from this historic meeting identified a set of issues for further debate, research, and political action—issues that centered on women's political participation and their role in production. These issues were framed within an orthodox Marxist paradigmatic understanding of the "woman question," a view shared by secular and religious opposition activists alike, including many women militants:

> The orthodox view might be summarized as follows: inequality between the sexes originates with private ownership of the means of production and the sexual division of labor; therefore, women's subordination can only be overcome through anticapitalist struggle and socialist transformation. The practical implications of this theoretical view can be characterized as *integrationist:* Women must be *integrated* into the paid work force so they can gain class consciousness and *incorporated* into the revolutionary struggle so they can eventually help secure their own liberation as women.[24]

In keeping with Singer and Muraro's admonitions, all proposed areas of action and research emerging from this groundbreaking meeting focused on the "vital problem of women's work." It presented the need for women to organize "within a more global social struggle," negating any need for women to organize as women and as workers.

The conclusions of the *encontro* centered almost exclusively on the economic dimension of the discrimination suffered by women.[25] This dimension became the focus of the Centro de Desenvolvimento da Mulher Brasileira (CDMB, or Center for the Development of Brazilian Women), the organization founded by some *encontro* participants to advance the proposals there formulated, as well as those of other middle-class–based feminist organizations in São Paulo during the ensuing months.

Also in October 1975, *Brasil Mulher,* the first women's newspaper of the contemporary movement in Brazil, was founded in the city of Londrina in the state of Parana. Linked to the Feminine Amnesty Movement and created by recently released female political prisoners, the newspaper's first issues focused on women's involvement in movements for general social and political change, most especially on the need for women to reorganize at the grassroots level for political amnesty. The editors, privileged working-class women, targeted the "third-class citizens" of Brazilian society as their audience:

> This is not a woman's newspaper. Its objective is to be one more voice in the search for and reconquest of lost equality. Work which is destined for both men and women. We don't want to take refuge in biological differences in order to enjoy small masculine favors, at the same time that the state, constituted in masculine form, leaves us in a place comparable to that reserved for the mentally incompetent. We want to speak of the problems that are common to all the women of the world. We also want to speak of the solutions which have been found both here and in distant places; nevertheless, we want to discuss them within the context of our Brazilian and Latin American reality.[26]

During late 1975 and early 1976, the CDMB held a series of debates on the "woman question" at the Journalists' Union in São Paulo. A group of university women and former student movement participants who were present at those debates founded the women's newspaper *Nós Mulheres* in early 1976. Nós Mulheres was the first group in contemporary Brazil to openly refer to itself as feminist. The group's newspaper, like *Brasil Mulher,* targeted poor and working-class women as its principal readership. But unlike the early organizers of *Brasil Mulher,* Nós Mulheres also insisted that women must organize their own political space within the general struggle for emancipation and stressed the need for a feminist press within the progressive alternative press.

After 1976, these two newspapers became the principal voices of the growing feminist movement in Brazil. Through the Feminine Amnesty Movement's political network, *Brasil Mulher* created subgroups in several major cities and later, in 1976, also openly identified itself with feminism.

Most of the feminists I interviewed in the early 1980s recalled the years from 1975 to 1978 as a time of very elementary, undefined feminism, essentially economistic and confined to established Marxist categories of analysis. The principal question confronting these feminists was how to link women's specific needs to the need for general social transformation (which Brazilian feminist activists typically referred to as the tension between *o geral* and *o específico*).[27] The question was largely resolved either by concentrating on the "general" and subsuming the "specific" until after the revolution, or more commonly, by trying to "feminize popular struggles":

> We thought we couldn't raise the issue of contraception, for example, and call it feminist. ... We thought the struggle was a struggle for "rights" because the women in the periphery were involved in the struggle for running water, for day care, for schools, etc., because they were working with the values they had in terms of their roles as women. So our role [in *Brasil Mulher*] in those struggles was to "feminize" them. ... That was our theory. ... Our role was to reflect upon why they, [working-class women], were involved in that type of struggle. ... We saw ourselves as the vanguard. ... We were the ones with the information, the ones who could reflect and theorize,

and our role was to support women's organizations wherever they emerged and help women develop an analysis about why it was women who were engaged in those day-to-day survival struggles.[28]

Early feminists saw themselves as the "vanguard" of what was to be a united, cross-class, mass-based Brazilian women's movement. The legacy of the Left led early feminists to conceptualize women's oppression exclusively in class terms and to promote the expansion of the grassroots women's movement, which by the mid-1970s was making its presence felt throughout the urban periphery. Moraes has termed this period of feminist activism in São Paulo "the other women's feminism" (*feminismo da outra*). Working from orthodox Marxist worldviews, feminists focused on the struggles of poor and working-class women rather than reflecting on their own lives or on the gender-specific issues they shared with working-class women, which might have constituted a more organic basis for cross-class alliance-building.[29] Both feminist newspapers from 1975 to 1978 featured interviews with women factory workers, domestic servants, metal workers, agricultural workers, and so on, in spite of the fact that, as Moraes points out, their principal organizational contacts were among mothers' clubs and housewives' associations whose participants did not usually work outside the home.[30] As the day care, cost-of-living, and feminist amnesty movements grew, so did feminist determination to capture the political significance of those struggles and to articulate them within the larger opposition.

But there was another important dimension of popular women's organizations, which some feminists began to perceive as they worked more closely with these groups over the course of the 1970s. Women's organizations in the urban periphery had provided a new context within which poor and working-class women could share their experiences not only as residents of the *periferia* but also as wives, mothers, lovers—as women. When given the opportunity or the "ideological space," participants in grassroots movement groups discussed problems they shared in their marriages, their sexual lives, their desire to control fertility, their desire for more information about the world outside the domestic sphere, and their relationships to family and community—subjects that feminists initially thought would be taboo among women of the popular classes.

Many women I interviewed at Jardim Miriam and in other peripheral neighborhoods in São Paulo told me, for example, that their husbands did not want them to participate in community activities. One woman explained to Teresa Caldeira that this was "because a woman who participates is the owner of her own nose" and that independence often generated new conflicts in their marriages.[31] The feminist press was trying to portray women's struggle as a part of the "united struggle of men and women of the popular classes for a better life," but the working-class women they interviewed continually demonstrated their awareness that gender constrained their lives in ways not shared by the men of their class. When *Brasil Mulher* published the results of the First Congress of Women Metalworkers, held in 1978, for example, the interviewees themselves stressed the specificity of

women's oppression within class exploitation more clearly than the feminist journalists who covered the event:

> There's no unity among the women. The men are stronger, and that's why women are
> on the bottom. ... They are all men and they protect one another. The owner of the
> factory is a man and he thinks men work more. ... Woman works in the factory and
> in the home, she gets more worn out, she ages. And he sits around looking like a doll.
> ... Men only do housework when they don't have a woman to do it for them. ... I
> think housework should be divided between husband and wife if the woman works
> outside the home.[32]

By 1977–1978, some middle-class São Paulo feminists were also beginning to
differentiate socialist feminist political analysis and practice from that of the orthodox Left to explain women's subordination in both class- and gender-specific
terms. In a 1977 editorial, the women of *Nós Mulheres* cautioned their readers not
to subsume the feminist struggle within the class struggle in their efforts "to demonstrate that we are not against men, that we are not against this or that." They
tried to define more positively the need for women's emancipation as "an integral
part of the struggle for a more just, democratic society."

The editorial also turned the question, How is feminism related to the class
struggle? so prevalent among left-wing activists, intellectuals, and some feminists,
on its head, asking also how the class struggle was related to the true liberation of
women.

> The fact is that the feminist struggle is not just that, it goes beyond that. Woman also
> suffers a specific oppression because of the simple fact of being a woman. She has
> more difficulty finding employment, especially if she married and has children, she is
> dismissed from work if she marries or gets pregnant, when she works outside the
> home, she works as a double shift, she is solely responsible for domestic work and for
> the education of her children (a task which should, in many cases, be assumed by the
> state, and in others, by the couple). She constantly suffers from sexual assault, in the
> home, in the street, in the workplace. In sum, woman is not treated as a being with
> the same rights and the same duties as men. There are many men who think that
> woman is and should be treated like a being equal to men. But it is only women, be-
> cause this affects them directly, organized and struggling for their specific
> revindication, who will have the necessary strength to change this situation. We know
> that only in a society that guarantees good conditions of existence, of work, of study,
> and liberty and independence to organize freely ... will the conditions be present to
> reach true emancipation for women. In that sense it can also be said that the struggle
> for that type of society is an integral part of the struggle for women's emancipation.[33]

The 1978 International Women's Day (IWD) celebration provided the basis for
an emerging women's political platform. Along with stressing the gamut of issues
concerning the feminine side of the Brazilian class struggle (women's important
role in the struggle for democracy, political amnesty, the rising cost of living, improved social services and urban infrastructure, the need for a more just distribu-

tion of income, the lack of equal pay for equal work, and so on), the women's movement began calling attention to the politics of the private sphere, the family, and reproduction. IWD participants demanded changes in the laws regulating marriage and state support for female heads-of-household; the socialization of domestic labor through the creation of day care centers, recreation centers, and schools that would operate full time and serve meals to children; public laundries and restaurants; and state-sponsored consumer collectives. They protested the government's proposed "family planning" programs an antinatalist and asserted that "the knowledge and use of contraceptive methods should be a conquest of women themselves."[34] New feminist groups emerged throughout 1978, reflecting the diversity of interests addressed by the expanded definitions of feminist struggle.

Other strands of the Brazilian women's movement had also emerged in São Paulo by 1978. Women in the newly militant trade union movement held congresses for women in various occupational categories. In January 1978 the First Congress of Women Metalworkers was held in Osasco, and in June women in the chemical and pharmaceutical industries held their first congress. Like the feminist-initiated March 8 commemorations, these congresses protested the general conditions of the Brazilian working class and decried the unjust and unequal conditions of women's work. Union women denounced the lack of equal pay, the lack of opportunity for women to ascend the occupational ladder, the fact that women were the last hired and the first fired (especially if they married or became pregnant), and the blatant disregard of gender-specific labor legislation that established female workers' rights to paid maternity leave and crèches in the workplace. They called for the establishment of women's departments within the unions.[35]

In 1978–1979, two new liberation movements joined feminists in proclaiming their right to articulate specific claims within the general struggle for democracy and social justice. Afro-Brazilians organized to challenge the myth of racial democracy and to contest the subsumption of the struggle for racial equality within the larger class struggle.[36] Brazilian gays also raised their voices against sexual oppression.[37] And women, of course, joined the ranks of both these struggles. But many Black women militants initially shunned feminist groups that were predominantly white and that seldom addressed the specificity of Black women's oppression during this early period of feminist organizing, even as they embraced the "other women's feminism" in class terms. Similarly, lesbians at first were reticent to openly discuss their lifestyles within existing feminist organizations because early feminist discussions of sexuality studiously skirted the question of lesbianism, partly due to efforts to placate male allies in the Church and on the Left and partly due to rampant (sometimes internalized) homophobia.[38]

In short, by the late 1970s, a panoply of social and political movements, all vocally opposed to the continuation of military rule, began remapping the terrain of Brazilian civil society. And this generalized social and political mobilization had

important consequences for women's movement organizations and helped redefine the political demands. As the political climate became more open to demands for social change, the focus of most women's movement organizations
narrowed. Part of the reason that early women's groups, feminist and nonfeminist
alike, had focused on general as well as gender-specific issues was that the number
of public forums for protest was extremely limited. When International Women's
Year offered the opportunity for women to organize as women, other issues of
great import for Brazilian society as a whole were, of course, addressed by the new
women's organizations.

By the late 1970s, however, important sectors of both the working class[39] and
the middle and upper-middle classes had begun pressuring for an end to military
authoritarianism and its repressive social and economic policies. Although wom-
en's movement organizations continued to oppose military rule and capitalist exploitation, feminists increasingly turned their attention to issues such as reproductive rights, violence against women, and sexuality—issues too often ignored
by the male-dominated opposition.

Many neighborhood women's groups also began focusing on gender-specific
issues such as day care and domestic labor (rather than gender-related issues such
as running water, sewage, etc.) after 1978. This shift was partially the result of the
changing political practice of those groups and the resistance they sometimes encountered from parallel, male-dominated community organizations and the
Church. By 1978, the politicization of gender among popular women's groups was
also partially attributable to their increased contact with middle-class feminist
groups. Several neighborhood women's organizations, such as the Associação das
Donas de Casa, which claimed over 400 members throughout São Paulo's Eastern
Zone by the late 1970s, worked closely with feminist groups after 1975.

The Consolidation of a Feminist
Political Identity, 1979–1981

According to most observers and participants, 1979 through 1981 were the peak
mobilizational years of the contemporary Brazilian women's movement. New
feminist groups proliferated throughout major Brazilian cities, numbering close
to 100 by 1981. Dozens of new neighborhood women's associations blossomed in
Brazil's urban periphery.

Feminist groups together with other strands of the women's movement organized citywide women's congresses that drew thousands of women of all social
classes and political affiliations. Those congresses and other movement activities
drew the attention of both the mainstream and the alternative media to women's
political mobilization and to their gender-specific political claims. The media as a
whole devoted a good deal of coverage to most women's movement events and
protests after 1979—from feminist academic lectures or symposia to popular protests for day care at the mayor's office. Television networks and radio stations created new women's programs, which, along with the traditional focus on cooking,

fashion, and makeup, also occasionally featured interviews with women active in feminist groups or the day care movement, or documentaries and editorials addressing such previously untouchable subjects as sexuality, virginity, contraception, and divorce.[40]

As the media extended its coverage of women's issues, the political opposition intensified its outreach to women's organizations of all types. As the women's movements grew, so did the male-dominant opposition's determination to take advantage of the political capital represented by organized female constituencies. By 1979, the women's movement was a burgeoning political movement that seemed to include women of all social classes, races, and ideologies. The 1979 International Women's Day celebrations symbolized its growing social and political reach. IWD events were held in Salvador, Rio de Janeiro, Belo Horizonte, and three events were organized in the city of São Paulo alone (other commemorations were held in Campinas and São Carlos in the state of São Paulo).

The 1979 First Paulista Women's Congress drew nearly 1,000 participants. The organizing commission's program highlighted issues of women's day-to-day lives: domestic labor, discrimination in the workplace and occupational training for women, fertility control, sexuality, the lack of day care centers, and women's political participation. In small consciousness-raising–like groups, participants discussed the issues that had become the standard banners of feminist groups, women's neighborhood associations, women trade unionists, and other strands of the women's movement—equal pay for equal work, better schools, urban infrastructure, and so on. But as the *Folha de São Paulo* noted, "For the first time the question of feminine sexuality was discussed, until now an issue which had taken second place as a function of problems such as work, day care, political participation."[41] For the first time at a large public gathering, women learned of their shared feelings of dissatisfaction or lack of fulfillment in their sexual relations, their common problems in controlling fertility, and they began to identify power relations between men and women as one of the principal sources of those problems.

Women of the popular classes also pointed to the inadequate living conditions in the urban periphery and to the exhausting labor that they and their spouses performed as reasons for their lack of sexual satisfaction. But all insisted that male and female social conditioning aggravated those material problems. The most radical gender-specific issues were raised by women of the popular classes, the very women who both the Church and the Left had insisted were unconcerned with such issues as sexuality or contraception.[42] Some of their declarations during the congress were reproduced in the alternative newspaper *Em Tempo*:

> Women suffer much more with problems of sex. I married when I was 14 years old. My father said that I was three years older on the documents. I have been living with my husband for thirty years. Sometimes I rebel and wonder why I ever got married. When the girls were born, I slept with them, after working like a dog all day long. He never helped me, slept in the other room. Then, when the girls were still, he would

come and get me. He would fulfill himself, and that was it. Me, never. I know I always repressed that side, sex. But because of my daughters I put up with everything. I live for them.[43]

Em Tempo also described the emergence of other "private" issues during the Paulista Congress:

> Then, sexual oppression appeared; of the double standard of morality which allows men the practice of nonmonogamy, and punishes women on the basis of stigma of single motherhood; of the sadistic doctors at the Hospital das Clinicas (among others) who practice curettage in cold blood, whenever they suspect that a patient interned for hemorrhaging had induced an abortion. The existence of machismo represented in the physical violence which many women suffer and the very existence of a professional category known as prostitution—that is, in women who sell their own bodies. ... Machismo which imposes the weight of contraception on women, which uses her as a sexual object, as an article for bed and table.[44]

And in summarizing the political significance of the congress, the same article proclaimed:

> The proposals presented were innumerable: they reflected the need for a cultural revolution, the inseparable complement of economic transformation. Declaring the Brazilian woman has no guarantees when she gets pregnant, given undernourishment, the lack of medical attention, many voices at the Congress declared that Brazilian woman has no right to choose and that in the face of an unwanted pregnancy, clandestine abortion is her only alternative, practiced by quacks in the case of women who lack resources (that is, the overwhelming majority of Brazilian women), or in clinics which charge exorbitant prices. ... The capacity to create a climate of enthusiasm, solidarity, and trust, and to also touch the emotions of participants ... led to spontaneous demands that "we cannot say good-bye now ... we cannot wait till the next Congress: we must continue to struggle together."[45]

The 1979 Paulista Congress thus set forth one of the women's movement's unique contributions to the struggle for a democratic Brazil, proclaiming that power relations in the family, in daily life, in civil society and not just in the State and political society, must also be democratized. After 1979, the movement began expanding the horizons of the feminist political project, moving beyond orthodox Marxist paradigmatic solutions to the woman question and demanding the cultural as well as political and economic transformation of Brazilian society.

An organization composed of São Paulo's women's groups, called Coordination, was formed to advance the conclusions of the First Paulista Women's Congress and consolidate the ties of solidarity established during that unprecedented event. The more radical issues raised during the Paulista Congress did not make their way into its final document, however, due to movement participants' fears of losing important allies in the Church and in the Left.[46] That document highlighted three areas that were to constitute the axes of concerted, unified movement actions during 1980—the struggle for publicly financed day care, the demand for equal pay for equal work, and the protest of a proposed Program for the Prevention of High-Risk Pregnancy—while claiming "the right and the social conditions which would really permit women to opt to have or not have children."[47]

The demand for day care immediately reverberated throughout São Paulo's urban periphery. The women from the new Coordination contacted all of the neighborhood women's associations that had been working for day care in an isolated fashion and called a citywide meeting, attended by hundreds of middle- and working-class women. Regional coordinations were formed, corresponding to the principal administrative regions of the city, and weekly meetings were held to develop a united strategy that would strengthen the heretofore disparate local efforts to secure public day care facilities. Women's confinement to the domestic sphere and their exclusive social responsibility for "caring for the workers of tomorrow" became the axis of the new united movement's political claims, and the State became the principal target of the demands of the Movimento de Luta por Creches (MLC, or Struggle for Day Care Movement).

The First Paulista Congress also encouraged the creation of new grassroots women's organizations in São Paulo. Twenty-nine new neighborhood women's associations were created in 1979–1980 in São Paulo's Eastern Zone alone.[48] The MLC helped new day care groups get started in the urban periphery and politicized the day care issue within existing mothers' clubs and housewives' associations. The number of core participants in existing feminist groups also grew considerably in the immediate aftermath of the 1979 congress. New feminist organizations were created as well. Among these was the Frente de Mulheres Feministas (Feminist Women's Front), a group growing out of women's professional and academic networks that worked to disseminate feminist ideas through the media, the arts, and academia. Also, lesbians active in both the gay and feminist movements founded Grupo Ação Lésbica-Feminista (Lesbian-Feminist Action Group, or GALF); sexuality and the right to sexual pleasure was featured prominently in GALF's political agenda, which also aimed to challenge the sexism prevailing among gay men and the homophobia found among many feminists in São Paulo. The Paulistas took their congress's proposals to the First National Women's Congress, organized by Rio feminists, which drew over 30 groups from several major cities. The National Women's Congress endorsed the political banners raised during the Paulista Congress, propelling Paulista women's organizations into the forefront of the nascent Brazilian women's movement.

In 1979, the regime's concession to opposition demands for political amnesty, spearheaded by the Feminine Amnesty Movement, and the Figueredo administration's expansion of Geisel's decompression (now termed *abertura,* or political "opening"), infused new energies into all opposition currents, including the feminist movement. As one of the feminists who had remained in Brazil put it, "Returning exiles literally flooded feminist groups in São Paulo." The feminists who had "stayed behind," sometimes enduring political persecution and internal exile,

expressed some resentment toward the "supposedly sophisticated European" re-
turnees. But resentment soon gave way to collaboration as the *exiladas* shared
their experiences of feminist activities unheard of in Brazil until the late 1970s.
The *exiladas* back from France and Italy, for example, had participated in
proreproductive choice movements in predominantly Catholic countries and had
confronted Church resistance to the more radical issues raised by feminism.

Returning exiles elaborated on the concept of movement autonomy, one that
readily caught on among Brazilian feminists struggling to define their relationship to the political opposition as a whole. In a 1979 booklet entitled "O
Movimento de Mulheres no Brazil," the Associação das Mulheres explained why
the women's movements' organizational autonomy came to be perceived as essential by Brazilian feminist organizations:

> When we say that the feminist movement searches for its own organizational forms,
> we have in mind the articulation of two essential and inseparable initiatives. On the
> one hand, the discussion—among women—of questions which speak to us directly,
> our sexuality and the image we have constructed of ourselves, as well as our role in
> the family and our insertion into the process of production. On the other hand, the
> generalization of those discussions—and the demands that emerge from them—
> within society as a whole. But, above all, we believe that this movement must be au-
> tonomous, because we are certain that no form of oppression will ever be overcome
> unless those directly interested in overcoming it take the struggle into their own
> hands.[49]

The São Paulo women's movement Coordination, established by the original
sponsoring groups of the First Paulista Congress, continued meeting on a weekly
basis throughout 1979. At first composed of some 15 or 20 women representing a
dozen or so feminist and other women's movement organizations, Coordination
welcomed from 150 to 200 women, representing 56 groups. By the beginning of
1980, it included groups engaged in any type of political, union, professional, or
community activity concerning women.[50]

Many of the union, professional, and community organizations that joined Coordination in 1979 were directly linked (ideologically and structurally) to the various leftist sectarian political tendencies, such as the Movimento Revolucionario 8
de Outubro, the Partido Comunista do Brasil, and others (many of which were
part of the MDB [Movimento Democrático Brasileiro, or Brazilian Democratic
Movement] electoral front), that had reemerged in full force after political amnesty was granted in 1979. These groups viewed the 1980 Second Paulista Women's
Congress and the expanding women's movement as a whole as opportunities to
recruit new militant members among a previously untapped constituency—
women's organizations.[51] According to one of the early members of the CDMB
(after 1980 the Centro da Mulher Brasileira—Setor São Paulo, or CMB), the feminists themselves "became the minority [within Coordination] even though we
[feminists] did the bulk of the infrastructural organizational work."[52]

Consequently, setting the agenda for the Second Paulista Congress became a political and ideological struggle among the multitude of political groupings and strands of the women's movement represented within Coordination. Feminists of all political stripes insisted that the second congress should advance the issues raised at the first congress and mobilize women around new issues that had emerged within the women's movements during the course of 1979–1980. Violence against women was one such issue. Several "crimes of passion" committed by male celebrities and assassinations of women by jealous husbands or lovers because of alleged infidelity and committed in the defense of male "honor" incited generalized outrage and vehement protests by feminist groups in several major Brazilian cities.[53]

But other mixed groups (i.e., male and female, like the MR-8, whose legal front was the newspaper *Hora do Povo*, or HP) insisted that the congress should mobilize women around such general, pressing political issues as the convocation of a national, sovereign constituent assembly to overturn authoritarian rule. In response, representatives of some grassroots women's associations and feminist groups argued that IWD was the only major forum for the articulation of the women's movements' specific political claims and that, moreover, by 1980 numerous political spaces existed within the opposition for women and men, together, to discuss such things as the Constituent Assembly.

In contrast to the more unified and politically homogeneous First Paulista Congress, clear political lines divided many of the discussions during the second. Members of the MR-8 and other political tendencies took over many of the discussion groups, even when group leaders had been designated by Coordination weeks in advance and pushed the discussions in the direction of their predetermined political agendas. The Church also intervened in an organized fashion, packing the discussions on contraception and abortion with members of Church-linked groups such as CEBs (Comunidades Eclesiais de Base, or Christian Base Communities), mothers' clubs, and Catholic Workers' Action who opposed any form of "artificial" family planning.

The events of the second day of the 1980 congress distinguished the orthodox Left's "woman question" from the "socialist feminist question" once and for all, with lasting implications for Paulista women's movements' political strategies. The agenda for the day was women's political participation. After the proposals of the discussion groups during the previous day were read by the chair, representatives from union groups, known to be linked to HP and other sectarian offshoots of the Brazilian Communist Party, demanded the floor. They claimed that "working women's voices had not been heard at the Congress," that "the women in the periphery are starving to death and nobody is paying any attention to that,"[54] and that the day's agenda therefore should focus on the Constituent Assembly, general unemployment, and other such issues that were featured in the platforms of their sectarian organizations. These women were booed by the vast majority of the congress participants, who were anxious to get on with the preestablished agenda. Accompanied by several men from their groups, sectarian women attempted to muscle their way toward the main microphone, and mayhem ensued in the auditorium as other women tried to prevent them from doing so.

In the aftermath of this chaotic incident, several Paulista feminist groups formulated a joint resolution, condemning the actions of the sectarian political tendencies, to be read at the closing session of the Second Paulista Congress.[55] The motion "against attempts at political-partisan manipulation and distortion of the Congress's objectives" was signed by the great majority of organizations present (including some of the ones responsible for the manipulation and distortion) and received a standing ovation during the final plenary. As journalist Maria Carneiro da Cunha noted,

> The purpose of this congress was the discussion of women's specific issues. But in bringing together such a large number of people, many of them with divergent political interests, it became practically impossible to avoid that there be attempts at manipulation on the part of diverse political-partisan currents, more preoccupied with propagandizing their 'slogans' than in discussing women's *problematique,* in spite of the efforts of various members of the coordination to impede this from happening. That is, that women serve once again as the *massa de manobra* (manipulable mass) for interests which are not their own.[56]

The consolidation of a distinct feminist political identity within the larger women's movement began as a direct consequence of the conflicts that occurred during the Second Paulista Congress. Where in the early 1970s, the Brazilian Left had identified two kinds of feminism—one acceptable and one unacceptable—Brazilian socialist feminists now began distinguishing between two kinds of Left—one acceptable, which acknowledged the specificity of women's oppression and respected the organizational autonomy of the movement, and another unacceptable, which subsumed women's struggle within the class struggle and attempted to instrumentalize and manipulate women's movement organizations.

After the second congress, this distinct feminist political identity was solidified at a statewide feminist meeting, attended by some 150 women, held at Valinhos in June 1980. After Valinhos, feminists undertook new types of political activities. The "generic" activities of earlier years gave way to more "genderic," issue-focused ones. Women from all existing feminist groups rallied around three political banners raised at the Valinhos meeting. They created an umbrella organization to provide counseling and social services to victims of sexual abuse and domestic violence, which later became a new feminist group, SOS-Mulher. A feminist commission for family planning and against population control was formed. And a new women's newspaper, *Mulherio,* which reflected the changed political perspective of the feminist movement, was founded.

During 1980, Paulista feminists staged protests in support of prostitutes and in solidarity with the Madres of the Plaza de Mayo in Argentina. They also joined the gay movement and the Black movement in a protest march against the police chief's efforts to remove from the streets of downtown São Paulo gays, Blacks, prostitutes, transvestites, and other "undesirables." SOSs were also created in seven other major cities in subsequent years. Women in Recife organized SOS-Corpo, which provided gynecological and contraceptive counseling to women in poor and working-class neighborhoods. And explicitly feminist groups emerged in cities in the regions outside the Brazilian industrial triangle, such as Goiania, Fortaleza, Porto Alegre, Curitiba, Florianopolis, Salvador, and many others.

Though the Cost of Living and Amnesty Movements had been absorbed by the political opposition after the 1978 elections, the Struggle for Day Care Movement continued to grow during 1989 and won significant concessions from local government officials. Grassroots women's organizations also proliferated throughout urban Brazil, and some initial steps were taken to organize rural women workers in the interior.

During 1980–1981, feminists in São Paulo asserted a political identity and purpose distinct from that of the orthodox Left, consolidated links to popular women's associations, and achieved wider public acceptability (reflected in more favorable media coverage of the movement).

En*gender*ing the Democratic Transition: Articulating Feminist Claims Within Political Parties and the State, 1981–1988

During the 1970s, the formal political arena was not perceived as relevant to the feminist transformational project. Feminist politics centered on working with popular women's organizations and on continuing to struggle in civil society against the authoritarian social, political, and economic order. But as the legal political opposition began gaining electoral strength after 1974 and especially after opposition parties gained control of some state and municipal governments in 1982, feminists had to rethink their posture vis-à-vis institutional politics. Suddenly, advancing some sort of feminist policy agenda appeared viable, at least at the state and local levels.

Some "autonomous" feminists, who after the Second Paulista Women's Congress and the Valinhos meeting had severed organizational, though not necessarily ideological, ties to militant leftist parties and extralegal opposition organizations, eagerly signed on to the legal electorally successful opposition parties in the early 1980s. Feminist party militants argued that if parties translated basic feminist demands such as equal pay for equal work, publicly financed day care, and safe, accessible, noncoercive family planning into programmatic objectives, they could perhaps (with the help of feminists) tap into this female base of political support. Because rigid authoritarian controls had been in effect during the 1960s and 1970s, opposition parties still had quite precarious social bases and therefore readily courted women's movement support by incorporating at least the more

digestible items of the feminist agenda into party platforms. The parties' courtship of women's movements confounded feminist activists who for the first time
since the inception of second-wave Brazilian feminism had to wrestle with the
question of whether parties and elections might prove to be useful vehicles in the
struggle against women's subordination.

The increased importance of electoral politics after 1980 had two important
consequences for the Brazilian feminist movement. Old political and partisan divisions among movement participants were reopened, resulting in new forms of
ideological struggle *within* the feminist movement. And as legal parties of the recently divided opposition scrambled to secure votes for the 1982 elections, there
was renewed partisan struggle *over* the organized constituencies and
mobilizational potential of the women's movement.[57]

The opposition party, the MDB, had been gaining electoral strength since 1974.
In an effort to stop its electoral ascent, President João Batista Figueredo decreed a
new party law in 1979, dissolving the two-party system in force in 1966[58] and thus
forcibly dividing the partisan opposition.

As the new parties moved rapidly to consolidate their social bases of support,
opposition sectors basically aligned themselves behind two distinct, and at times,
antagonistic, strategies: (1) maintaining the unity of an ideologically diverse opposition front for the purpose of defeating the regime electorally in 1982 and ensuring the transition to liberal democracy or (2) creating ideologically distinct
opposition parties whose programs would address the substantive concerns of diverse social groups and thus would consolidate the full spectrum of oppositional
tendencies in civil society. Among women's organizations and other social movement groups in São Paulo, these two distinct political strategies congealed into
support for either the Partido do Movimento Democrático Brasileiro (PMDB, the
Party of the Brazilian Democratic Movement), the "democratic" front and the direct political heir of the MDB; or the PT (Partido dos Trabalhadores, or the Workers' Party), a new political party with roots in the new trade unionism of the late
1970s.

By late 1981, partisan rivalries had exacerbated a number of underlying political
tensions within feminist movement organizations.[59] In March 1981, for example,
two competing International Women's Day celebrations were held simultaneously
in São Paulo. One was organized by party activists and women linked to the sectarian groups who had disrupted the proceedings at the Second Paulista Congress
(now labeled the "the políticas"), the other by autonomous women's organizations. Ideological and strategic differences also generated splits in some groups
and led to the eventual dissolution of others. The divisions within the feminist
movement after 1981 were not necessarily based either on partisan differences or
on differing conceptions of feminism (except in the case of groups tied specifically to the various communist parties). The real basis for the divisions appears to
have been over the most appropriate short-term strategy for the pursuit of gen-

der-based social change given the enforced fragmentation of the political opposition and the upcoming elections.

Some feminists believed that liberal democracy must first be consolidated before any further gains could be made in securing women's rights and that feminists could promote significant change only from within a democratically elected state government. These women tended to support the PMDB in São Paulo, which appeared to be the most pragmatic political vehicle through which to complete the democratic transition. Many women who had come into the movement through professional or academic networks were among the principal feminist supporters of the PMDB.

Other feminists, many of whom had previous political experience in the New Left and student movements of the late 1960s and early 1970s, saw the PT as the potential expression of social movements at the level of institutional politics, as the *"retomada dum sonho"* (the resurgence of a dream) of class struggle, which had been crushed by the repressive apparatus of the State during the early 1970s. Still other feminist movement participants mistrusted either partisan option, fearing the subordination of the women's movement to the goals of political parties.[60] They fiercely defended the absolute political, ideological, and organizational autonomy of the women's movement.

As partisan rivalries intensified, several feminist movement organizations began to feel the strain. Some groups—such as the Centro da Mulher Brasileira, Frente de Mulheres Feministas, and Sociedade Brasil-Mulher—were almost completely demobilized, and partisan tensions contributed to the total dissolution of other groups such as the Associação das Mulheres. The feminist organizations most adversely affected by partisan rivalries were those generic feminist groups that could be described as federations or umbrella organizations for a wide variety of political activities, each informed by distinct conceptions of general social transformation.

The groups that survived partisan tensions were those with specialized projects or with a single-issue focus, such as Centro Informação Mulher, SOS-Mulher, Grupo Ação Lésbica-Feminista, and Sexualidade e Política. These groups were better able to resist partisan polarization as a consequence of shared, concrete organization goals—such as combating violence against women in the case of SOS-Mulher or combating heterosexism in the case of Grupo Ação Lésbica-Feminista.[61]

Partisan tensions were also less acute within neighborhood-based women's movement organizations. In fact, parties made little effort to recruit women into the local party cells established in the urban periphery. Those that did met with limited success, as working-class movement women expressed their continued belief that party politics was "men's business."

As middle-class feminists claimed political space within the new political parties of the opposition, many increasingly relied on traditional lobbying and interest-group tactics. Their ties to neighborhood-based women's groups gradually weakened. As a result, one critical source of Brazilian feminism's political leverage and legitimacy—its gender-based alliance with mothers' clubs and other working-class women's organizations—was partially eroded. The movement-oriented feminism of the mid- to late 1970s was beginning to give way to the interest-group feminist strategies that would prevail in the 1980s.

After 1982, the arenas of gender struggle rapidly multiplied as movement activists began articulating their demands in a wide variety of institutional and noninstitutional settings. In the mid- to late 1970s, the women's movement had attempted to centralize and unify its political work through such ill-fated mechanisms as Coordination. Women's concurrent participation in militant organizations of the Left or other progressive organizations, referred to as *dupla militância,* or "double militancy," was viewed as a double political load. One worked in political organizations for general social change, and then one worked separately in women's groups to ameliorate women's specific oppression. In the early 1980s, feminists took their gender-specific political demands into their work in community organizations, Black and gay liberation groups, the ecology movement, professional associations, and political parties. After 1983, many would take this revised understanding of double militancy into their work in the new opposition-led state and municipal governments.

Significantly, other movement activists organized exclusively in women-only groups around women's issues. After multiple confrontations and years of struggle around feminist issues within sexist "progressive" organizations, they mistrusted male-dominated parties and insisted on organizational and ideological autonomy both from parties and the State. This posture ensured that the women's movements would not be fully absorbed or institutionalized by the democratic opposition. The persistence of autonomous feminist organizing provided women working within parties and the State with a legitimating political constituency.

By the early 1980s, the full spectrum of opposition parties had endorsed, if not fully embraced, core aspects of the feminist agenda. As the new political parties courted the hundreds of grassroots women's organizations and competed for the allegiance of the female electorate, they turned for help to the middle-class feminists who had been working with popular women's organizations since the early 1970s. Interest-group feminism gained newfound political clout.

During the 1982 electoral campaign, all the opposition parties paid unprecedented attention both to the female electorate and to organized female constituencies.

Acutely aware of the free-floating political currency represented by the hundreds of grassroots women's groups and dozens of feminist organizations, opposition candidates for local, state, and national office featured issues such as day care, family planning, women's health, equal pay for equal work, domestic labor, and other women's issues in their campaign materials.

Even the reconstituted government party, the PDS (Partido Democrático Social, or Democratic Social Party), jumped on the prowoman bandwagon. It created a national women's division, coopted feminist discourse, and purported to be a longtime ally of the feminist cause. In the State of São Paulo, PDS gubernatorial candidate and former mayor Reynaldo de Barros, for example, claimed to be a champion of the working woman's struggle for day care. Indeed, by the end of the de Barros administration, 141 day care centers (the so-called *creches diretas* entirely financed by the municipal government) had been constructed in the county of São Paulo. De Barros made crèches a rallying cry of his campaign, stating in numerous campaign materials that "when Reynaldo de Barros came into office São Paulo only had three day care centers. Now São Paulo has 333! The 333 were in the planning stages, at best, though de Barros had further serviced his political aspirations—in classical neopopulist fashion—by preappointing the directors of all unconstructed day care centers.

Most opposition parties also formed women's divisions. But thanks to the efforts of feminists active in the opposition, these did not resemble mere women's auxiliaries created by the government party and other political parties in the past. Several parties, most notably the PMDB and the PT, presented women candidates for the elections of 1982—and several of these candidates had extensive experience in or links to women's movement organizations.[62]

Taking Feminism into
the State, 1983–1985

During the 1982 campaign, a subgroup of the PMDB Women's Division, the Grupo de Estudos da Situação da Mulher (Study Group on Women's Situation), had formulated a specific "Proposal of PMDB Women for the Montoro/Quercia Government." The proposal was to be implemented and supervised by a Conselho da Condição Feminina (Council on Women's Condition), a new state consultative council that would "serve as an instrument for a global policy destined to eliminate the discriminations suffered by women.[63] The four proposed areas of action included women's work and the elimination of salary and employment discrimination, women's health and reproductive rights, day care, and the protection of women against violence.

After the overwhelming victory of the PMDB in São Paulo, discussions of how the Council on Women's Condition would in fact be constituted, whether a women's department would be preferable to a council, and which areas of gender-specific government policy would take precedence under the new administration remained a closed, partisan discussion within the PMDB. Those sectors of the women's movement that had supported the PMDB during the campaign were now in power and the opposition women (members or sympathizers of the PT) and nonpartisan women's movement activists saw themselves as marginalized from the decisionmaking process, which was to define the new state administration's policy toward women.

The result was that even before the PMDB had officially announced its plan of action, strong opposition to the council was already emerging among the ranks of grassroots-based feminist groups, the more politicized neighborhood women's groups, and the day care movement. This incipient position criticized the plan for the council as co-optation of the women's movement by the state and labeled the feminists involved in policy formulation "unrepresentative" of the women's movement as a whole.

Created by Governor Franco Montoro on April 4, 1983, the Conselho Estadual da Condição Feminina (State Council on Women's Condition) was granted broad advisory powers but had no executive or implementation powers of its own. Nor did it have an independent budget, being totally dependent on the governor's civilian cabinet for financial and technical assistance. The decree made no mention of the State Program in Defense of Women's Rights, developed and proposed by PMDB feminists. Instead, the council was granted the power to "propose measures and activities which aim at the defense of the rights of women into socioeconomic, political and cultural life … ; incorporate preoccupations and suggestions manifested by society and opine about denunciations which are brought before it … support projects developed by organs, governmental or not, concerning women, and promote agreements with similar organizations and institutions."[64]

The avowed purpose of the council was to give women influence over several areas of state administration rather than isolate them in a women's department. The council's inclusion of representatives of civil society and representatives from several key executive departments made it an innovative government mechanism for promoting gender-based social change. However, since the council was given no executive power, its influence on policy was necessarily limited, though its very creation unquestionably represented an advance for women relative to the previous PDS administration.[65]

The women who made up the original council were aware of the problematic nature of the council's relationship to both the male-dominated state apparatus and the autonomous women's movement. In one of its earliest official publications, Eva Blay, then president of the council, addressed the contradictory character of this new "women's space" within the State apparatus.

> Another question to be profoundly considered refers to the political-administrative form chosen [to represent women's interests within the new government]: a Council. Social movements, and among them, women's movements, desire and should guarantee their autonomy vis-à-vis the state. To be part of the state apparatus in order to be able to utilize it from within but at the same time maintain the freedom to criticize it is an extremely complex question. Nevertheless, this difficulty must not constitute an obstacle which paralyzes the participatory process. The [political-administrative] form devised to avoid the reproduction of vices typical of the traditional [political] structure is the creation of a Council which has a majority representation of sectors of civil society. The mechanisms of selection [of said representatives] have yet to be

defined as it is hoped that organized groups or independent feminists will pronounce their opinions on the subject.[66]

The creation of the council in and of itself remobilized the women's movement in São Paulo. Feminist groups and other women's movement organizations had to recast their political priorities so that they could be effectively channeled through the council or else risk having their demands manipulated by the PMDB administration for its own political gain.

In response to the new, more democratic climate, women's movement activists developed a dual political strategy. These seemingly divergent feminist strategies instead proved to be complementary. Though initially emerging from significant tactical disagreements among feminist activists—some took their struggle into parties and the State and others continued to focus their energies on combating gender power imbalances in society—in effect, a dual, or two-pronged, political strategy took shape over the course of the mid- to late 1980s that enabled Brazilian feminism to achieve considerable policy influence. The women who won minimal access to the State through PMDB party activism moved to consolidate and institutionalize political gains made during the preelection period. They pursued an interest group–oriented strategy akin to that which typifies liberal feminist pressure groups in the United States and Western Europe. The council became their principal access point to state policymaking arenas.

Though a small sector of the organized movement continued to view the council as an instance of State co-optation, most activists reformulated their policy goals and rethought the movement's relationship to the State. They focused on new strategies for influencing council policy and preventing state co-optation. After 1983, feminists "outside" the State put pressure on both the council and the PMDB São Paulo administration to advance the movement's more radical goals. This pressure kept council members responsive to a grassroots constituency (and indirectly legitimated the claims of women working within the State). They continued engaging in grassroots-based or movement-oriented politics, relying on protest actions, petitions, rallies, and other forms of autonomous organizing rather than on direct contact with policymakers or politicians.

As a result of this two-pronged strategy, feminism had a subversive impact on some state policies affecting women during the mid- to late 1980s.[67] For example, in 1983, under pressure from the International Monetary Fund (IMF) and the international aid and financial communities, the still-military-controlled federal government began formulating what the opposition (both feminist and nonfeminist) perceived to be a comprehensive population control program. As a counteroffensive, the autonomous women's movement organized a series of study groups, protest actions, and conferences aimed at preventing contraceptive abuses such as the arbitrary distribution of birth control pills to poor women.

In July 1984, the Fourth National Feminist Meeting, held in São Paulo and attended by 97 women from 33 feminist organizations, focused on the issues of women's health and family planning to develop a feminist position on reproductive rights in order to contest antinatalist policy proposals at the state and national levels. The feminist position began to take definitive shape during the remaining months of 1984.[68]

In September and October 1984, follow-up regional meetings were organized in Rio and in São Paulo, and in November of that year, several feminist groups in São Paulo organized the First National Meeting on Women's Health, held in the city of Itapecirica and attended by over 400 women from 19 Brazilian states. The *Carta de Itapecirica,* elaborated by conference participants, called for "the participation of women's groups in the elaboration, execution, and inspection of women's health programs, sex education for all the population, the reclaiming of popular and feminist wisdom against the excessive medicalization [of women's health], and a revalorization of natural forms of life and health."[69]

The São Paulo Council on Women's Condition supported the movement's initiatives and steadfastly opposed State population control while advocating safe, accessible, noncoercive family planning. The council's Commission on Women's Health argued that if São Paulo's Women's Health Program (which emphasized contraception) was properly administered and accompanied by popular education, it would advance the status of women by enabling women of all social classes to make informed reproductive choices. As a direct consequence of the council's sustained efforts, the São Paulo Health Department made the Women's Health Program one of its programmatic and budgetary priorities for 1985.

After months of deliberation within the council, it was agreed that family planning representatives, trained and supervised by the Department of Health in conjunction with the council's Commission on Women's Health, would supervise the implementation of the Program for Women's Health in all 17 subdivisions in the state of São Paulo. The council also helped the women's movement gain access to the policy implementation process, urging the Department of Health to hold monthly public forums to bring State health policy planners, employees of the public health network, and movement participants active in grassroots sex education together to discuss the progress of the program.[70] The Council on Women's Condition also pressured the Ministry of Health to create a commission on reproductive rights to help promote a safe, accessible, and noncoercive federal family planning policy.

In supervising the implementation of family-planning policy at the state level, the original council accomplished what the autonomous women's movement could never have accomplished on its own due to its position outside the State power structure. The women's movement in turn organized numerous discussions on family planning and closely monitored the council's and the Department and Ministry of Health's deliberations and policy proposals. Unquestionably, such consistent, gender-conscious political pressure from within civil society made the PMDB state government more responsive to the council's proposals.

The council in turn devised and oversaw a number of innovative public policies that addressed the needs and concerns of Paulista women, maintaining consistent, organized, and gender-conscious political pressure within the local state apparatus. In addition to the policy initiative discussed previously, for example, the council's Commission on Violence Against Women persuaded the São Paulo secretary of justice to create the first *delegacia da mulher* (DDM) in August 1985—a police precinct staffed entirely by specially trained female officers to process cases of rape, sexual abuse, and domestic violence.[71] The State's groundbreaking recognition of this gender-specific aspect of crime was unprecedented in Brazil, and indeed the women's-precinct structure is unparalleled elsewhere in the world. Again, on this issue the council's effectiveness in promoting policies that directly address the concrete needs of Paulista women as women was partially due to the São Paulo women's movement's constant protest actions and public education campaigns around the issue of violence against women.

Due to the fluidity of the transitional political conjuncture, a number of innovative policies of benefit to women were implemented at the state and local levels after 1983. After the installation of 11 opposition-led state governments in March 1983, feminists secured "women's spaces" within local government structures—Councils on the Status of Women were established not only in São Paulo but also in Minas Gerais in 1983 and subsequently in 34 other states and municipalities. On December 19, 1986, the São Paulo State Assembly voted to institutionalize the State Council on Women's Condition, making it a permanent organ of the state's government.

When the first civilian president in 21 years, José Sarney, took office in 1985, a National Council on Women's Rights (Conselho Nacional dos Direitos da Mulher, or CNDM) was created within the Ministry of Justice, and women with long-standing ties to Brazilian feminist groups and other women's movement organizations secured the majority of seats within this new government body.

Though in some cases these councils were created as political showcases intended to shore up support for male politicians, in others they represented legitimate concessions to women's movement organizations that were able to gain access to State policymaking through the councils. These transitional feminist inroads into formal politics were extremely important to the relative policy success of Brazilian women's movements in the mid- to late 1980s. And from 1985 to 1988, it was through such access points to the State and political society that feminists waged new policy battles.

From 1985 through 1988, the National Council on Women's Rights intervened in favor of women in federal agrarian reform deliberations, promoted a national day care policy, implemented antisexist educational reforms, and expanded its outreach to women in civil society through its access to government-controlled media.

From 1986 to 1988, when Brazil's new democratic constitution was being formulated in Congress, the CNDM worked with independent feminist and other women's movement organizations throughout Brazil to develop a women's agenda to be included in the constitution. In 1986, the widely circulated "Letter from Women to the Constituent Assembly" called for an expanded definition of democracy that encompassed the democratization of both public and private life:

> For us, women, the full exercise of citizenship means, yes, the right to representation, a voice, and a role in public life, but at the same time, it also implies dignity in daily life, which the law can inspire and should ensure, the right to education, to health, to security, to a family life free of traumas. Women's vote brings with it a double exigency: an egalitarian political system and a non-authoritarian civilian life.
>
> We, women, are conscious of the fact that this country will only be truly democratic and its citizens truly free when, without prejudice of sex, race, color, class, sexual orientation, religious or political creed, physical condition or age, equal treatment, and equal opportunity in the streets, the political stage, workshops, factories, offices, assemblies, and palaces, are guaranteed.[72]

In short, in the mid- to late 1990s, the CNDM and some state and municipal councils worked to strengthen the autonomous women's movement, providing direct and indirect subsidies to independent women's groups, coordinating national campaigns on women's issues, and providing the movement with new access points to State policymaking arenas. During the early years of civilian rule, the CNDM became the principal staging ground for a 1980s Brazilian brand of pressure-group feminist politics, and the CNDM advanced a fairly radical and successful policy agenda.[73] For example, through intensive CNDM lobbying, combined with women's movement–organized mass mobilizations, petition drives, and even sit-ins at Congress, many items from the women's agenda made their way into the new constitution. It provides for formal equality between the sexes and extends new social rights and benefits to women, including increased maternity leave (from 90 to 120 days); provides for paternity leave (though its duration is left unspecified); expands social benefits and workers' rights to women workers and domestic workers; and "extends provisions for childcare beyond the already existing obligation of employers so that it is now the general responsibility of the State to provide 'free care to children from zero to six years of age, in nurseries and preschools.'"[74] Moreover, the constitution engenders important rights in the realms of the family and reproduction, as Florisa Verucci notes, in that it "at long last revokes the notion of the husband's leadership (chefia) of the conjugal unit" and makes family planning "a constitutional right" while respecting individual decisions over reproduction.[75]

Despite the tireless efforts of both the CNDM and the feminist reproductive rights movement, both of which lobbied the Constitutional Congress, proposed several "popular amendments" on abortion and family planning,[76] and countered the Catholic Church's and the Right's opposition by pointing to the risks illegal abortion posed for women's health, the constitution's respect for individual reproductive decisions did not extend to abortion rights.

The right to safe, legal abortion has been a long-standing demand and an increasingly pressing concern for Brazilian feminists. Brazil is a world leader in illegal abortions: One study placed the number at 1.5 million per year, approximately the same number as are legally performed in the United States, whose population is about 100 million more than that of Brazil. This same study found that "curretage was the fourth most frequent medical procedure conducted in Brazilian public hospitals in 1991, where the operation was performed on 342,000 women."[77]

In light of these disturbing indices, it was not surprising that feminists, undaunted by the likelihood of conservative and religious opposition, struggled to persuade the Constituent Congress that this egregious situation must be redressed. As Leila Linhares recounts,

> In 1987, during the early stages of discussion on the elaboration of the new Federal Constitution, women's groups began to articulate nationwide to set a strategy for approaching members of the Constitutional Congress on the issue of abortion rights. At first, the feminists intended for the right to abortion to be declared in the new constitution. In opposition to this proposal, the Catholic Church and Evangelical Congressmen intended for abortion to be declared a crime.[78]

These propregnancy lobbies ultimately proved unshakable, but in a strategic move to prevent a retrogressive development in abortion rights,

> the feminist lobby, organized by the National Council for Women's Rights and autonomous groups from all over the country, succeeded in changing the wording proposed by the religious groups for article 5 of the Constitution, which defended "the inviolability of the right to life beginning at conception." The final wording of the article as it was approved in the Constitution merely reads "the inviolability of the right to life, liberty. ..."[79]

Feminists' ability to block this conservative assault on women's reproductive rights and to secure significant gains for women in the 1988 constitution was the outcome of the coordinated actions of feminists working within and outside the State; these gains did not emanate from the largesse or enlightenment of the politicians. They were achieved through sometimes fierce political battles waged by feminists active within the State and in opposition parties. But these battles were not mere intraparty affairs; because of enduring links between women working in parties and in the government and independent feminists, the latter could be mobilized to persuade parties and policymakers of the importance of women's claims.

From 1985 to 1988, this dynamic interaction between feminists active within and without the State was of pivotal importance. The inroads made by feminists into the State and the political parties, coupled with the continued vitality of women's organizations in civil society, enabled feminists to advance a fairly successful policy agenda and prevent any serious rollbacks in gender policy. Brazilian feminists responded flexibly and with considerable agility to a rapidly changing political context in which, in just a few years, their once-ridiculed demands became principles of constitutional law and featured prominently in party platforms.

The Closing of a Gendered Political Opening? Current Dilemmas in Brazilian Feminist Politics

The reformist euphoria of the first few years of civilian rule gave way to widespread disillusionment by the late 1980s. The new women's institutions proved sources of disappointment for Brazilian feminists, even for some of the founding mothers of the councils and *delegacias.* The gendered political opening provided by the first phase of transition politics was partially closed off during the democratic consolidation phase.

To the dismay of feminists who during the transition assiduously labored to conquer "women's spaces" within the State apparatus, by the late 1980s, many of these women's institutions appeared to have fallen prey to partisan manipulation and had lost most of their already limited political clout. In São Paulo from 1986 to 1990, the Center-Right PMDB administration of Orestes Quercia appointed women from his political machine to the Paulista Council on Women's Condition, significantly reduced its staffing and resources, and marginalized it from policymaking arenas. The turn to the right at the federal level in the late 1980s also subjected the CNDM to the vagaries of clientelistic politics as usual and similarly reduced its policy effectiveness. As former CNDM president Jacqueline Pitanguy wrote in 1990:

> As of 1988, the complex of governmental organs which, at the beginning of the so-called New Republic, presented unstructured and highly flexible political profiles, have adapted to the predominantly conservative character of the executive branch. The CNDM suffered a series of pressures ... especially after February 1989, with the arrival at the Ministry of Justice of an extremely conservative new minister. ... Paralyzed since then ... the CNDM symbolizes simultaneously the relevance of transformative actions from within the State and the fragility of the establishment of medium- and long-term policies in societies dominated by conjunctural political arrangements.[80]

To be sure, women's institutions tied to the executive branch proved highly vulnerable to shifting political-partisan alignments, and their efficacy in the policy realm declined in proportion to their shrinking influence within the State apparatus.

Executive-centered strategies also proved less than efficacious for implementing progressive gender policy in the almost three dozen municipal administrations governed by the PT from 1988 to 1992. PT feminists had long been critical of the PMDB-inspired women's councils and sought to redesign the mechanism through which gender-sensitive public policies might be promoted at the local level. In São Paulo, as in several of the other PT municipal administrations, the mechanism devised was the Coordenadoria Especial da Mulher, an organ typically linked directly to the mayor's cabinet and made up of women with ties to different sectors of the autonomous women's movement. Unlike their PMDB counterparts, they would be paid municipal government employees, thus abandoning what the PT saw as the "pretense" of representation embodied in the "hybrid" composition of the councils: "The [PT] experience proposed to overcome the proposals of Councils on Women's Rights which were instituted in many cities and in some state governments, looking to advance in the recognition of the discrimination of women and in making governments responsible for the implementation of policies for women. It tried to radically surpass the [PMDB's] vision that it is up to women's movements to organize and demand and that women in instances of the government represent the movements."[81] These were to be explicitly executive organs, not institutions putatively representative of the women's movement. They would work "in articulation with different action-oriented programs ... in municipal departments and other municipal organs" to "formulate, coordinate and accompany policies and directives, as well as develop projects, aimed at combatting sex discrimination, defending women's rights, and guaranteeing the full realization of women's capabilities."[82]

But the *coordenadorias* also soon found themselves marginalized from larger policy debates within most PT administrations. Often understaffed and poorly funded, they struggled to obtain recognition and executive support for many long-standing feminist policy goals. As one São Paulo *coordenadora* put it in late 1991, "It wears one down working in here, you have to fight for everything, you have to fight in order to work. ... For example, the last meeting we had with a *secretario* we told him: we even have to fight to get a spoon for the Casa Abrigo [battered women's shelter], you know, that one spoon is obtained through fighting."[83] The relegation of gender-related policy initiatives to a secondary plane within the still male-dominated radical democratic leftist party prompted PT feminists in 1991 to seek (and ultimately secure) the establishment of 30 percent quotas to ensure that women would be represented in leadership at all levels of the party organization.

PT feminists were not alone in criticizing the recalcitrance of their party to embrace more fully the feminist transformational project. By the late 1980s, parties' courtship of organized female constituencies continued, but feminists were now less readily wooed. After the liberalization of party legislation and the enfranchisement of illiterates in 1985, over 30 parties vied for the support of the greatly expanded Brazilian electorate. Most new parties added women's issues to their platforms and created women's branches or caucuses. There is some evidence that parties also allotted more slots to women candidates; for example, 15 times as many women ran for office in the state of São Paulo in the 1986 congressional elections than in 1982.[84]

But feminist activists still faced sexist obstacles within party organizations, according to party militants I interviewed in the late 1980s and early 1990s. Most contended that the parties remained ideologically resistant to the feminist political agenda and still viewed women's organizations only as electoral fodder. Many also complained that parties were reluctant to fully support feminist-identified candidates and failed to grant real power to women's caucuses or divisions. In new and old parties alike, the political space conceded to women and women's issues remained minuscule.

Several feminist activists noted that it was now in vogue for politicians and parties to pay lip service to issues of gender inequality, that speaking of women's concerns conferred democratic legitimacy on politicians in the New Republic. Yet the marginalization of women and women's issues and their manipulation for electoral purposes characterized the full spectrum from left to right. At a June 1988 statewide meeting of PT women activists, I heard many of the same complaints expressed by PT feminists in the early 1980s: "Too many activists view the woman question as secondary." "The Party does not support or subsidize the women's movement." "The women's commission is not consulted on key programmatic issues." "The Party must create a space for political reflection of feminist issues and train cadres on the specificity of gender oppression."[85]

In light of continued contradictions experienced by PT feminists, the 30 percent quota is indeed an important advance for women party militants, and despite the multiple constraints confronting feminists working in the PT municipalities, they achieved some notable accomplishments. In Santo André, the Assessoria dos Dircitos da Mulher established special educational programs to sensitize municipal employees and the *guarda civil* (civil guard, a security force charged with protecting municipal facilities) to women's issues, provided the local women's police precinct with trained social workers to assist women victims of violence, and set up a battered women's shelter under municipal auspices.[86] In São Paulo, the *coordenadoria* persuaded the health department to provide abortion services to women in one municipal hospital as permitted by law (abortion is legal in cases of rape, incest, or danger to the women's life) and, as in Santos and Santo André, also established referral and counseling services (such as the Casa Eliane de Grammont) and two shelters for female victims of domestic violence.[87]

This focus on services to victims of domestic and sexual violence was in turn inspired by feminists' growing dissatisfaction with the women's precincts or DDMs, which numbered 53 in the state of São Paulo and totaled over 80 nationwide by 1991. Though staffed by women police officers, the *delegacias* often replicated many of the sexist practices of regular police precincts in dealing with female victims of violence. Whereas in the mid-1980s, feminist scholars and activists were involved in training female police personnel at these specialized precincts, by the late 1980s, feminists had been marginalized from most and the women's officers who staffed the DDMs received no special training. As Sara Nelson notes, "Reporting a rape or beating to a woman officer in a private office will not ensure that a female victim will receive better treatment at a women's police station than she would at an all-male precinct. What is crucial is that victims are attended by officers who are trained to be sensitive to the specific issues inherent in violence against women."[88] Furthermore, the same contradictions that constrained other women's spaces within the masculinist State also plagued the *delegacias.* Nelson argues that "the capacity for the DDMs to fulfill many of their original objectives is *necessarily* limited by their problematic position within the police bureaucracy—problematic because the DDMs were created in resistance to the very male-dominated criminal justice system in which they themselves are located."[89]

The limitations of the DDMs, coupled with the extremely low prosecution and conviction rates for perpetrators of violence against women, incited renewed feminist activism on this vital issue. In March 1993, the Coletivo de Mulheres Negras de Baixada Santista (Santos Black Women's Collective) and the União de Mulheres de São Paulo (Union of São Paulo Women) organized the First National Conference of Popular Organizations Against Violence Against Women, held in Praia Grande, São Paulo, and attended by over 300 women. The conference launched a national mobilization campaign under the slogan "Impunity is the accomplice of violence," a new twist on the feminist campaign initiated by SOS-Mulher in 1980 ("Silence is the accomplice of violence"), which reflected the 1990s feminist awareness of the circumscribed effectiveness of State actions in this and other realms of critical importance to women. This new awareness is aptly captured in the manifesto approved by this Praia Grande conference, which merits citing at some length:

> "Silence is the accomplice of violence" has been our plea since 1980. And in this decade women denounced sexual and domestic violence. The numbers, even if underestimated, reveal the quotidian tragedy: 500 thousand Brazilian women yearly file complaints of beatings, rapes and death threats to the police delegacias. Black women react to racial discrimination and register the violations they suffer. They would like to make us believe that only Black and poor men beat, rape and murder women. We reveal the truth. Violence against women occurs in all social classes. White men also practice acts of violence.
>
> But the reality of the numbers of incidents of sexual, domestic and racial violence has not moved the public authorities. The State remains immutable and omissive, thus permitting the perpetuation of acts of violence against women.
>
> The impunity for crimes of violence against women has remained. Batterers, assassins, and rapists of women rarely are taken to the tribunals and condemned. And, when they are, they remain free and pose a constant threat to society.
>
> We women have changed our attitude. We have left silence behind to engage in public denunciation. We had the courage to expose ourselves and to bare the marks of our torture. But the public authorities and, in particular, the Judiciary, have not changed. They continue to absolve the criminals. And the onus of proof still falls heavily upon us.

> From here on, we issue a cry: Impunity is the accomplice of violence. With this
> campaign, we enjoin all of society to also demand that the State fulfill its role in guar-
> anteeing our right to life with dignity.[90]

Feminist attorneys also stepped up efforts to improve prosecution rates and
redoubled their long-standing struggle to promote reforms in the civil and penal
codes because these reforms, "which follow from the 1988 Constitution, are
stalled in the National Assembly, leaving Brazilian women in the precarious state
of having constitutional rights which are not reflected in the codes designed to
enforce those rights."[91] The penal code, for example, still defines rape "as a crime
against custom rather than a crime against an individual person—society rather
than the female victim is the offended party." It enshrines the "defense of [male]
honor" as a legitimate defense for wife murderers, and deems most other sex
crimes "crimes only if the victim is a 'virgin' or 'honest' woman."[92]

But in the early 1990s, independent feminists seldom looked to the considerably weakened women's councils and *coordenadorias* as domains in which to pursue these and other reforms. One might argue that this political posture inadver-
tently deprived these women's institutions of a legitimizing constituency within
civil society and thus further eroded their leverage within State policymaking arenas. And, indeed, though independent feminists continued to mobilize around
sexual and domestic violence, reproductive rights, and other issues crucial to
overcoming gender power imbalances, as the gendered political opening snapped
shut, many of the policy initiatives launched by the CNDM and other councils on
the status of women in the mid-1980s were blocked or, at best, stalled in the increasingly conservative political conjuncture of the late 1980s and early 1990s.

Instead of seeking new gender-related legislation and public policies, some
feminists, working within and without these precarious State "women's spaces,"
turned their energies toward securing the implementation of existing gender-related policies and laws. Under the slogan "Respect: We conquered it in law, we
will conquer it in practice," for example, the São Paulo Council on Women's Condition revitalized somewhat under the Fleury administration (1991–1995), proclaimed 1991 the Year of the Application of Legislation for Equality. It promoted
dozens of events and discussions throughout the state to sensitize the public and
the local government officials to the disparities between legally mandated gender
equality and the glaring inequalities that continued to confine women's lives.[93] In
September 1992, the council promulgated the Paulista Convention on the Elimination of All Forms of Discrimination Against Women, ceremoniously signed by
dozens of mayors during a gala official event presided over by Governor Fleury.[94]

Some feminists, many of whom worked within the State's "women's spaces"
during the 1980s, established feminist nongovernmental organizations (NGOs),
feminist lobbies, and policy think tanks in the early 1990s. For example, several
women who left the CNDM after the conservative takeover of the National Council of Women's Rights by women from the Center-Right's clientele networks,
founded the Centro Feminista de Estudos e Assessoria (Feminist Center for Re-

search and Consulting, or CFEMEA) in Brasília to monitor the regulation of constitutionally guaranteed rights through the formulation of ordinary and complementary laws in the national Congress.[95] Former CNDM president Jacqueline Pitanguy now works with the Rio-based feminist NGO Cidadania, Estudos, Pesquisa, Informação e Ação (Citizenship, Study, Research, Information and Action, or CEPIA), which among other projects is conducting a nationwide study of judicial response to crimes against women and is systematically evaluating possible strategies for the expansion of reproductive rights.

The Transformation and Multiplication of Feminisms in Postauthoritarian Brazil

Pressure-group-oriented feminist politics, once lodged almost exclusively within parties and the State, is now also being pursued through "professionalized" feminist nongovernmental organizations that seek to influence public policy. And the shrinking of the limited political spaces conquered by women during the transition also inspired other feminists to renew and redouble their efforts to promote a feminist transformational project beyond the State in the realms of society and culture.

Several movement-oriented feminists I interviewed in 1991 and 1992 were wary of the potential "NGO-ization" of the feminist movement, just as some were once troubled by its institutionalization or co-optation by parties or the State. They were critical of what they viewed as elite-centered and excessively State-centric strategies that underplayed the importance of continued feminist efforts to foment gender consciousness and challenge patriarchal cultural norms. Many of these women were again eschewing the State as a privileged arena for feminist struggle and were devoting their efforts principally to building feminist counterhegemonic cultural projects. As feminism became increasingly officialized, professionalized, and institutionalized in postauthoritarian Brazil, growing numbers of feminist activists came to understand genuine feminism as a worldview or vantage point on all aspects of life, culture, and politics, and not just as a political struggle, which would require involvement in either formal institutional or conventional revolutionary politics. The recent profusion of feminist video collectives, alternative publications, bookstores, a feminist publishing house, and an explicitly feminist scholarly journal; the over two dozen women's studies nuclei (*núcleos*) now found in Brazilian universities; the yearly national feminist "encounters," or conferences; the regular issue- or group-specific gatherings of Afro-Brazilian women, feminist ecologists, lesbians and popular feminists; the new national and regional feminist networks established formally among reproductive rights and women's health activists and among other feminists working on specific issues such as violence; and revitalized mobilizational efforts such as the Impunity is the Accomplice of Violence campaign all attest to the vitality of autonomous society-centered feminist thought and action in postauthoritarian Brazil.

In the 1990s, these feminist incursions into the societal, cultural, and academic realms, like the policy-focused activities of the growing numbers of feminist NGOs, seldom made the headlines of the mainstream or the alternative press as they had during the heady days of transition politics in the late 1970s and early 1980s. Feminists were less visible and perhaps less militant than in the turbulent years of the now infamous First, Second, and Third Paulista Women's Congresses, when many other sectors of Brazilian civil society had also loudly voiced their claims and staged mass mobilizations against military rule. However, in democratizing Brazil, new modalities of feminist organizing, new forms of articulating strategies, and new strands of feminism have multiplied.

Growing numbers of poor and working-class women are claiming feminism as their own. Grassroots women's groups affiliated with Rede Mulher, União de Mulheres de São Paulo, women's sections of the trade union centrals like the PT-influenced Central Unica dos Trabalhadores, or CUT, and several *casas da mulher* (women's centers) in São Paulo's urban periphery, for example, have expanded the feminist agenda to (re)affirm the interrelatedness of class and gender oppression in poor and working-class women's lives, a focus of historical feminist discourse and organizing in the era of the "other woman's feminism" now being appropriated and rearticulated by its subjects.

Popular feminism was in many ways the outgrowth of the politicization of women active in the neighborhood-based and trade union struggles discussed earlier. Empowered by their involvement in community and workplace struggles, many poor and working-class women increasingly challenged gender power imbalances in their families, neighborhood groups, and trade unions. Whereas most of the mothers' clubs and women's associations created in the 1970s focused on gender-related issues such as the cost of living or urban services, popular feminist political discourses critically examine why it is women who lead survival struggles. This distinctive class-centered feminist political identity was forged in dynamic interaction with nonfeminist neighborhood women's struggles, and popular feminists criticized "historic" feminists who, according to the self-defined "popular" feminists I interviewed in 1991, had focused more of their energies on influencing parties and the State and worked less directly with poor women in the grassroots struggles (which "popular" feminists want to make more feminist).

Black feminist organizations are also growing and are expanding the feminist political agenda. As noted previously, Afro-Brazilian women have always been integral participants in the larger Black movement and in Black religious and cultural associations. And Black women activists were also among the founders of the predominantly white second-wave feminist movement. In the early 1980s, some began to realize that their needs and concerns were not being adequately articulated by either the male-dominated Black movement or the white-dominated feminist movement. Racism in the women's movement and sexism in the Black movement led them to found autonomous Black women's groups in Rio, São Paulo, and Santos in the early to mid-1980s.

By the early 1990s, the growing Black women's movement, like the Brazilian women's movement as a whole, was ideologically quite diverse. Many active in Black women's groups rejected the feminist label. Their repudiation of feminism stemmed from a variety of sources: Some feared losing crucial allies among Afro-Brazilian men who, like some white men on the Left, still viewed gender as a "secondary contradiction" and believed feminism was a bourgeois, white woman's issue. Others believed Black women must work together with Black men to combat racial oppression. And for many, the racism found in early feminist groups had irreparably damaged feminism's credibility.[96] Still other Afro-Brazilian women were reclaiming the feminist label and were working to expand the parameters of feminist struggle, arguing that there could be no hierarchy of oppressions, that race, class, and gender shape the lives of Black women in inseparable ways. This awareness made their struggle distinct from that of Black men and white women.

In the coastal city of Santos, Black feminists founded the Coletivo de Mulheres Negras da Baixada Santista in 1986, with the aim of "combatting all types of discrimination based on color, sex, age, religion or race, and at the same time, encouraging Black women to participate, occupy spaces, conscious of her condition as a woman and a Black person in a *machista* and racist society which doubly discriminates against them."[97] The *coletivo* focused on disseminating information about gender and racial discrimination and about Black culture to schools, unions, and popular movements. It developed a library-archive and produced a number of publications on the history and status of Afro-Brazilian women. Though members often lobbied legislators and policymakers on issues of particular concern to women (e.g., sterilization abuse), the *coletivo*'s concurrent focus on cultural struggle was reflected in several of its activities: It ran a restaurant featuring African and Afro-Brazilian cuisines to subsidize its political activities and coordinated a women's *pagode* musical group, a Black women's theater group, a children's choral called Coral Infantil Omo Oya, Children of Iansã, and an African dance ensemble, Grupo de Dança Afro Ajaína.

Founded in São Paulo in 1988 by Afro-Brazilian women active in the feminist or Black consciousness movements, several of whom also had worked in the Black women's commissions of the São Paulo Council on Women's Condition and the CNDM, Geledés-Instituto da Mulher Negra was centrally concerned with extending meaningful sexual, cultural, and gendered citizenship to Afro-Brazilian women. One of its projects, SOS-Racismo, provided legal assistance to victims of racial discrimination, the first service of its kind in Brazil. Geledés also mounted an extensive program in the area of Black women's health, arguing that "Black women's health results from the real conditions of our existence. Poverty, inadequate education, unemployment, racial and sexual discrimination are conditions that favor the development of illnesses. As human beings, we Black women get ill like women from any other racial group. But what differentiates us is the pro-

cesses of getting ill, which stem principally from the intensity of oppression unleashed by racism and sexism, experienced in our daily lives."[98] Their activities in
this realm ranged from promoting self-help groups and workshops for Black
women to pressuring the public health system to incorporate the specific needs of
Afro-Brazilian women.

Geledés also worked on reproductive rights and the issue of sterilization abuse,
the latter focus inspired by the disturbing results of a 1986 study that revealed that
female sterilization was the most widely used contraceptive method in Brazil
(used by 44 percent of all women). Taking the controversial and distinctive stance
that some women choose sterilization, that medical abuses and coercion are the
real problems, and that sterilization is not exclusively about population control
targeted at the Black community (as the Black movement has historically contended), in contrast to some other sectors of the feminist health movement,
Geledés advocated the passage of specific federal legislation to regulate sterilization abuse, coupled with continued political mobilization to denounce widespread abuses:

> Massive sterilization of women in Brasil has been systematically denounced by the
> women's movement and the Black movement over the course of the last 15 years.
> From this action resulted innumerable studies, diagnoses, pamphlets widely divulged
> nationally and internationally but which unfortunately have not prevented that the
> sterilization of women reach the alarming indices which we confirm today. Perhaps
> we can suppose that these indices would be higher had it not been for the political
> battles waged by the women's movement and other social sectors during this period.
> … We want to emphasize that the construction of a legal instrument, together with
> continued *denuncia* activities will work toward changing the current situation of
> abuse and impunity.[99]

Geledés, the Santos *coletivo*, and other Black feminist organizations sponsored
national and regional Afro-Brazilian women's conferences and also regularly participated in and collaborated with other feminist networks and *encontros*. Since
the late 1980s, the specificity of Black women's oppression also has increasingly
been incorporated into Brazilian feminist discourses and politics. The inclusion
of racial violence and discrimination in the Praia Grande manifesto (cited earlier)
is exemplary of the incipient but growing awareness of and attention to racism
within most strands of the feminist movement.

Sexual preference and the specific discriminations afflicting lesbians have also
found greater resonance in Brazilian feminist politics in recent years, and the
struggle against homophobia has been openly assumed by growing numbers of
feminist organizations. Several new lesbian feminist groups were founded in the
late 1980s and early 1990s: Women from six lesbian feminist groups from the state
of São Paulo, including a group of young women from the working-class city of
Santo André who proclaimed themselves "anarchist lesbian feminist punks," organized a regional meeting in early 1993; several lesbian feminist newsletters such
as the São Paulo–based *Lesbertária* were being published; and lesbians were

loudly denouncing heterosexism in movement events and public forums. At the Praia Grande conference, for example, lesbian participants drafted a manifesto that was read at the closing plenary "denouncing that *obligatory heterosexuality,* imposed as a sexual model on women is *sexual violence* which is exercised against all women. Because it is absolutely indispensible to attack the bases of sexual violence, we call upon all women to deny that heterosexuality is the only valid sexuality for all of us."[100]

In the 1990s, the existence of many feminisms was more widely acknowledged, and the diversity of feminist visions, approaches, organizational forms, and strategic priorities appeared to be increasingly respected within the movement. With the growth of "popular feminism," the dichotomy between feminine and feminist struggles was also increasingly being abandoned or blurred. The various pieces of this feminist mosaic combined and recombined in a variety of forms and forums: Periodic national and regional meetings brought together all strands of feminism and other sectors of the larger women's movement. Groups working on women's health and reproductive rights created the Rede Nacional Feminista de Saúde (National Feminist Health Network) to coordinate their activities. Feminist ecologists coordinated their input into the 1992 UN Conference on the Environment, held in Rio in June 1992, sponsoring a series of activities in a separate women's space, the Planeta Femea (Women's Planet), during that important global summit, and formalized their growing network in December 1992, forming the Coalizão de ONGs de Mulheres Brasileiras para o Meio Ambiente, a População e o Desenvolvimento (Coalition of Women's NGOs for the Environment, Population, and Development). Women's studies *núcleos* in the North and Northeast formed a regional feminist studies network and feminist documentation centers planned to form their own computerized information network. These more fluid forms and forums of feminist organizing and the articulation of a multiplicity of feminist transformational projects in the 1990s appeared to be replacing the more formalistic and tension-ridden movement coordinations of the First and Second Paulista Women's Congresses.

Concluding Reflections

Even though the patriarchal barricades had again been erected in the realms of parties and the State, Brazilian feminism remained alive and well in the civil society. Still, in the 1990s, the *desencanto,* or disenchantment, with the formal political terrain that generally afflicted many progressive forces in Brazilian society extended into gender politics as well. The limitations, contradictions, and vulnerabilities of women's spaces in a patriarchal, racist, and neoliberal capitalist State became increasingly evident. Though during the 1980s, some women's councils proved to be effective vehicles for the articulation of gender-based demands within the state, the 1990s showed that women's spaces could also readily be relegated to bureaucratic obscurity and become mired in the vicissitudes of masculinist politics as usual. As of the early 1990s, few of the progressive policy proposals advocated by feminists during the 1980s had been effectively implemented. Perhaps even fewer of women's hard-won rights had been effectively enforced. And, of course, there remained serious limitations to gendered citizenship in a context where the exercise of meaningful social, political, civil, cultural, and sexual citizenship continued to be restricted to the privileged few.

During the 1980s, the State went abruptly from being what I have called women's worst enemy to representing itself as women's best friend[101] by appropriating selective elements of historical feminist discourses and political demands. Responding to feminists active in the opposition parties, governments translated many core items of the feminist political agenda into public policy proposals. New women's spaces such as the Councils on the Status of Women and women's police stations were created within the State apparatus at the local, state, and federal levels, and women also acquired new social and political rights in postauthoritarian Brazil. Indeed, with respect to women's rights, Brazil's 1988 federal constitution may well be one of the most progressive in the world today. Thanks to the tireless efforts of feminist activists working both within and outside parties and the State, a veritable windstorm of progressive gender legislation was enacted during the 1980s, and it appeared that Brazilian women had secured pathbreaking advances during the transition and the initial stages of civilian rule.

But as the dust settled on transition politics and Brazil returned to politics as usual, the Brazilian State began looking less like women's best friend and a lot more like, at best, an estranged acquaintance—somebody you once thought you knew well but rarely call on or count on anymore.

Many Brazilian feminists are again reassessing their relationship to the State. Some of the vexing questions confronting them include How can feminists continue to depend on an increasingly undependable State? Which aspects of feminist politics might still be launched from the State? And where in the State (i.e., the executive, the bureaucracy, the legislatures, the judiciary) should feminist advocacy efforts be focused? What strategies would be necessary to secure the implementation and enforcement of the rights women conquered in theory during the 1970s and 1980s? How can women of all ethnic groups, social classes, and sexual orientations come to enjoy more meaningful political, social, cultural, and sexual citizenship?

I highlighted three promising developments within the feminist movement that might ultimately alter or at least counterbalance this infelicitous state of gendered state affairs. They include influencing policy from outside the State and forming feminist policy think tanks, policy-oriented NGOs, and independent feminist lobbies, as well as revitalizing efforts to secure rights and promote gender consciousness in the realms of society and culture. Feminisms have multiplied since the late 1980s; Black feminist organizations, "popular feminist" groups, lesbian feminists, and other strands of feminism imploded the feminist political identity forged dur-

ing the transition period and infused new life and brought new dynamism to Brazilian gender politics in the terrains of both State *and* society.

Notes

1. The original version of this chapter was written in 1986 and was based on field research conducted principally in metropolitan São Paulo during November–December
1981, October 1982 to October 1983, and July–August 1985. This research was supported by
doctoral dissertation research grants from Fullbright-Hays, the Inter-American Foundation, and the Social Science Research Council. This revised and updated version draws on
further field research carried out in São Paulo and Brasília during July–August 1988; in São
Paulo and several other Brazilian cities during August–September 1991 and July–December
1992; and during a brief trip to Rio and São Paulo in May 1993. Research in 1988 and 1991
was supported by grants from the University of California and in 1992 by a lecturer-re-
search award from Fulbright-CIES. For a more detailed discussion of many of the issues
discussed in this chapter, see my *Engendering Democracy in Brazil: Women's Movements in
Transition Politics* (Princeton, N.J.: Princeton University Press, 1990). Many movement activists, friends, and colleagues in Brazil have provided invaluable information and support
over these many years, and I would like to acknowledge my deep thanks to one and all. In
particular, I want to recognize here my most profound debt of gratitude to those friends
who have closely accompanied my research on Brazilian women's movements and gender
politics for more than a decade and without whose boundless generosity and steadfast encouragement my work would have been far less intellectually productive and personally re-
warding: Miriam Bottassi, María Teresa Aarão, Roberto Ronchezel, Vera Soares, María
Amelia de Almeida Teles, Regina Stella, Silvia Artacho, Sonia Calió, Ruth Cardoso, and
Teresa Caldeira.

2. I borrow this metaphor from Fernando Calderón, Alejandro Piscitelli, and José Luis
Reyna, who discuss the "mosaic of Latin American diversity" manifest in the region's varied forms of contemporary collective action. "Social Movements: Actors, Theories, Expectations," in Arturo Escobar and Sonia E. Alvarez, eds., *The Making of Social Movements in
Latin America: Identity, Strategy, and Democracy* (Boulder, Colo.: Westview Press, 1992),
22.

3. For the best discussion of the dynamics of state-opposition relations under authoritarian rule and the *abertura* process, see María Helena Moreira Alves, *State and Opposition
in Brazil, 1964–1984* (Austin: University of Texas Press, 1985); see also Alfred Stepan, ed., *Democratizing Brazil* (New York: Oxford University Press, 1989). For an analysis of the intra-
elite negotiations that narrowed the scope of Brazilian democratization, see especially
Frances Hagopian, "'Democracy by Undemocratic Means'? Elites, Political Pacts, and Regime Transition in Brazil," *Comparative Political Studies* 23, 2 (July 1990): 147–170; María
Helena Moreira Alves, "Dilemmas of the Consolidation of Democracy from the Top: A Political Analysis," *Latin American Perspectives* 15, 3 (Summer 1988): 47–63; and William C.
Smith, "The Political Transition in Brazil: From Authoritarian Liberalization to Elite Conciliation to Democratization," in Enrique Balorya, ed., *Comparing New Democracies: Transition and Consolidation in Mediterranean Europe and the Southern Cone* (Boulder, Colo.:
Westview Press, 1987).

4. For incisive analyses of the political and institutional transformation of the Brazilian Catholic Church, see Scott Mainwaring, *The Catholic Church and Politics in Brazil, 1916–1985* (Stanford: Stanford University Press, 1986).

5. A distinction between "feminine" and "feminist" women's movement organizations is commonly made by both movement participants and social scientists in Latin America. Paul Singer clarifies the usage of these concepts: "The struggles against *carestia* or for schools, day care centers, etc., as well as specific measures to protect women who work interest women closely and it is possible then to consider them *feminine* revindications. But they are not *feminist* to the extent that they do not question the way in which women are inserted into the social context." "O feminino e o feminismo," in P. Singer and V. C. Brant, eds., *São Paulo: O povo em movimento* (Petrópolos; Vôzes, 1980), 116–117.

6. Moema Viezzer, *O problema não está na mulher* (São Paulo: Cortez, 1989), 60.

7. According to a participant-action-research study of mothers' clubs in São Paulo conducted by Rede Mulher between 1983 and 1985, "Four principal institutions organized women in mothers' clubs and women's groups: the Catholic Church (67 percent); the Legão Brasileira de Assistência (Brazilian Legion of Charity [LBA]) (13.8 percent); the Health Movement (5.1 percent) and the municipal prefecture, through its health centers. Only two (2.1 percent) of the clubs registered considered themselves autonomous. The rest (7.2 percent) were linked to political parties, Societies of Friends of the Neighborhood, and private philanthropic organizations." Ibid., 61.

8. On the Movimento Feminino pela Anistia, see Therezinha Godoy Zerbini, *Anistia: Semente da liberdade* (São Paulo: Escolas Professionais Salesianas, 1979). On the Movimento Custo de Vida, see Tilman Evers, "Os movimentos sociais urbanos: O caso do Movimento do Custo da Vida," in J. A. Moises et al., eds., *Alternativas populares da democracia* (Petrópolis: Vôzes, 1982). On the Movimento de Luta por Creches, see María da Gloria Marcondes Gohn, "O movimento de luta por creches em São Paulo: Reconstitução histórica e algumas consideraçoes teóricas," paper presented at the V Encontro Anual da Associação Nacional de Pós-Graduação e Pesquisa em Ciências Sociais, Nova Friburgo, Rio de Janeiro, October 1981; Carmen Barroso, *Mulher, sociedade e estado no Brasil* (São Paulo: Brasiliense, 1982), especially 151–154 and 167–168; and "Creche," *Supplemento dos Cadernos de Pesquisa* 43 (November 1982).

9. A more nuanced analysis of the complex dynamics of grassroots women's organizations in Brazil is beyond the scope of this chapter and has been discussed extensively elsewhere. See, especially, Sonia E. Alvarez, "Women's Participation in the Brazilian 'People's Church': A Critical Appraisal," *Feminist Studies* 16, 2 (Summer 1990); and *Engendering Democracy in Brazil* (Princeton: Princeton University Press). For a general discussion of this phenomenon, see also Eva Alterman Blay, "Movimentos sociais: Autonomia e estado: Uma analise teórica dos movimentos de mulheres entre 1964–1983," paper presented at the VI Reunião Anual da Associação Nacional de Pós-Graduação em Ciências Sociais, Aguas de São Pedro, Brasil, October 24–27, 1983, and "Mulheres e movimento sociais urbanos: Anistia, custo de vida e creches," *Encontros com a Civilização Brasileira—Mulher Hoje,* special issue (1980). See also "A luta das mães por um Brazil melhor," *Cadernos do CEAS* 58 (November-December 1978): 19–27. For a discussion of changes in the domestic political economy of the working classes under authoritarianism, see Ana María Q. Fausto Neto, *Familia operaria e reprodução da força de trabalho* (Petrópolis: Vôzes, 1982). For an especially insightful and provocative reconceptualization of popular women's organizations and poor and working-class women's interests in Latin America, see Amy Conger Lind,

"Power, Gender, and Development: Popular Women's Organizations and the Politics of Needs in Ecuador," in Escobar and Alvarez, *The Making of Social Movements in Latin America*. On the personal transformative dimension of women's participation in community struggles, see Teresa Caldeira, "Women, Daily Life, and Politics," in Elizabeth Jelín, ed., *Women and Social Change in Latin America* (London: UNRISD and Zed Books, 1990).

10. For a critique of Church-linked women's organizations, see Jany Chiriac and Solange Padilla, "Carateristicas e limites das organizações de base femininas," in Maria Christina, A. Bruschini, and Fulvia Rosemberg, eds., *Trabalhadoras do Brasil* (São Paulo: Brasiliense, 1982). See also Alvarez, "Women's Participation in Brazilian 'People's Church.'"

11. See, for example, Che Guevara, *Guerrilla Warfare*, with an introduction and case studies by Brian Loveman and Thomas M. Davies, Jr. (Lincoln: University of Nebraska Press, 1985), 132–134.

12. Testimony in *Memorias das mulheres do exilio* (Rio de Janeiro: Paz e Terra, 1980), 248, cited by Anette Goldberg, "Feminismo em regime autoritário: A experiência do movimento de mulheres no Rio de Janeiro," paper presented at the Twelfth Congress of the International Political Science Association, Rio de Janeiro, August 9–14, 1982, 10–11.

13. Ibid., 11.

14. Most of the preceding information on women in the militant Left, both in Brazil and in exile, is based on extensive formal and informal interviews with former female militants who are presently active in the feminist movement. And though therefore they are not representative of women in the Left in general, their analysis of their experiences within resistance organizations was key to the development of the feminist movement. Since many of the women interviewed might be compromised politically if their names were revealed (even in the New Republic), their names will not be mentioned here or hereafter. See Angela Neves-Xavier de Brito, "Brazilian Women in Exile: The Quest for an Identity," *Latin American Perspectives*, 13, 2 (Spring 1986): 58–80. On women's participation in Brazilian *guerrilhas* and the implications of such involvement for feminism, see also María Amelia de Almeida Teles, *Breve historia do feminismo no brasil* (São Paulo: Brasiliense, 1993), chapter entitled "A luta armada: Um aprendizado para a mulher."

15. Alfred Stepan, "State Power and the Strength of Civil Society in the Southern Cone of Latin America," in Peter B. Evans, Dietrich Rueschemeyer, and Theda Skocpol, eds., *Bringing the State Back In* (New York: Cambridge University Press, 1985), 334–338.

16. Doug McAdam, *Political Process and the Development of Black Insurgency, 1930–1970* (Chicago: University of Chicago Press, 1982), 11.

17. See Michele Mattelart, "Chile: The Feminine Side of the Coup d'Etat," in June Nash and H. I. Safa, eds., *Sex and Class in Latin America* (New York: Praeger, 1976), 279–301, on a similar dynamic in Chile in 1973. For a comprehensive and provocative analysis of gender politics under authoritarian rule in Chile, see Patricia Chuchryk, "Protest, Politics and Personal Life: The Emergence of Feminism in a Military Dictatorship, Chile 1973–1983," Ph.D. dissertation, York University, 1984.

18. This is not to say that women have been spared the brutality of the repressive apparatus of the state. On the gender-specific aspects of state repression, see Ximena Bunster-Burroto, "Surviving Beyond Fear: Women and Torture in Latin America," in June Nash and Helen Safa, eds., *Women and Change in Latin America* (South Hadley, Mass.: Bergin and Garvey, 1986). Alves argues that within the process of political liberalization certain social sectors were considered more politically problematic than others. Thus although the regime increasingly negotiated with elite sectors of the opposition (MDB politicians, the

Brazilian Bar Association, etc.), it continued to repress the militant working class and progressive opposition. See María Elena Moreira Alves, *Estado e oposição no Brasil (1964–84)* (Petrópolis: Vôzes, 1985).

19. Much of the ensuing discussion of Brazilian feminism(s) draws on field research, archival research, and formal and informal interviews with movement activists, party militants, politicians, and policymakers conducted between 1981 and 1993 and is elaborated more fully in my *Engendering Democracy in Brazil*. On the development of the Brazilian feminist movement, see also Almeida Teles, *Breve historia do feminismo no Brasil;* Viezzer, *O problema não está na mulher;* Elizabeth Souza Lobo, *A classe operaria tem dois sexos* (São Paulo: Brasiliense, 1992); Elizabeth Sussekind, "The Brazilian Woman During the 1980s: A View from Feminist Groups," *Beyond Law/Más Allá del Derecho* 2, 5 (July 1992): 11–74; Heleieth Iara Bongiovani Saffioti, "Feminismos e seus frutos no Brasil," in Emir Sader, ed., *Movimentos sociais na transição democrática* (São Paulo: Cortez, 1987); Cynthia Sarti, "The Panorama of Feminism in Brazil," *New Left Review* 173 (January-February 1989): 75–90; María Lygia Quartim de Moraes Nehring, *Mulheres em movimento* (São Paulo: Nobel and Conselho da Condição Feminina, 1985), and "Familia e feminismo: Reflexões sobre papeis feminismos na imprensa para mulheres," Ph.D. dissertation, University of São Paulo, 1981; Goldberg, "Feminismo em regime autoritário"; and Ana Alice Costa Pinheiro, "Avances y definiciones del movimiento feminista en el Brasil," master's thesis, Colégio de México, 1981.

20. Among those that received considerable attention in Brazilian leftist circles were Juliet Mitchell's "Women: The Longest Revolution" (pamphlet), and Simone de Beauvoir's *The Second Sex.*

21. Cited in Goldberg, "Feminismo em regime autoritário," 14–15. As Goldberg argues, "The idea that there existed two feminisms began to take shape among intellectuals: one acceptable, which could be invited to take its seat among the forces of the left which attempted to reorganize the country; another, totally unacceptable, alien, the struggle of bourgeois lesbians against men," 23.

22. Paul Singer, "Caminhos Brasileiros para o movimento feminista," *Opinião* 24 (April 16, 1973), cited in Goldberg, "Feminismo em regime autoritário," 17–18.

23. "Commissão Organizadora, "Encontro para o diagnóstico da mulher Paulista," *Cartá-proposta da mulher Paulista,* São Paulo, December 1975.

24. Alvarez, *EnOCgendering Democracy in Brazil,* 93. For a critical account of the evolution of Marxist thought on the women's emancipation, see Zuleika Alambert, *Feminismo: O ponto de vista Marxista* (São Paulo: Nobel, 1986).

25. Moraes Nehring argues that this economistic focus was the result of the fact that the "political space [of the *encontro*] was occupied by the orthodox communist political current ... which had been saved from the repressive terror precisely because of its opposition to the armed struggle and which did not reject, as the new left had incorrectly rejected for a period of time, the legal opportunities for political work." See María Lygia Quartim de Moraes Nehring, "Familia e feminismo."

26. Editorial, *Brasil Mulher* 1, 10 (October 1975).

27. Given government censorship and state repression, "general social transformation" served as a widely used code phrase for radical democratic or socialist revolutionary change.

28. Interview with one of the early participants of *Brasil Mulher,* São Paulo, August 18, 1983.

29. Moraes Nehring, "Família e feminismo," provides an excellent, detailed analysis of the evolution of feminist political thought and practice in São Paulo that highlights this "other" aspect of early Brazilian feminism. Most major documents of the early years of the feminist movement in São Paulo are fully reproduced in her dissertation.

30. Moraes Nehring, "Família e feminismo," 201–203. Moraes devotes a section of her dissertation to the analysis of the feminist press—286–305.

31. Teresa Caldeira, personal communication to author. See also Caldeira, "Women, Daily Life, and Politics," and *A política dos outros: O cotidiano dos moradores da periferia e o que pensam do poder e dos poderosos* (São Paulo: Brasiliense, 1984).

32. *Brasil Mulher* 11 (March 1978).

33. Editorial, *Nós Mulheres*, August 1977.

34. "Encarte especial—Por liberdades democráticas," *Brasil Mulher* 3, 12 (May 1978).

35. For a description of these two congresses, see *Nós Mulheres* 7 (March 1978): 8, and 8 (June-July 1978): 10; *Brasil Mulher* 3, 11 (March 1978): 4–10, and 3, 13 (June 1978): 13.

36. On the Brazilian Black movement of the 1970s and 1980s, see Hamilton B. Cardoso, "Limites do confronto racial e aspectos da experiência negra do Brasil: Reflexões, in Emir Sadir, ed., *Movimentos sociais na transição democrática* (São Paulo: Cortez, 1987); Leila Gonzalez, "The Unified Black Movement: A New Stage in Black Political Mobilization," and Michael Mitchell, "Blacks and the *Abertura Democrática*," in Pierre-Michel Fontaine, ed., *Race, Class and Power in Brazil* (Los Angeles: University of California at Los Angeles, Center for Afro-American Studies, 1985); and Howard Winant, "The Other Side of the Process: Racial Formation in Contemporary Brazil," in George Yudice, Jean Franco, and Juan Flores, eds., *On Edge: The Crisis of Contemporary Culture* (Minneapolis: University of Minnesota Press, 1992). For a compelling and comprehensive political history of Brazilian race relations and Afro-Brazilian movements, see George Reid Andrews, *Blacks and Whites in São Paulo, Brazil, 1888–1988* (Madison: University of Wisconsin Press, 1991).

37. On the gay movement, see Edward MacRae, "Homosexual Identities in Brazilian Transition Politics," in Escobar and Alvarez, *The Making of Social Movements in Latin America;* see also James N. Green, "The Emergence of the Brazilian Gay Liberation Movement: 1977–1981," paper presented at the Fourteenth International Congress of the Latin American Studies Association, Los Angeles, California, September 1992.

38. The terms Black, feminist, homosexual/lesbian, or working-class, for that matter, are, of course, hardly mutually exclusive. Indeed, the most painful contradictions within the new liberation movements were experienced by nonwhite or working-class lesbians and gays who often felt marginalized from or silenced within both the feminist and Afro-Brazilian movements.

39. For an excellent discussion of the labor movement and the new trade unionism in Brazil, see Margaret Keck, "Workers in the Brazilian Abertura Process," in Stepan, *Democratizing Brazil.* See also María Herminia Tavares do Almeida, "O Sindicalismo Brasileiro entre a Conservação e a Mudanca," in B. Sorj and M. H. Tavares de Almeida, eds., *Sociedade e política no Brasil pós-64,* (São Paulo: Brasiliense, 1983).

40. The heightened media attention to women is partially attributable to the efforts of Brazilian feminist journalists such as Carmen da Silva, Irede Cardoso, and María Carneiro da Cunha, who pressured major newspapers and networks to grant more space to women's voices and women's issues.

41. *Folha de São Paulo,* March 8, 1979.

42. *Brasil Mulher* had dedicated a special issue to the Congress that included a feature on "sexual pleasure, contraception, and marital relations. ... Besides, rice, beans, day care and salaries, these things also concern working women, housewives, mothers." See *Brasil Mulher,* special issue (March 1979).

43. *Em Tempo,* March 1979, cited in Moraes Nehring, "Familia e feminismo," 246.

44. Ibid.

45. Ibid.

46. Moraes argues that some of the women directly tied to extreme-left political tendencies "cleansed" the final document of its more radical, gender-specific content. See Moraes Nehring, "Familia e feminismo," 250.

47. "I Congresso da Mulher Paulista," final document, March 1979. Also reprinted in *Brasil Mulher,* April 1979.

48. Rede Mulher, "Retrato dos clubes de mães" (São Paulo, 1980), mimeo, 17.

49. Associação das Mulheres, "O movimento de mulheres no Brasil," *Cadernos da Associação das Mulheres* 3 (August 1979): Six other groups also raised the issue of autonomy at this time. This important movement document, widely distributed among opposition sectors and movement organizations in São Paulo, contains position papers on the nature, content, and direction of women's struggle as conceptualized by feminist and feminine organizations in São Paulo and Rio de Janeiro.

50. By early 1980, Coordination's weekly meetings included representatives from 9 explicitly feminist organizations, 21 neighborhood women's associations (including organizations such as the now-united Struggle for Day Care Movement, the Cost of Living Movement, and the Housewives Association, each of which represented dozens of groups throughout the city), 11 unions and union opposition groups, 5 professional associations, 2 community organizations, 3 student associations, 2 women's divisions of political parties (the only legal opposition party, the MDB, and the Trotskyist Convergência Socialista), 2 health movement groups, and the women's division of the Unified Black Movement.

51. Many of the feminists I talked to believed that there were several "phantom organizations" among the 56 represented in Coordination, groups with no actual social base and formed with the exclusive intent of flooding Coordination with additional members of a particular tendency.

52. Interview with founding member of CMB, participant in Coordination for the First, Second, and Third Paulista Women's Congresses and member of Centro Informाção Mulher, São Paulo, August 10, 1983.

53. For an analysis of the sanctioning of violence against women in the name of honor in Brazilian law, see Mariza Correa, *Morte em familia: Representações jurídicas de papeis sexuais* (Rio de Janeiro: Graal, 1983) and *Crimes de paixão* (São Paulo: Brasiliense, 1981). See also Danielle Ardaillon and Guita Grin Debert, *Quando a vitima é mulher: Analise de julgamentos de crimes de estupro, espancamento e homicidio* (São Paulo and Brasília: CEDAC and Conselho Nacional dos Direitos da Mulher, 1987); and Americas Watch, *Criminal Injustice: Violence Against Women in Brazil* (New York: Americas Watch, 1991).

54. Quoted in *Jornal do Brasil,* March 10, 1980, this claim was made in spite of the fact that poor and working-class women constituted the majority of participants and that representatives from women's neighborhood groups and union organizations formed part of the presiding panel of the Paulista Congress. When the Domestic Workers Association and women from the Unified Black Movement asked for representation in the panel, a repre-

sentative of each was immediately invited to take a seat among those presiding over the Paulista Congress.

55. Moraes Nehring, "Familia e feminismo," 265–277, provides a detailed discussion of these controversial events. My own recounting of the Second Paulista Congress relies principally on innumerable conversations with women's movement participants in São Paulo and interviews with women involved with one of the political tendencies held responsible for the disturbances, as well as a thorough review of media coverage of the events and of internal organizational documents of Coordination.

56. Maria Carneiro da Cunha, "Tumultos e polemica no. 2.o congreso da mulher," *Folha de São Paulo,* March 10, 1980.

57. This crucial distinction regarding struggles "over" and struggles "within" social movements in the Brazilian context is developed by Margaret Keck in her incisive analysis of the dynamics of the new trade unionism of the 1970s. See her "Labor in the Brazilian Transition," in Stepan, *Democratizing Brazil.*

58. The military had dissolved the precoup parties in 1965 and created two new parties— ARENA (Aliança de Renovaçao Nacional, or National Renovating Alliance), the official government party, and the MDB (Brazilian Democratic Movement), the "official" opposition party. On the role of parties and elections in the Brazilian transition, see Bolivar Lamounier, "Authoritarian Brazil Revisited: The Impact of Elections on the Abertura," in Stepan, *Democratizing Brazil.* See also David Fleischer, "De la distensión a la apertura político-electoral en Brasil," *Revista Mexicana de Sociologia* 44, 3 (July-September 1982), 961–998.

59. These tensions were deliberately fueled by the regime, which in November 1981 decreed that straight-ticket voting would be mandatory. Thus, movement participants could not support candidates from different parties.

60. As many of my interviewees who did engage in party politics suggested, many of these women were nevertheless active sympathizers of either the PT or the PMDB even as they fiercely defended the movement's autonomy.

61. Movement polarization differed in other Brazilian states where the PT did not emerge as a significant political force. For example, women's movement allegiances were divided among the PMDB, PT, and PDS (Partido Democrático Social, or Democratic Social Party, headed by Leonel Brizola) in both Rio de Janeiro and Rio Grande do Sul. The PP, the center-right opposition party that later incorporated into the PMDB, also exerted some influence in Minas Gerais. In most other states, the polarization between MDB and ARENA was largely transposed onto their renamed political reincarnations—PMDB versus PDS.

62. On the relationship between women's movements and political parties, see Iara Maria Ilgenfritz da Silva, "Movimentos de mulheres e partidos políticos: Antagonismos e contradições," paper presented at the V Encontro Anual da ANPOCS, Nova Friburgo, Rio de Janeiro, 1981; Fanny Tabak and Silvia Sanchez, "Movimentos feministas e partidos políticos," paper presented at same *encontro,* 1981; Silvia Pimentel, "A necessaria participação política no Brasil," paper presented at the Twelfth International Conference of the Latin American Studies Association, Albuquerque, New Mexico, April 1985. For a full discussion of party mobilization of women and partisan "women's platforms," see Alvarez, *Engendering Democracy in Brazil,* chaps. 6, 7.

63. "Proposta das mulheres do PMDB para o governo," 1982.

64. Governo do Estado de São Paulo, Decree 20,892, *Diário Oficial,* April 5, 1983.

65. Montoro appointed *no* women to any of the 24 posts in his state cabinet, and only two were appointed to the municipal cabinet—in posts that have traditionally been held by women in liberal democracies, the Municipal Department of Social Welfare and the Family *(Secretaria Municipal da Familia e Bemestar Social)* and the Municipal Education Department *(Secretaria Municipal de Educação)*.

66. Governo do Estado de São Paulo. Conselho da Condição Feminina, untitled newsletter, 1984.

67. A full discussion of post-1983 policy developments is beyond the scope of this chapter. See my "Politicizing Gender and En*gendering* Democracy," in Stepan, *Democratizing Brazil*, for an in-depth discussion of gender and public policy in the Brazilian transition.

68. Coletivo Feminista Sexualidade e Saúde, "Brasil: Mujeres y salud," in ISIS International, ed., *La salud de las mujeres: La experiencia de Brasil, reflexiones y acciones internacionales* (Santiago: ISIS, 1985) 11.

69. Ibid., 13.

70. Informal interview with Ana María P. Pluciennik, coordinator of the Women's Health Program, Secretaria da Saúde, São Paulo, August 21, 1985.

71. Since its creation, the *delegacia* has been reportedly receiving 200–300 complaints per day, for a total of over 6,000 in its first year of operation. Similar "women's precincts" have been installed elsewhere in greater São Paulo and in over 80 other Brazilian cities.

72. "Carta das mulheres aos constituintes de 1987," Conselho Nacional dos Direitos da Mulher, pamphlet, December 1986.

73. For a detailed analysis of gender policy developments in the 1980s, see Alvarez, *Engendering Democracy in Brazil*, chaps. 8–10.

74. Florisa Verucci, "Women and the New Brazilian Constitution," *Feminist Studies* 17, 3 (Fall 1991): 559.

75. Ibid., 562.

76. On CNDM and feminist movement strategies to influence the Constituent Assembly and the popular amendment process, see my *Engendering Democracy in Brazil*, 251–255.

77. James Brooke, "Ulcer Drug Tied to Numerous Abortions in Brazil," *New York Times*, May 19, 1993.

78. Leila de Andrade Linhares Barsted, "Legalization and Decriminalization of Abortion in Brazil: Ten Years of Feminist Struggle," *Estudios Feministas* 0, 0 (1992): 180.

79. Ibid., 181.

80. Jacqueline Pitanguy, "Politicas públicas y ciudadania," in ISIS International, ed., *Transiciones: Mujeres en los procesos democráticos* (Santiago: ISIS International, 1990), 21. On the multiple contradictions confronting the councils and the *delegacias,* see my *Engendering Democracy in Brazil*, chap. 10. See also Danielle Ardaillon, "Estado e mulher: Conselhos dos direitos da mulher e delegacias de defesa da mulher," unpublished manuscript, 1989, and Sonia E. Alvarez, "Contradictions of a 'Woman's Space' in a Male-Dominant State: The Political Role of the Commissions on the Status of Women in Postauthoritarian Brazil," in Kathleen Staudt, ed., *Women, International Development, and Politics: The Bureaucratic Mire* (Philadelphia: Temple University Press, 1990).

81. Jorge Bittar, ed., *O modo petista de governar* (São Paulo: Secretaria Nacional de Assuntos Institucionais, 1992), 188.

82. Coordenadoria Especial da Mulher, Secretaria de Negocios Extraordinários, Prefeitura do Municipio de São Paulo, pamphlet, 1990.

83. Interview with Teresa Verardo, coordinator of the Violence Against Women sector of the São Paulo Coordenadoria, São Paulo, September 11, 1991.

84. *Mulherio* (December 1986-February 1987).

85. Based on participant observation at the Encontro Estadual das Mulheres do PT, organized by the Comissão de Mulheres do PT, São Paulo, June 25, 1988.

86. Interview with Ivete Garcia, director, Assessoria dos Direitos da Mulher, Gabinete do Prefeito, Prefeitura Municipal de Santo André, September 19, 1992; and with Sonia Calió, consultant for the Assessoria, September 17, 1991.

87. Interviews with Liege de Pauli and Teresa Verardo of the Coordenadoria Especial da Mulher, Prefeitura Municipal de São Paulo, September 11, 1991, and with Cibele Simão Lacerda, director, Coordenadoria Especial da Mulher, Prefeitura Municipal de Santos, September 4, 1991.

88. Sara Nelson, "Women's Police Stations in Brazil: The Dynamics of Institutional Resistance," paper presented at the Forum on Women and the State in Brazil, University of California at Berkeley, February 19, 1993, 19.

89. Ibid., 17.

90. Reproduced on the back cover of *Enfoque Feminista,* a publication jointly produced and issued by six São Paulo feminist groups, 3, 4 (April 1993).

91. Americas Watch, *Criminal Injustice,* 4.

92. Ibid.

93. Conselho Estadual da Condição Feminina, *Respeito: Conquistamos na lei. Conquistaremos na Prática* (São Paulo: CECF, 1991). This discussion also draws on formal interviews with María Teresa Augusti, president, Conselho Estadual da Condição Feminina, and members of the CECF'S Commission on Violence, São Paulo, September 18, 1991.

94. Conselho Estadual da Condição Feminina, *A lei e a vida: Convenção paulista sobre a eliminação de todas as formas de discriminação contra a mulher* (São Paulo: CECF, 1992).

95. In 1993, CFEMEA published a comprehensive study of pending congressional legislation in the areas of violence, work, welfare, health, and education with the aim of enjoining women's movement activists to pressure Congress on these bills and other stalled policy areas of interest to women. See CFEMEA, *Pensando nossa cidadania: Propostas para uma legislação não discriminatória* (Brasília, F.D.: CFEMEA, 1993).

96. This discussion draws on formal interviews with Edna Roland, member of the São Paulo Black Women's Collective and of the Black Women's Commission of the São Paulo State Council on Women's Condition, São Paulo, June 24, 1988; Sueli Carneiro, also a member of the collective and director of the Black Women's Program of the CNDM, Brasília, June 29, 1988; Nilza Iraci, member of Geledés-Instituto da Mulher Negra, São Paulo, September 27, 1991; and two members of the Coletivo de Mulheres Negras da Baixada Santista and the Casa de Cultura da Mulher Negra, Santos, October 6, 1991.

97. Coletivo de Mulheres Negras da Baixada Santista, *Boletim* 0, n.d.

98. Geledés-Instituto da Mulher Negra, "Programa de Saúde," pamphlet, n.d.

99. Geledés-Instituto da Mulher Negra, Programa de Saúde, *Cadernos Geledés 2; Esterilização: Impunidade ou Regulamentação?* (São Paulo: Geledés, 1991).

100. *Lesbertária* 1, 1 (May 1993): 3, emphasis in the original.

101. For a theoretical elaboration on gender and the state in Brazil and the Southern Cone, see my *Engendering Democracy in Brazil,* especially chaps. 1, 10, 11.

THREE

From Dictatorship to Democracy: The Women's Movement in Chile

PATRICIA M. CHUCHRYK

In 1983, it appeared possible that the unprecedented numbers of Chileans who participated in the national days of protest might succeed in focusing international and national attention on their political situation such that Pinochet would feel pressured to begin the progress of democratic transition—but military repression and strategic divisions within the opposition diminished the momentum of these protests. The Chilean people would have to wait until the October 5, 1988, plebiscite in which 56 percent of the voters voted no to the continuation of the Pinochet government and initiated the beginning of the transition to civilian democratic rule. And on December 14, 1989, after 19 years without presidential and parliamentary elections, Chileans voted 55 percent[1] in favor of Patricio Aylwin, the Christian Democratic candidate of the Concertación de Partidos por la Democracia (United Parties for Democracy).[2]

During the period of military dictatorship, which began with the 1973 coup d'état, Chileans were engaged in the difficult and laborious process of building an opposition and reconstructing political networks. Remarkably, in building this opposition, Chilean politics appear to have gone through a kind of democratization process. This has nothing to do with the mechanisms of access to political decisionmaking and power. Rather, it has to do with a "process of inclusion"[3] signified by the emergence in Chile of new social and political actors and of a new consciousness and conceptualization of politics, the political process, and the role of authoritarianism in civil society. This process involved the emergence of a changing political vocabulary and resurrected the concept of social movement, in part due to the absence of an institutionally legitimated role for political parties, and in part due to the emergence of new social movements during the period of military rule that transcended traditional party links.[4] Political parties, therefore, have been obliged to construct new kinds of relationships with the nonpartisan opposition.[5]

One of the most important new political actors to emerge was the women's movement. Women's groups and organizations, however, were not new. As early as 1913, in the northern mining regions of Chile, working-class women organized the Centros de Belén de Zárraga to address the exploitation of women workers. By the 1920s, there were a variety of women's political organizations devoted to expanding women's political and economic rights. The growth in women's suffrage organizations during the 1930s and 1940s gained momentum until 1949, when women were enfranchised and the women's movement appeared to withdraw from the political arena.[6] Since 1973 and the imposition of military rule, however, there has been an impressive growth in women's groups. Some were created to facilitate women's participation in the opposition to the dictatorship. Others renewed the legacy of the suffrage struggle and, most important, began to raise gender issues within the context of that opposition and Chilean society in general.

By the late 1980s, the women's movement had achieved a level of political articulation and visibility that demanded a response from the different parties and alliances of the opposition. The presence, for example, of María Antonieta Saa, a prominent and well-known feminist leader in the Asamblea de la Civilidad (Civilian Assembly), formed in April 1986, meant that for the first time, gender issues were raised and represented in an important body of the opposition. Later that year the "Pliegue de Mujeres," a list of gender-based demands, was incorporated into the assembly's "Demandas de Chile" (Demands of Chile). In 1988 the Feminist Movement of Chile published "Demandas de las mujeres a la democracia" (Women's Demands of Democracy) in a major Santiago daily, *La Epoca*, with 22 organizations and 11 prominent women as signatories.[7] By the end of 1988 there were at least two new broadly based organizations with considerable convocatory power, the Coordinator of Women's Social Organizations (Coordinación de Organizaciónes Sociales de Mujeres), which launched a major campaign in 1989, "I am woman and I have rights" *(Soy mujer ... tengo derechos)*[8] and the Concertación Nacional de Mujeres por la Democracia (National Coalition of Women for Democracy) a broad-based group of women from a variety of political parties and women's organizations dedicated not only to developing a women's agenda for the 1989 elections but also to taking it to the arena of national politics. Twenty thousand women, an unprecedented number, participated in the March 8, 1989, celebration of International Women's Day.[9] What had been viewed as a relatively diffuse social movement with little experience with formal political participation had become an important social actor.

This chapter has three objectives: to examine the emergence of an autonomous women's movement in authoritarian Chile, to explore the relationship between this movement and the opposition, and to assess the prospects and potential of a feminist politics in a democratic Chilean context.[10] In order to situate a discussion of the emergence of feminism in Chile, it is necessary to look first at the broad-based mobilizations of women that have occurred in response to the political and economic consequences of the imposition of military rule.

Filling the Vacuum: The Political and Economic Crises

It would be difficult to overestimate the social, economic, cultural, and psychological destruction wrought by more than 16 years of military rule in Chile.[11] It was, without a doubt, a reign of terror, not only in the sense of political repression—concentration camps, torture, disappearances, and executions—but also in the imposition of a monetarist economic model that, as many economists have argued, effectively crippled the Chilean economy.[12]

The essential features of this model are privatization, the free play of market forces, and comparative advantage—the latter being the military's response to the previous import substitution model. Industrial and financial firms acquired by the state during the socialist Unidad Popular (Popular Unity) government were sold, often at below-market value. Most restraints on foreign investment were lifted in an attempt to attract foreign capital.[13] In 1982 alone, there were 810 commercial bankruptcies in Chile.[14] The consequences of these policies, with few exceptions, were devastating for the population and for the economy. Real wages declined, growth rates dropped (except during the so-called boom period, 1976–1979), prices rose continuously, and official unemployment in 1987 was 20 percent of the labor force.[15] The official unemployment rates, however, were somewhat deceiving. If those who participated in the military government's make-work programs[16] and those who became chronically unemployed due to a greatly reduced industrial sector were included, the official rate would have been considerably higher. Indeed, in many poor neighborhoods, the unemployment rate reached 80 percent.[17] Generally speaking, the military's new economic model left massive poverty, a disproportionately large unemployed and demoralized labor force, and deteriorating wage levels in its wake.[18]

For the working class, this situation was exacerbated by the government's anti-union policy. Trade unions were among the first political organizations targeted for repression. The 1979 Labor Plan, one of the government's seven "modernizations," decentralized and effectively dismembered the union structure in Chile. Under this plan, some worker's rights were recognized, such as collective bargaining and the right to strike. But the new law was designed to atomize and weaken unions so that, for example, collective bargaining could occur only at the plant level (to divest unions of their "monopoly" power) and companies had the option to postpone negotiations.[19] Strikes could not last longer than 60 days (after 30 days the companies had the right to hire workers to replace the strikers), at which time the strikers had to either accept the company's offer or lose their jobs. Union elections were permitted, but the new law stipulated that candidates for election

could not have held office in the previous 10 years.[20] Union membership decreased from roughly 41 percent of the labor force in 1972 to 10 percent in 1987.[21]

One of the key features of Chile's new economic order, and especially of the
strategy to combat inflation, was a drastic reduction in government spending. By
1979, government expenditure on social services, in real terms, was 10 percent below 1969 levels.[22] Education and health, two of the areas most affected by this reduction, were also subject to the military's strategy of privatization. The policy
papers of 1979 imposed a concept of a free market supply-demand system of education and health based on the ability to pay. Thus, the military regime's economic policies created a devastatingly poor populace while at the same time re-
moving from their reach the social services that could have served to lessen the
extent of that poverty. As Jorge Leiva, a Chilean economist, has pointed out, the
military included hunger in its list of repressive tactics.[23]

Unemployment, combined with poverty, had a dramatic impact on women. It
forced many women, especially those from the lowest income sector, into the informal (and sometimes, but less frequently, the formal) labor market for the first
time.[24] Women's labor force participation steadily increased from 25.2 percent of
all women aged 15 and over in 1976 to 28.2 prevent in 1985 and 32 percent in 1990.[25]
Women were 27.6 percent of the total labor force in 1976, 34.6 prevent in 1985,[26]
and 31 percent in 1990.[27] Women are concentrated in the low-wage sectors of the
economy, primarily in service occupations. In 1987, roughly 25 percent of all
women who work for wages are domestic servants.[28] In the 1980s women have
also had slightly higher rates of unemployment than men,[29] in part a reflection of
the number of women looking for work for the first time. Women's wages continue to be considerably lower than men's even if education is taken into account.
In contrast to the trend in industrialized countries where male-female wage dif-
ferentials tend to decrease as the level of education increases, women with university education in Chile made 49 percent of the average male wage in 1985, whereas
women with eight years or less of formal schooling made 59 percent.[30]

The military's market-oriented approach led it to rescind all protective labor
legislation for women. Employers were no longer required to provide or subsidize
child care for female employees, although day care has rarely been accessible to
working-class women. A new law made it possible for employers to fire pregnant
employees. Indeed, one of the issues on the agenda of a conference organized by
women unionists in June 1987 was the subjection of prospective female employees
to gynecological examinations to ascertain that they were not pregnant.[31] The
privatization of education reduced the number of day care centers and increased
the costs of those that did exist. Furthermore, the laws that govern working hours
have never been extended to the realm of domestic service, the single largest
group of exploited women workers.

Poverty, massive unemployment, and a greatly diminished industrial sector
forced women, especially the growing urban working-class poor, to join the ranks
of street vendors, beggars, and prostitutes. At the same time, women devised new

and often creative strategies for economic survival. Poor and working-class women, whose husbands were often demoralized and chronically unemployed, were forced to figure out ways to feed their children. One of the byproducts of this process was the amount of (undesired) role reversal that occurred, especially among the urban working-class poor.

New survival strategies emerged out of the poverty. Popular economic organizations (*organizaciones económicas populares,* or OEPs) were set up, mainly by women.[32] Women knit together, made tapestries (the well-known *arpilleras*), collected and sold old clothing, tended collective gardens, and operated the hundreds of *ollas comunes,*[33] which provided many of the poor with at least one hot meal, as meager as it might be, per day. Women also formed shopping collectives, called *comprando juntas.* Given the tremendous increases in the prices of basic foodstuffs, it was often impossible for many people to purchase, for example, a whole liter of cooking oil. To deal with this problem, women organized centers where people were able to buy food essentials at lower prices.[34] In 1982, there were 495 OEPs in greater Santiago and the surrounding area.[35] In 1985, there were 1,125 in Santiago alone.[36] In metropolitan Santiago, there were 34 *ollas comunes* in 1982 and 232 in 1985. In 1982, there were 57 *comprando juntas.* These had increased to 232 by 1985. The 151 artisan workshops in 1982 had increased to 331 by 1985.[37] These figures clearly reflect the poverty that existed in Chile during the period of military dictatorship.

It might be tempting to view these as housewives' organizations having purely economic goals, but that would be incorrect. They provided these women with a focus for political organizing and self-education, as well as a means of self-empowerment. Chilean popular educator Horacio Walker's study of one such all-woman *olla común* provides us with a dramatic example of the importance of such organizations.[38] The women of the María Goretti *olla común* in a Santiago shantytown insisted on doing all the work themselves. They made a conscious decision to exclude men from their organizing activities in order to prove they were just as capable as men. When the roof needed fixing, for example, one of them climbed up and fixed it herself. Walker suggested that even though in many respects the women were simply extending domestic roles into the public realm, at the same time their work significantly represented collectivization of those roles.[39] Furthermore, "by engaging in the operation of an all-woman soup kitchen, they are criticizing traditional gender relations from the bottom to the top, they are raising doubts; they are prompting questions; they are seeing themselves differently."[40]

The women in Walker's study often saw their work as somehow outside of that which is conventionally considered political. Walker disagreed, distinguishing between consciousness in discourse and consciousness in action.[41] The language used by these women was not the language of conventional political discourse but rather the language of their reality—of daily life. But their language and practice, he suggested, challenged authoritarianism in a way that conventional political discourse could not, precisely because their resistance to the regime, expressed in daily life survival strategies, was their discourse.[42] Because these women "saw themselves differently," they were capable of moving beyond the limits a patriarchal society imposed on them by collectivizing and thereby transforming women's traditionally defined roles. As Walker pointed out, they discovered that they were capable of much more than raising children and cooking and cleaning, that indeed they were capable of political action.[43] This recognition and growing self-awareness is one of the most common consequences of participation in a women's group, regardless of the kind of group. By creating the need for alternative economic survival strategies, the regime's economic policies impelled women to organize. Similarly, the political crisis mobilized women around human rights issues.

The new authoritarian state was designed to restructure Chilean society in its totality. As pointed out by Humberto Vega and Jaime Ruiz-Tagle, one of the central characteristics of Chile's authoritarian-capitalist model was "a *political system* in which political life is reduced to control by military power. This political system is not legitimated by popular will, lacks mechanisms and channels for citizen participation by which it could be legitimated, and seeks support through the individualistic and materialistic values of the economic model in order to sustain itself."[44]

The authoritarian-capitalist model is based on values often referred to as Catholic traditionalism, that is, a firm belief in religion, family, private property, and nation.[45] Thus, any attack on traditional capitalist values such as private property are seen as attacks on Christian values and the Chilean family and nation.[46] The Doctrine of National Security, a geopolitical strategy favored by Latin American generals, especially those trained in the United states, reinforces this ideological project. Based on the notion of "internal threat," it permitted the Chilean military to declare war on the Chilean citizenry, and without a doubt, it *was* open war that was declared on September 11, 1973.

There is probably little need to recount the atrocities that were committed by the Chilean military and its secret police, now the CNI (Central Nacional de Inteligencia).[47] Thousands were executed, tortured, and imprisoned. Hundreds of thousands were exiled and many others sent into internal exile *(los relegados)*. Literally countless others, probably numbering in the thousands,[48] disappeared without a trace.

Given the particular circumstances of this reign of terror, it is not surprising that women, as the mothers, wives, sisters, daughters, and grandmothers of the victims of repression, were the first to mobilize in opposition to the dictatorship. Men were the victims of repression more often than women in part because women had tended to play what were considered marginal or secondary roles in the targeted organizations, principally political parties and trade unions. In this sense, it was precisely women's traditional public invisibility that allowed them to become political actors at a time when it was extremely dangerous for anyone to do so. Furthermore, this political involvement was legitimated by traditional roles as wives and mothers.[49]

Less than three weeks after the coup, on October 1, 1973, the Association of Democratic Women (Agrupación de Mujeres Democráticas) was formed to do solidarity work[50] with political prisoners and their families. Over the years, their activities included the provision of basic foodstuffs for prisoners and their families, strike support work, the delivery of food to the *ollas comunes* in poor neighborhoods, and political self-education. Especially during the early years, much of their work had to be done clandestinely. Participants suggest that it was easier for women to work in the underground in part because the military itself tended to ignore women.[51] In the beginning, they used traditional female activities to camouflage their meetings. Tea parties and group knitting sessions enabled them to get together to organize their activities.

During the late 1980s the Agrupación de Mujeres Democráticas expanded not only its sphere of political activities but also its self-definition—although its principal task was always defined principally as solidarity work with the victims of political repression. As an organization, it participated in the general struggle for democracy; it also saw itself as having important political roles after the return to democratic rule, such as encouraging the political education of women so that women could begin to participate in traditional political organizations on an equal footing with men. Members of this group have pointed out that women have held few leadership positions, in part due to women's familial responsibilities and in part due to machismo.[52] Many of the women involved in this group are older, middle-class housewives and professionals. Many had never before engaged in political activity. Although in one sense, the work of this group can be seen as a kind of Ladies Auxiliary, it is the context itself that made this work politically significant as well as politically dangerous. During the first months after the coup, the group played an important role in taking the first tentative steps toward rebuilding political networks, often just by acting as a liaison among political leaders forced underground. Many of the women, especially wives and sisters of political leaders who were dead, imprisoned, or "disappeared," were forced by circumstances to take on leadership roles for the first time.

Groups seeking the whereabouts of detained and disappeared family members have unfortunately become a fixture in Latin American political life. Perhaps the most internationally well known of these is the Madres of the Plaza de Mayo, formed in 1977 in Argentina. The Chilean Association of the Relatives of the Detained and Disappeared (Agrupacución de los Familiares de los Detenidos y Desaparecidos) was formed in 1974.[53] Later, the Associations of the Relatives of Political Prisoners (Agrupación de los Familiares de los Presos Políticos), of the Exiled (Agrupación de los Familiares de los Exiliados), and of the Politically Executed (Agrupación de los Familiares de los Ejecutados Políticos) were also formed. As was the case in other countries, in Chile the same women kept running into each other outside prisons, in hospitals, and in government offices, all seeking information on the whereabouts of a loved one. With the help and support of the Church, they formed organizations to coordinate their search. Initially, they sought the emotional support of the group, seeing themselves as individual, accidental victims of historical circumstances. Many, if not most, of the women who founded these organizations had never been politically active. The overwhelming majority of the members of the *agrupaciones* are middle- and working-class housewives and mothers, some of whom are also professionals.

At first, their efforts focused on the traditional mechanisms of the criminal justice system, such as habeus corpus. When these strategies proved ineffective (if the military denied having detained someone, then a writ of habeus corpus was meaningless), they began to use more unconventional methods such as hunger strikes. As early as 1975, these women were, in fact, the first to take to the streets to protest the military regime. As a result of their activities, many were arrested numerous times. Moreover, members of the *agrupaciones* were active in the general struggle for a return to democracy.

Beginning in 1976, other, more formally structured women's organizations equally concerned with rights issues began to emerge. In 1979, the Women's Committee of the Chilean Human Rights Commission (CDM) was formed and in 1982 began to publish a newsletter called *Hojita,* which has since ceased publication. The work of these women, among them professionals, housewives, union leaders, and representatives of other organizations, includes solidarity work (especially with women who have been imprisoned or tortured), popular education, and public consciousness-raising around women's rights issues. They have done a considerable amount of work documenting the legal situation of women in Chile, although during the latter part of 1980s they did not appear to be as active as during the 1983–1984 period.

Another of these groups was the Women's Department (Departamento Femenino, or DF) of the National Trade Union Coordinator (Coordinadora Nacional Sindical, or CNS), a proscribed organization at the time, which attempted to unite women union leaders and the women's departments of the various unions affiliated with the CNS. Its objectives were to organize women workers, to encourage women (both workers and wives of workers) to actively participate in the Chilean trade union movement, and to struggle for the rights of women workers both in the workplace and in the union. By encouraging the wives of workers to participate in the trade union movement, the Women's Department was addressing two very important issues: the development of a partnership of women and men in class struggle and the assumed political conservatism of women, particularly housewives. In 1978, the DF organized the First National Women's Conference, attended by over 300 women. It organized the first large demonstration to be held after the imposition of military rule—a demonstration to commemorate International Women's Day, March 8, 1978. In 1979, it took up the struggle against Decree 2,200, which effectively eliminated the few workplace protections of women workers. In June 1987, the DF organized a conference on women's rights in the workplace, taking up such issues as sexual harassment and equal pay.

Motherhood and Politics:
A Contradiction?

The political and economic crises of authoritarian rule in Chile propelled many women to take on new roles in the public sphere. Much of this activity was organized around traditionally defined political goals and was reinforced by women's traditional roles. What is interesting is how some women, politically active for the first time, justified their participation in terms of being good wives and mothers. At the same time, the process of engaging in political activity often encouraged women to begin to question those very same roles that provided the initial impetus for political organizing.

> Breaking away from the private world ... is at first done in the name of preserving its order. [Women's] entrance into the public world is initially presented as temporary, its objective is a solution which will permit the return to the natural course of the sexual division of labor. The appropriation of men's struggle is revindicated as a struggle for family. But the entrance of women into these struggles creates a potentially contradictory dynamic. If women, reaffirming their family responsibilities, enter the public world invested in a role which oppresses them as women, objectively this foray into the social and political struggle can place them in contradiction, at the same time, with that oppression.[54]

Ironically, Pinochet used an exaggerated version of the ideology of traditional motherhood in an attempt to *depoliticize* women. Immediately after the coup, in October 1973, Pinochet created the National Secretariat of Women (Secretaría Nacional de la Mujer, SNM). Also during October, he reorganized the Mothers Centers (Centros de Madres, CEMAs), which had been community-based, grassroots organizations formed during the government of Christian Democrat Eduardo Frei. Pinochet's wife, Lucía Hiriart de Pinochet, became the director of both organizations. It appeared that the government wanted to capitalize on the success of El Poder Femenino (Woman Power, EPF), a group of primarily middle- and upper-class housewives who had mobilized against Allende and the "dangerous threat of communism" in 1971.[55] In 1979–1980, the SNM reported a membership of over 10,000 volunteers.[56] In 1983, CEMA-Chile had over 10,000 centers throughout Chile with 6,000 volunteers and over 230,000 members.[57]

Pinochet assigned to women, as mothers, the sacred duty of defending the integrity of the Chilean family, promoting the values essential to the "new Chile," and saving the fatherland. Through their self-sacrifice and self-abnegation, through their suffering, through their dedication to the family, and through their unwavering loyalty to the *patria*, women—in Pinochet's plan—would ensure that Chile's sons and daughters grew up to be patriotic citizens, which meant progovernment and nonpolitical.[58] These two organizations, SNM and CEMA-Chile, promoted this image—an image defined exclusively in terms of women's reproductive function.[59] Women were conceived of as pillars of the society who defend and transmit spiritual values. Sacrifice, abnegation, service, honesty, diligence, and responsibility were women's chief characteristics, according to the Pinochet government's official discourse.

The government's control of SNM and CEMA enabled the military to manipulate the ideology of motherhood for its own purposes.[60] By focusing on motherhood and the family, Pinochet was, in effect, using the state to manipulate women's reproductive roles for its, and his, own purposes in an attempt to depoliticize women and situate them outside of politics. Not surprisingly, this strategy backfired in some significant ways.

Among those who first recognized the contradictions in Pinochet's ideological project were middle-class women, especially academic and professional women who had occupied important political roles during the Unidad Popular government.[61] When the military took power, many academic women, like academic men, lost their university jobs. There was an abrupt decline in university enrollments due to the military's reduction of the number of students permitted to register. After the coup, roughly 2,000 faculty were dismissed and more than 20,000 students expelled.[62] In 1983, it was estimated that a university system that accommodated 140,000 students in 1973 would serve only 20,000 by 1985.[63]

Furthermore, the state effectively militarized the university system by rewriting and controlling the curriculum and installing military officers in key university administrative posts. Many women were forced into exile (or accompanied husbands forced into exile), where they did obtain degrees. In the absence of domestic servants, they were obligated to take on domestic roles and responsibilities and often, for the first time, were confronted with the contradictions of female roles. For those who stayed, employment opportunities were also greatly reduced. The privatization of education and health, for example, resulted in fewer jobs for women. One study found that in 1982, 17 percent of all employed women were professionals. Of these, 57 percent were teachers and 24 percent were nurses and midwives, thus constituting 82 percent of all those women classified as professionals by the Chilean census.[64]

Many of these women were personally uncomfortable with Pinochet's ideological political project for women. Coming from the tradition of the Marxist Left and a history of personal political activism, they began to recognize their own political marginalization not only in political parties but in their own political discourse on global liberation.[65] As participants in the popular project of Allende's government, they had engaged in the struggle of the poor and the working class[66] without recognizing their own oppression as women. Similarly, they began to recognize that the Left shared with the military its traditional view of women.

Almost all of the aspects of the junta's policies have been abundantly criticized by the Chilean left. Nevertheless, there has been a curious silence regarding the retrogressive policy of the junta on women. What's more, no one has seriously investigated why women were the Achilles heel of the Popular Unity government.[67]

For many women, it soon became clear that authoritarianism, for them as women, did not begin on September 11, 1973, and in fact was a central feature of Chilean society and characterized the nature of women's experience in the family, in the private sphere to which they had been relegated. As pointed out by Julieta Kirkwood, "Now, confronted by [military] authoritarianism, women, in a certain sense, are faced with a phenomenon well known to them: authoritarianism in their daily experiences."[68]

Some of these women began to raise important questions regarding their previous and future roles as political activists. They joined alternative research centers,[69] eventually forming one of their own. They began to raise issues of women's participation in their political parties. And, most significant, they began to form women's groups and took the first tentative steps toward constructing a feminist politics—in a society now generally hostile to politics and within an opposition specifically hostile to feminism.

The Women's Movement in Chile to 1987

In her discussion of authoritarianism in Brazil, Fanny Tabak has observed that, ironically, "authoritarianism and repression served to develop many women's intelligence, creativity and political capacity."[70] Military rule led many women to question their marginalization in the public, political sphere and to reject their relegation to the private sphere, where their roles were defined exclusively in terms of their reproductive potential. By joining their voices in opposition to the dictatorship, a historically specific phenomenon, they found themselves struggling to be heard as equal partners in that opposition, fighting an ideology that transcended military rule. It was this contradiction that provided the context in which feminism emerged in Chile.

With increasing frequency and visibility, a wide variety of women's political organizations began, in the late 1970s and early 1980s, to dot the Chilean political landscape. Many of these groups were part of the growing *movimientos de mujeres* or *movimientos femeninos* and eschewed the feminist label. In his study of women's groups in São Paulo, Brazil, Paul Singer clarified the distinction:

> The struggles against the rising cost of living or for schools, day care centers, etc., as well as specific measures to protect women who work interest women closely and it is possible then to consider them *feminine* revindications. But they are not *feminist* to the extent that they do not question the way in which women are inserted into the social context.[71]

In the Chilean case, "feminine" groups would include all of the housewife-organized OEPs, the human rights groups, as well as the multitudinous *talleres* (workshops) *de reflexión* that sprang up in shantytowns throughout Chile. Among those groups that raised gender issues, it is possible to distinguish between what I call integrationist groups and feminist groups. The former generally had a traditional political focus and emphasized integrating women into existing political organizations and projects *(que la mujer participe)*. Women were seen as politically backward people who had to be adequately educated to take their rightful place in existing organizations. Feminist groups, however, emphasized instead the need for women to create a politics based on their own needs rather than incorporating themselves into organizations that were created for other purposes and in which women's needs and demands historically had been ignored. By using women's experience of oppression as a point of departure for an analysis of women's reality, Chilean feminists recognized and articulated women's needs as a legitimate point of departure for political action. In this way, they challenged traditional structures of political participation and laid the groundwork for a reconceptualization of what constitutes politics and political action. What follows is a brief description of some of these groups, both integrationist and feminist.

In the early 1980s, three women's federations were formed: the Committee for the Defense of Women's Rights (Comité de Defensa de los Derechos de la Mujer—CODEM), Women of Chile (Mujeres de Chile—MUDECHI), and the Movement of Shantytown Women (Movimiento de Mujeres Pobladoras—MOMUPO). The first two of these were born out of left-wing political party traditions. All three emerged as grassroots organizations uniting and coordinating the activities of smaller neighborhood groups.[72]

CODEM and MUDECHI both emerged directly as a response to the political and economic crises, focusing their activities around survival issues and defining as their central priority the struggle against the dictatorship. Over the years, however, both of these groups increasingly incorporated a growing concern for the specific situation of women. They defined their constituency as women precisely because women have been marginalized in and by the political process and hence are assumed to lack the education and skills required to become active political participants. Although MUDECHI did not define itself as a feminist organization (viewing feminism as antimen), it nevertheless emphasized the importance of women taking on public roles and participating in politics on equal footing with men. For many years, CODEM, too, self-consciously defined itself as nonfeminist, if not antifeminist. After a long internal process and struggle, however, CODEM resolved to politically identify itself as a feminist organization. This was particularly significant given this group's earlier position, borrowing from left-wing orthodoxy, that feminism is a middle-class movement divisive of the working class.

Whereas CODEM and MUDECHI were federations involving groups in a large number of Chilean cities, MOMUPO's activities focused on working with *pobladoras* from the northern area of Santiago. The initial thrust of the organization was motivated by the need to devise economic survival strategies. Later, self-education, self-development, and consciousness-raising were added to their list of priorities. They organized workshops on parenting skills, sexuality, women's legal rights, women's history, and political self-education. In 1984, MOMUPO founded a women's center whose objective was to meet some of women's most urgent needs, for example, in the area of health and legal information. In 1985, MOMUPO began to define itself as a feminist organization and began to combine inner-directed activities with public activism.

In addition to these federations, a wide variety of different organizations emerged.[73] In 1981, a collective of socialist feminist women began to publish a magazine called *Furia.* Through an analysis focused on patriarchy, they hoped to put women's issues on the socialist agenda. In part due to lack of funding and in part due to the untimely death of one of the members of the collective,[74] the last issue appeared in 1985. But in this collective's place other socialist women's groups have emerged. In fall 1983, a group of small "s" socialist women united across class and sectarian lines to discuss issues important to them as women and to define the role that feminism might play in the political process. In 1984, they formed the Movement of Women for Socialism (Movimiento Mujeres por el Socialismo— MMS), a group that combined an analysis of capitalism and the need for major socioeconomic transformation with an analysis of patriarchy and the need for women's autonomy and self-determination in the political process. This group was very active in moments of intense political crisis, giving public visibility to feminist analyses of opposition strategies.[75]

By far one of the most significant groups to emerge was the Women's Studies Circle (Círculo de Estudios de la Mujer). Its roots go back to 1977 when a small group of primarily professional middle-class women began to meet to discuss their situation as women. Later, after organizing an unexpectedly successful forum on the situation of women, the *círculo* was admitted to the Academy of Christian Humanism (Academia de Humanismo Cristiano, AHC), an important umbrella organization instituted by the Church to provide a safe "space" for alternative research centers, political expression, and the articulation of dissent. The activities of the *círculo* focused on generating knowledge about women and generating consciousness of women's oppression. In addition to a core group of feminist researchers, there were grassroots activists, ongoing consciousness-raising groups, a feminist theater group, courses on women's history, a documentation center, and public forums on a wide variety of issues.

Despite careful self-censorship, which consisted of avoiding the issues of abortion, divorce, and sexuality in their published documents and public forums, the contradiction of being a publicly feminist group protected by a Church umbrella group eventually resulted in the expulsion of the *círculo* from the AHC in December 1983. Nevertheless, as Chile's first feminist groups, it left the Chilean movement with an important legacy. During the early part of 1983, largely owing to the efforts of some *círculo* members, the Feminist Movement (Movimiento Feminista, MF) was organized. Women wanted to participate, *as feminists,* in the Days of Protests, which were initiated by the copper workers' union in May 1983 when the regime successfully intimidated it to cancel a strike it had called. On August 11, 1983, the fourth day of protest, approximately 60 women staged a five-minute sit-on the steps of Santiago's National Library under a banner that read, "Democracy Now! The Feminist Movement of Chile." This was the first public demonstration by a feminist group (as opposed to a women-led demonstration) and, in a real sense, put feminism on Chile's political map. To celebrate International Women's Day, March 8, 1987, feminists organized a women's lunch, attended by approximately 1,000 women.[76]

When the AHC withdrew its support of the *círculo,* two groups emerged: the Women's Studies Center (Centro de Estudios de la Mujer—CEM), a feminist research organization fashioned after other alternative research centers (but independent of the AHC); and the Center of Analysis and Information on the Status of Women (Centro de Análisis y Difusión de la Condición de la Mujer—La Morada). La Morada took on the political, activist, consciousness-raising activities. The work of La Morada consisted of a wide variety of ongoing workshops and the provision of a meeting place for a variety of feminist groups, including the MF and the Frente de Liberación Femenino (Women's Liberation Front), a shantytown women's group.

In 1983, two other important organizations emerged: MEMCH83, an umbrella group established to coordinate the activities of the women's opposition, and Mujeres por la Vida (Women for Life). The former, which took its name from a group originally formed in 1935, is an important example of how a concern for women's rights gradually became incorporated into a program for political change. As an umbrella group, MEMCH83 included a variety of women's organizations, both feminist and nonfeminist. The original intention was to create a united women's front against the military government and to facilitate the flow of information among the various groups. The specificity of women's situation was not, at first, considered a fundamental part of this opposition. Later on, however, demands for women's rights, such as equal pay and the right to work, were incorporated. On November 28, 1983, for example, MEMCH83 organized a successful women's demonstration not only to oppose the government but also in the name of peace and women's rights. During the late 1980s, MEMCH83 operated out of a house in central Santiago, focusing its activities on giving greater visibility to its activities and providing opportunities for dialogue among various constituencies of the opposition and for the coordination of women's oppositional activities. During this period there was a great coming and going of organizations. New groups such as Acción Femenina (Women's Action) joined the movement; others, such as MOMUPO and the Feminist Movement, withdrew.

Mujeres por la Vida began as a group of 16 women—many of whom were well-known political figures representing a wide political spectrum—who organized a demonstration (in December 1983) in the name of peace and unity. These women were deeply concerned over the lack of unity among the various forces of the opposition—a lack of unity, they felt, due to political party sectarianism. Determined to show the (male) opposition that it is possible to form a united opposition, approximately 10,000 women turned out at the Caupolicán Theatre. Men were not permitted to attend, not even male journalists, for the simple reason that these women wanted to demonstrate to the men of the opposition how unity could be achieved. Until the late 1980s, despite a sometimes troubled existence, Mujeres por la Vida continued to play an important convocatory role in the women's opposition, joining with other groups to call for demonstrations and raise the issue of women's rights within the context of the struggle for democracy.[77]

What bound *all* of these groups and enabled them to work together was the struggle for the return to democracy. But within this struggle, however, feminists began to reconceptualize democracy, which, they argued, never really existed for women.[78] This argument is fundamentally related to the analysis of the relationship between the public sphere (of work and traditional politics) and the private sphere (of women's unwaged work and the family). Historically, women have been excluded from those structures that give them some degree of self-determination and some possibility of controlling their own destiny. Thus, democratization for women has come to mean the democratization of daily life, self-determination, autonomy, and freedom from violence and oppression.[79] A struggle for democracy, it was argued, must include a struggle for women's liberation or it will not eliminate authoritarianism.[80]

Feminist Democratic Politics

One of the most important contributions of Chilean feminism to opposition politics was the analysis of the link between state authoritarianism and authoritarianism in Chilean society generally. To fully appreciate the significance of this contribution, it is necessary to explore the work of Chilean sociologist Julieta Kirkwood.[81] Kirkwood's work, by linking authoritarianism and patriarchy, uncovered the connections between the underlying authoritarianism structures that govern political (in the traditional sense) and personal (also political but in a nontraditional sense) relationships. Only in this way, she argued, is the construction of a truly liberating and democratic political project possible.[82]

From 1980 to 1985, her work focused on three areas: the recovery of women's history, the relationship between the Chilean Left and women's struggle, and the political content of feminism in an authoritarian context. She sought the answers to a great many questions. Why is the history of women's political activism invisible? Why have left-wing political parties ignored women's issues? Why have women political party activists fought everyone else's struggle but their own? What was the nature of the relationship between the left-wing political parties and the women's suffrage organizations of the 1930s and 1940s? Why have women never been very receptive to the Left's political project? Are women essentially politically conservative? What is the role of authoritarianism in the development of feminism in Chile? Is feminism revolutionary?

In her study of the history of feminist movements in Chile, "Ser política en Chile: Las feministas y los partidos," Kirkwood found that historically there have been two lines of reasoning regarding the relationship between women's groups and political parties; rejection (and the formation of women's parties) and incorporation (based on the belief that political parties have no gender).[83] The former has generally manifested itself in autonomous women's groups and the latter, in women's abandoning women's issues and participating in male politics where women generally occupy secondary roles.[84] As she pointed out, this was not unlike the situation during the 1980s in Chile.

Kirkwood argued that the democratization process that was occurring in Chile during the 50 years preceding the coup was a process involving the incorporation into the political community of those who were not previously incorporated, such as the middle classes, workers, peasants, youth, and women. However, the only group not addressed in terms of its specificity was women. This accounts, in part, she argued, for women's conservative political behavior. They were left off the political bandwagon.[85] Women's political participation had traditionally been seen in terms of the *obstacles* that *impede* the integration of women into existing political organizations such as political parties. "These 'obstacles' more often than not appear ... rooted in biological determinist arguments which end up reaffirming the separate—and necessary—existence of the two spheres of existence: the public and the private."[86] The focus on obstacles to women's political participation, she suggested, obscured underlying political agendas. Women's political participation thus was often sought to support particular agendas rather than to improve the situation of women. Political parties, for example, would seek

> to bring the vast majority of women into a particularly political project, even if this is done only sporadically or by involving symbolic images—"the Chilean woman," "the mother of Chile," "the protector of the great family that is the nation," "the defender of our children," and "woman rise up and fight for what is yours."[87]

Feminism does not impose these images or limitations on women's political participation. It is not a question of determining "what and how much of it women lack in order to become incorporated into an already predetermined political process."[88] She argued that women must determine for themselves the nature of their political process and that feminists must construct a nonsexist concept of what is political—a concept that includes daily life and the private sphere.[89]

One of the major problems with a concept of politics based only on the public sphere is that it neglects the structure of domination and subordination in the family. This narrow focus, which excludes the private sphere, has led the Left to accept the ideology of traditional family, an ideology generally found in all social classes.[90] However, at the same time, the Left generally sees itself as a champion of the "proletarian family as the basic revolutionary unit," ignoring the complex authoritarian structures within that unit.[91]

These kinds of arguments led Kirkwood to an analysis of authoritarianism that moves beyond a focus on the public sphere. She argued that military rule politicized daily life, that it only made visible an authoritarianism embedded in the Chilean social structure. It has enabled us to see that the family is authoritarian, that the socialization of children is authoritarian, that education, factories, and even political parties are based on authoritarian relationships and structures.[92] She argued that a feminist perspective also enables us to see that authoritarianism emerges not only from the bourgeoisie and the military but that "the authoritarian discourse can also be found in the middle classes, including professionals and intellectuals, and even among workers and peasants. In reality, it can be found throughout society."[93]

Given that the roots of authoritarian culture can be found in the family, she argued, it is logical that one of the three political orientations regarding women since the 1973 coup is the military's (de)mobilization of women, that is, the reinforcement of authoritarian structures by activating the traditional ideology of women's place in society. Another is the Left's "integrationist" approach—also traditional—which focuses on incorporating women into the general struggle against the military regime. The third perspective, she argued, is the feminist perspective, which is based on the attempt to develop a critical analysis of society that moves beyond an economistic analysis.[94] The feminist perspective, sustained Kirkwood, is a truly revolutionary perspective because "in its elaboration of the concept of patriarchy, it transcends the differentiation and struggle based on social classes at the one and only root of the social relations of oppression, and by pointing out the existence of sexual oppression, it underlines the domination and cultural and material oppression of one sex by the other."[95]

The feminist political project is first and foremost the negation of authoritarianism.[96] It also involves the negation of the separation of existence into two spheres of activity, the public and the private; the negation of women's work being treated as nonwork; the negation of women's condition of political, economic, social, legal, psychological, and sexual dependence; the negation of being the "other"; the negation of women's issues always being treated as outside the historical context; and the negation of women's problems always seen as *women's* problems and thus outside the social realm.[97]

Another important issue is the relationship between a politics constructed from class contradiction and one based on gender issues. Chilean feminism, as with Latin American feminism generally, is extremely class conscious, and clearly, the debate regarding the relative importance of class struggle versus gender issues has formed much of the development of the women's movement. Many integrationist groups, among them especially the shantytown and trade union organizations, view class struggle as the central struggle. Machismo and women's oppression are often seen as divisive of the working class and as impediments to working-class organizing. This is an interesting variation on the argument that feminism, and an analysis of gender, is divisive of the working class, such that confronting machismo is transformed into a strategy to make class struggle more effective by eliminating the barriers that prevent women and men from working *together*. Feminist groups, which focus on women's oppression as the point of departure for women's political participation, refuse to establish a hierarchical relationship between the two. Rather, their analysis attempts to merge class struggle with gender issues.[98]

Kirkwood argued that an exclusive focus on class oppression (based on exploitative relations in the public sphere) only perpetuates the public-private distinction, continues to exclude the process that determines women's lives, and, furthermore, ignores the fact that men have personal lives too.

> It is not part of the [feminist] project to deny the reality and the validity of the analysis of class domination. On the contrary, a feminist analysis, which exposes the economistic bias of class analysis, enriches it. ... In fact, feminism truly constitutes a social movement for liberation in Chile because it successfully links the struggle ... against class and sex oppression simultaneously.[99]

Indeed, Chilean feminists see no contradiction between class struggle and the struggle for women's liberation.[100] However, they do argue that women's oppression transcends class oppression. Despite the fact that women of different social classes experience oppression in different ways, they are all subject to the same structures of patriarchal domination. Poor and working-class women suffer more under the double burden of capitalist exploitation and sexual oppression; all women suffer from domestic violence, economic dependence, sexual aggression, discrimination in the workplace, lack of reproductive control, and clandestine abortion.

Clearly related to the feminist rejection of traditional class analysis is the focus on praxis. Because a feminist perspective begins with women's understanding of their own experience of oppression, the "political" enters their daily lives. In other words, change begins at home. Women's political activity should be defined by them on the basis of their concerns and their needs.[101] Women's political activity is born of their oppression. Thus, middle-class women, generally neglected in the traditional political discourse, constitute an important new political constituency. Contrary to a traditional class analysis that sees only the working class as exploited and oppressed by capitalist relations of production, feminists argue that all women are subject to patriarchal domination (although this takes different forms, according to the economic system).

When the military dismantled the institutional structures for political participation, Chileans were obligated to invent new ways of "doing politics" *(hacer la política)*. By exacerbating the contradictions in Chilean society, the military unwittingly ensured that new forms of social movement mobilization would emerge.[102] New concepts of politics and political activity, the reconceptualized articulation between political parties and social movements, as well as the daily practical struggles to create a viable opposition to the military, have played an important role in the emergence, growth, and development of a feminist democratic politics in Chile.

As Kirkwood's research pointed out, historically the relationship between political parties and women's organizations has been problematic. During the 1930s and 1940s, in the heyday of the struggle for women's suffrage, women's groups consistently and stubbornly attempted to maintain their autonomy from political parties, traditionally *the* structure of political participation. What is curious is why, after the vote was won in 1949, women abandoned their organizations and became absorbed into political parties.[103] Most of the women's groups active in the 1980s were cognizant of the tendency of political parties to co-opt women's struggles. For this reason, movement autonomy was one of the most important issues for the Chilean women's movement during the pre-transition period. In practice, this emphasis on autonomy was reflected in the strategy of double militancy *(doble militancia)*, that is, actively participating in traditional political organizations such as parties and unions while at the same time building a strong feminist movement independent of those organizations. The argument was that if a strong women's movement exists outside of the traditional institutional mechanism of political participation, women will be in a much stronger position to avoid letting things go back to the way they were after the struggle for a representative parliamentary democracy has been won.

In the 1980s there was some indication that political parties, forced by circumstances to redefine their role in Chilean political culture, responded to the need to address gender concerns. The Socialist Party-Núñez, the Christian Democratic Party, and the dissolved Socialist Convergence (Convergencia Socialista) all made such attempts. Adriana Muñoz argues that traditionally political parties have tried to build "women's fronts," which simply reproduce the party line. She suggests that even though political parties began to resurrect women's departments and commissions, the strength of the women's movement will foster new kinds of relationships between the parties and their female membership.[104] What was not clear at the time was whether these responses represented yet another attempt to incorporate and thus co-opt women, adding gender issues to the long list of sectarian conflicts. On the positive side is the extent to which groups like MUDECHI and CODEM, originally founded on partisan connections, were able to distance themselves from their respective parties and function independently and autonomously. During the 1980s the visibility of women and of gender issues in newspapers, news magazines, on the radio, in alternative research centers, and in the elections of professional associations[105] increased considerably.

However, on the negative side, partisan splits, sectarian conflict, and shifting political alliances in the opposition were often reflected in women's movement organizations such as the umbrella group MEMCH83 and the Women's Department of the National Trade Union Coordinator (Coordinadora Nacional Sindical). Acrimonious debates within the movement on the role of Mujeres por la Vida, perceived as co-opting the feminist movement, did little to strengthen the autonomous base of the women's movement. Mujeres por la Vida had tremendous convocatory and legitimating power that transcended party alliances, but some saw it as co-opting the energies, organizational base, and public visibility of the feminist movement. Similarly, there was concern that the Federación de Mujeres Socialistas (FMS), a feminist partisan group linked to the Partido Socialista-Núñez, would rekindle sectarian struggles. This type of conflict emerged around International Women's Day, March 8, 1988, when many women's groups, both feminist and nonfeminist, declined to participate in the commemorative act given the partisan agenda of the group that organized it.[106]

Democratic Transition, the State, and the Women's Movement in Chile, 1987–1992

Recent analyses have distinguished 1987 to 1990[107] as the period in which the various elements of the women's movement, along with other social and political actors, were singularly dedicated to mobilizations around the plebiscite and the subsequent presidential and parliamentary elections.[108] Not only were women's organizations participating in the "no" campaign in 1988, they were, at the same time, trying to develop strategies to carry their agenda and their demands into the national political arena.

Beginning in 1986, with the "Demandas de las Mujeres" presented to the Asamblea de la Civilidad, women's groups interceded in a variety of ways, attempting to develop an awareness among political leaders of the constituency they represented. For example, the First National Conference of Rural Women (July 1986), the Second National Conference of Working Women (July 1987), and the Subcommission on Women and Legislation of the Study Group on the Constitution all developed a series of demands that they proposed be carried forward in a new democracy. These demands converged on issues related to human rights, human dignity, and a decent standard of living and specified a number of gender-related demands: legislative reform, an end to labor force discrimination against women, and reproductive rights.[109] On July 1, 1988, 22 feminist groups and 11 well-known individuals took out a full-page ad in a major Santiago daily, *La Epoca*, calling upon all Chilean women to participate in the construction of a democracy in which women and men would be equals.

> As feminist women, we are aware of the times we are living in. To all Chilean women, young and old, organized and independent, we would like to propose that we unite to express our own demands of democracy. We further propose that these demands become part of the democratic project to which the majority of us aspire. We think that

the series of basic demands we propose below represent justice for all women. We invite you to support them and propose that together we take them to democratic political parties, to social organizations and unions, to religious institutions and the Chilean Human Rights Commission. Our objective is that these organizations develop a commitment to include our demands as a non-negotiable part of the democracy that all of us, women and men alike, are constructing.[110]

The four basic demands consisted of the following: (1) immediate ratification of the UN Convention on the Elimination of All Forms of Discrimination Against Women, (2) the creation of a national government office with ministerial rank on women's issues, (3) the elimination of the reproduction of sexism and inequality in the educational system, and (4) the requirement that 30 percent of all government decisionmaking positions be held by women. In addition there were a number of gender-specific demands related to women as citizens, women as mothers, and women as workers.

Not long after the victory of the no vote on October 5, 1988,[111] the Concertación Nacional de Mujeres por la Democracia (National Coalition of Women for Democracy) was formed to mobilize women for the 1989 elections and to intercede in an autonomous way in the opposition.[112] According to the executive secretary of the *concertación*, Josefina Rossetti, the main objectives of the organization were to take the women's agenda to the national political arena, formulate a program for the new government to improve the situation of women, and work in the presidential and parliamentary campaigns.[113] Approximately 150 women from a variety of political parties[114] as well as independent feminists, most of whom had long-standing involvements in a variety of women's movement organizations, were actively engaged in the work of the *concertación*. Eleven commissions were organized in the areas of education, health, family, communications, art and culture, work, political participation, rural women *(campesinas)*, poor working-class women *(pobladoras)*, legislation, and the National Office for Women. Each working commission, composed of women with professional expertise in the area, developed not only a diagnostic gender-specific analysis of the problems confronting women but also a series of demands that would hopefully prove the basis for policy development for the new government. For example women working in the area of education developed a set of principles and objectives designed to inform a gender-sensitive educational policy that would focus on the elimination of discrimination and inequality.[115]

The Concertación de Mujeres also worked energetically to raise awareness of women's issues among candidates of the opposition coalition as well as to encourage women themselves to become candidates for the parliamentary elections.[116] They distributed their own election and educational pamphlet, in which six main demands were specified: (1) the allocation of 30 percent of decisionmaking government positions to women, (2) the creation of a National Women's Office with ministerial rank, (3) the elimination of sexist education, (4) the development of a program of education and advertising to promote equality, (5) the elimination of sexism in advertising, and (6) the ratification of the UN Convention on the Elimination of All Forms of Discrimination Against Women.[117] In the pamphlet the *concertación* also advocated legal reform, for example, penalization for domestic violence; social responsibility for maternity and the right of women to decide if, when, and how many children they would have; legislation to assist women working in paid domestic service; pensions for housewives; and the elimination of all forms of discrimination against women, especially in the labor force.

One of the results of their efforts was that "women" was added to the constituency of social actors to whom Aylwin's presidential campaign was addressed. One of the campaign pamphlets, "Mujer: Chile te quiere" ("Women: Chile Cares About You," cowritten by Alicia Frohmann, the coordinator of the Commission in charge of the Presence of Women in Public Life of the Concertación de Mujeres), promises equal rights for women and men, legal reform, increased opportunities for women in the labor force, a national women's office and the ratification of the UN convention.[118]

The political opening up *(apertura política)* during the latter part of the 1980s dramatically increased the opportunities for political participation, and as a result, women were able to clearly and successfully put their concerns, issues, and demands on the national political agenda during the election process. Importantly, the creation of the opposition coalition and the Concertación Nacional de Mujeres por la Democracia left little room in the women's movement for the exacerbation of partisan tensions, which have the tendency to fragment and atomize the movement. Indeed, according to one commentator, the Concertación de Mujeres represents the first time in Chilean history that women have attempted a sustained mobilization effort of such magnitude.[119]

Another consequence of the women's movement's efforts to carry its agenda to the arena of national politics is the extent to which political parties have responded to the need to incorporate women's issues. Even right-wing parties such as National Renovation (Partido Renovación Nacional, PRN) and the National Party (Partido Nacional, PN) have had to develop or at least make known their position on women's rights.[120] For example, in its declaration of principles, the PRN states that it will "energetically sustain the principle of equality of rights for women in all activities, both labor-related and others in which women carry out duties similar to men, monitor the opening of more opportunities for women, and oppose all forms of unjust economic or social discrimination that affects women."[121] Of course the passage continues by pointing out that women also have a special calling as givers of life and transmitters of moral values and tradition, and as the backbone of the family.

The various parties of the Center and Left, for example, the Humanist-Green Party (Partido Humanista-Verde, PHV), Christian Democratic Party (Partido Democracia Cristiana, PDC), Socialist Party (Partido Socialista, PS), Party for Democracy (Partido por la Democracia, PPD), and Communist Party (Partido Communista, PC), have all articulated positions that incorporate, to a greater or lesser extent, a critical and sometimes feminist analysis of the situation of women in Chilean society. Some have instituted practices to facilitate the greater participation of women. For example, both the PS and PPD have affirmative action programs in place such that 20 percent of all high-level decisionmaking positions must be occupied by women. In fall 1992, the PS created a vice presidency in charge of women's issues. In 1991, the rates of female representation in executive positions in some parties appeared to have reached an all-time high. In the PHV, 38.5 percent; in the PPD, 25 percent; and in the PS, 21.1 percent of executive positions were held by women.[122] The PHV was the first political party in Chilean history to propose a female presidential candidate, Laura Rodríguez, who was later elected to the Chamber of Deputies.[123]

Political parties, Left, Center, and Right, have often appealed to the female electorate for support on the basis of woman's traditional roles of wife, mother, and guardian of hearth and home.[124] During the 1989 election campaign, however, the parties of the *concertación* also expanded this narrow definition to include women as citizens, as workers, and as participants in the creation of the new democracy. Furthermore, the existence of inequality and discrimination against women was formally and publicly recognized. This is clearly a direct consequence of women's movement mobilization against the dictatorship, the Concertación de Mujeres' support of the opposition coalition candidates, and especially intensive lobbying on the part of feminist activists inside party structures.[125]

With the victory of the opposition and of President Patricio Aylwin on December 14, 1989, women's groups held their breath to see whether or not the new government would incorporate any of their demands. Unfortunately, women continued to be underrepresented in the formal structures of political decisionmaking. Only 10 of 167 parliamentarians, 3 of 27 vice ministers, 1 of 15 mayors appointed by the president, and, until January 1991, no cabinet ministers were women.[126] But Aylwin made good on at least one of his promises. In May 1990 he presented to Parliament the legislation that would create the Servicio Nacional de la Mujer (National Women's Service, SERNAM). It was passed in December 1990 and SERNAM officially began to function in January 1991.[127]

SERNAM represents an important government initiative as well as a significant accomplishment of the women's movement. It has ministerial rank, and its director is the only woman currently in the cabinet. It has a budget, an infrastructure, and it is not dependent on the current government for its continued existence. Its objectives, laid out in a pamphlet published in July 1990, include the following:

> to dignify and to value the role played by women in society; to develop and propose social policies to strengthen the family; to promote programs which would dignify and value domestic labor and its indispensable role for the functioning of the family and of society; to support and create channels of participation for all women in Chile; to review current law and to promote legislative change and other policies designed to end discrimination against women; and to comply with Chile's commit-

ment when it signed the UN's Convention on the Elimination of All Forms of Discrimination against Women.[128]

Hagamos un nuevo trato (Let's make a new social contract), SERNAM's slogan, is intended to encourage mutual respect between women and men, the recognition of women's contribution to development, and the elimination of the barriers to equality in order to create a just, free, and integrated society.[129] By the end of 1992, SERNAM had established offices in all of the 12 regions of Chile, in addition to the metropolitan region of Santiago; published or copublished numerous documents and pamphlets;[130] established formal links with other government agencies and ministries;[131] facilitated the presentation of proposals for legal reform;[132] established a program for female heads of households in conjunction with the municipality of Santiago; established a network of women's information centers; and created a national commission on domestic violence.[133]

Although the establishment of a national office to deal with women's issues (rather than a ministry to protect the family as right-wing parties demanded) has been lauded as a major accomplishment of the women's movement, it has not been viewed uncritically. Raquel Olea, director of La Morada, suggested that "today, after two years of democratic rule, SERNAM has become established in public opinion as an agency which develops and monitors social policies dealing with women, policies which, in terms of official discourse, tend to reinforce the traditional roles of women as wife-mother and modern housewife, albeit with the right to a professional education."[134]

Natacha Molina of the Instituto de la Mujer (Women's Institute) points out that SERNAM represents little more than the fulfillment of a measure taken by most other legislatures in the contemporary world.[135] Claudia Serrano, a sociologist working with the municipality of Santiago, asks whether SERNAM represents the state's co-optation of the feminist agenda.[136] There is also a problem with SERNAM's credibility, at least in the women's movement. Although there are a few well-known women's movement leaders in key positions in SERNAM, the majority of the other appointees as well as its director, María Soledad Alvear, are women who have little history or experience working in or with women's organizations.[137]

Unfortunately, SERNAM has replaced the women's movement as the key interlocutor in the public discourse on women's issues. It is a government agency that consistently frames women's issues in the context of the need to preserve and harmonize family life and has focused public discourse almost exclusively in terms of three basic themes: legal reform, women as heads of households in the lower socioeconomic strata, and domestic violence. But domestic violence is constructed as an issue on the grounds that "the family is the basic unit of society. Healthy families make a healthy society. A healthy family is a family in which there is affection and respect among its members, where each person can develop himself [sic] as an individual."[138] SERNAM's conservative discourse may very well reflect its sensitivity to right-wing opposition and the need to move cautiously, yet its failure to engage the women's movement as an important interlocutor cuts it off from its major constituency.

Since the election, several proposals for legal reform have been presented to Parliament.[139] Proposed divorce legislation would provide the possibility for the dissolution of the marriage contract. There is no such possibility currently in Chile. Marriages can be formally dissolved only by annulment.[140] In November 1991, a new law was proposed that would reinstate therapeutic abortion in the case of danger to the mother's health, rape, or incest. Until 1988, when Pinochet criminalized abortion under all circumstances, therapeutic abortion was permitted only if the mother's life was in danger. Legislation was presented in May 1991 to modify the labor code to give men and women the right to take a day off to attend a sick child under the age of one, and men the right to take three days off for the birth of a child. The article that prohibits women from doing certain kinds of work would be eliminated. A new proposal, presented to Parliament in September 1990, would make domestic violence a crime, specify sentencing practices, and facilitate the lodging of complaints.[141] All of these proposals, with the exception of the latter, are still being studied by various parliamentary commissions and committees.[142]

Given the sociopolitical changes occurring in contemporary Chilean society, it is not surprising to find that the women's movement itself is experiencing a period of transition. Many of the movement organizations active in the 1980s have disappeared; others demonstrate a remarkable resiliency. New groups have emerged, the number of nongovernmental organizations working with women has mushroomed,[143] and support institutions such as women's studies programs appear to be flourishing.

Two examples of women's movement organizations that have become important feminist *institutions* are La Morada and the Instituto de la Mujer. Despite its shaky beginnings in 1983, La Morada appears to be one of the most stable, enduring, and visible faces of feminism in the country. The work of the women of La Morada is organized in four areas: (1) health, focusing specifically on mental health and the consequences of domestic and sexual violence; (2) organizational support, particularly to women in the lower socioeconomic strata; (3) education and culture; and (4) Radio Tierra, a feminist radio station. La Morada provides courses and workshops attended by approximately 240 women per year and in August 1992 cosponsored a two-day seminar focusing on education and gender with the Ministry of Education and the Metropolitan University of Santiago. The Instituto de la Mujer, formed in 1987 primarily by *retornadas* (women returning from exile), continues to combine research with grassroots activity in a number of areas: women's health; a women's center; and workshops for grassroots women's leaders, victims of domestic violence, and legal aid. It is an organization whose objectives are to contribute to the struggle against discrimination and women's subordination in Chilean society.

The work of both these institutions is consistent with the typically professional and service-oriented work of nongovernmental organizations (NGOs), defined by José Abalos and Rodrigo Egaña as "non-profit institutions, with paid staff sometimes supplemented by volunteers, that emerge to assist other social groups, but without seeking their own social or political representation. Their work is focused on direct social action, like the satisfaction of basic needs, or on academic work, or on a combination of both activities."[144] Significantly, their focus is much less on activism and much more on lending professional, technical, and educational support to other women and groups of women.

During 1991–1993 changes occurred in other organizations as well.[145] CODEM (Committee for the Defense of Women's Rights) has transformed itself from a militant feminist and leftist organization into a facilitator of self-help activities, offering courses and workshops in everything from relaxation to adolescent sexuality. MOMUPO (Movement of Shantytown Women) participated actively in the elections, but since that time its activities appear to have diminished significantly. The Chilean Human Rights Commission has recently established a Women's Program, primarily in response to new funding prerequisites. The focus of this program is on providing services to other women's groups and nongovernment organizations. The Association of Democratic Women, originally formed to do solidarity work with political prisoners, now focuses on defending women's rights, ecological issues, violence against women, and women's political participation. What used to be the Women's Department of the National Trade Union Coordinator has become the Women's Technical Committee (Secretaría Técnica de la Mujer) of the Central Unitaria de Trabajadores (United Worker's Center). The objectives of this committee include trying to get more women into positions of power on the governing bodies of the union federation, facilitating the inclusion of women's issues in collective bargaining, and lobbying the government for the reform of labor laws and the way in which they discriminate against women. MEMCH has ceased to be a body dedicated to coordinating the efforts of women's groups and now operates as a nongovernmental organization out of a new women's center. Most of its member groups have now dissolved, with the exceptions of CODEM and the Association of Democratic Women, many of whose members now participate in the newly regrouped MEMCH. Their work consists of developing awareness in women of gender issues, violence against women, issues related to women and aging, and women's health.

Although CEM (Women's Studies Research Center) continues to thrive, a second women's studies research organization was formed in 1990, the Center for Studies for the Development of Women (Centro de Estudios para el Desarrollo de la Mujer—CEDEM). During the early 1990s women's studies courses and programs were established at a number of Chilean universities, most notably at the University of Chile and the University of Concepción. The first National Women's Studies Conference was held in November 1992 at the University of Santiago. The women's bookstore La Librería Lila continues to be a fixture in the women's community; Radio Tierra, the feminist radio station, recently celebrated its first-year anniversary; *Marea Alta,* a women's monthly newspaper, has been publishing for almost two years; and Cuarto Propio, a women's publishing house established in 1987, has been steadily increasing the number of titles it publishes. Isis Internacional, with headquarters in Geneva and Santiago, continues to be a major source of support to the women's movement, providing Chile's most comprehensive documentation center on women as well as coordinating two international networks, one on women's health and one on women and violence.

One of the most significant aspects of the changes during 1991–1993 is the extent to which an NGO discourse and framework permeates and characterizes many women's movement organizations. This discourse constructs key organizations of the women's movement (both feminist and nonfeminist) as professional and technical service organizations rather than as grassroots activist organizations. In some ways, it is both a cause and effect of the professionalization and institutionalization of the Chilean women's movement. Two factors are probably responsible for this change. First, there is a renewed emphasis in Chile on using the conventional language and methods of development, a consequence of the return to civilian rule. Second, international funding agencies have decreased their support for Chilean social movement organizations. Ironically, funding agencies appear significantly less likely to underwrite social movement organizations in a democratic state than they were when Chile was living under military rule. Structured organizations that provide professional and technical support to the less-advantaged social sectors seem to have greater funding possibilities. Furthermore, programs organized and coordinated by SERNAM, an agency of the state, are competing for the same considerably diminished resources.[146]

There is concern among women's movement activists that the women's movement is disappearing or at least is in a seriously weakened state.[147] Two of the areas that have been especially problematic in recent years are the relationship between social movements and what has traditionally been defined as politics in Chile, and the relationship between the women's movement and the state.

An important element of the construction of a feminist politics during the period of military rule was the reconceptualization of what is political. The politicization of daily life refocused the nature of political life and also the ways in which women "do" politics. The shift in the locus of political activity away from the workplace and to the home and neighborhood[148] also entailed a new conception of *lo político,* that is, those areas of human life and social organization that are considered political.[149] Military rule also weakened the traditional hegemony of political parties over political activity given the repression and criminalization of party activity and the dismantling of the institutions of political participation. Women's movement activists believed that the strength of their autonomous movement would keep them from being absorbed into the traditional exclusionary political process after the return to democracy, but it appears that the business of politics is business as usual. Speaking of the period of mobilization for the election process, Ana María Arteaga, a sociologist with CEDEM, comments: "In fact, neither our active and permanent public presence nor our evident capacity for political intervention and social resistance, developed during these years, have been sufficient to alter our marginal and scarce representation in those decisions which define not only strategies for struggle and mobilization against the military regime, but also the orientation and content of what will constitute Chile's future democracy."[150]

During the preelection period, the women's movement revisited earlier debates around autonomy and integration in an attempt to develop a strategy for participation in the national political arena. According to Claudia Serrano, the victory of the no vote in the plebiscite opened up new opportunities for political participation such that feminists entered the political game, demanding spaces for women's participation.[151] She further argues that during this time, the traditional division between *las feministas* and *las políticas* (women active in political parties) reversed itself with feminists entering electoral politics and proposing public policy and *las políticas* becoming involved in feminism.

At the same time, many expressed a concern that political parties would co-opt the feminist discourse.[152] Adriana Muñoz, a socialist feminist later elected to the Chamber of Deputies, argued that one of the most important aspects of the plebiscite was the extent to which women "actively incorporated themselves into the processes unleashed in the political-institutional system."[153] The implication is that the women's movement would need to find ways not only of engaging the traditional political process but also of integrating its struggle and its discourse with the traditional ways of "doing politics." The women's movement continues to struggle with this issue, more so now, perhaps, because of the transformation of many movement organizations into NGOs.

There seems to be general consensus among women's movement activists, particularly feminists, that their marginalization in the areas of formal political decisionmaking belies the massive mobilization of women and feminists that occurred in the opposition to the dictatorship.[154] This leads Natacha Molina, for example, to suggest that it is no longer enough that the women's movement work to construct a mass base of grassroots organizations but that it must find ways to participate more effectively in national political decisionmaking structures, both in the state and in the political parties.[155] "Social democratization has to do with the constitution of a women's movement, sufficiently strong both quantitatively and qualitatively, to demand an effective participation in the transition. Political democracy, on the other hand, refers to practices directly related to the State, and as a result, to the presence of women in the formal structures of the political system, and the formulation of public policies that incorporate gender in state activities."[156] Molina is arguing for a strategy of both autonomy and integration and implies that the debate about autonomy versus integration is no longer a helpful one. It is also clear that the relationship between the women's movement and the state, and the articulation of a feminist agenda within the state and political parties, is probably one of the key challenges currently facing the Chilean women's movement.

The key state institution that has the potential to mediate a relationship between the women's movement and the state is, of course, SERNAM. As indicated earlier in this chapter, however, SERNAM is not at all effectively responsive to the women's movement or the feminist agenda. Clearly, a national women's office with ministerial rank whose mandate is not only to propose and develop programs to improve the lives of women but also to monitor the policies of other state agencies is in a difficult position. It is dependent upon and of the state; at the same time it is expected to be the state's key interlocutor and critic. This role would be less problematic if it were connected to a strong and independent women's movement. Yet SERNAM seems deliberately to antagonize the constituency to which it ought to be accountable.[157] And the women's movement and feminists in particular seem not to have taken advantage of the opportunity SERNAM affords to gain access to state decisionmaking; that is, they have not constructed *themselves* as the key interlocutor for SERNAM; they have not made SERNAM accountable to the women's movement.

Another way in which the relationship between the state and the women's movement is constructed is through the NGOs. Ana María Arteaga argues that the state has neither recognized nor adequately utilized the impressive amount of professional and technical expertise on women's issues developed by the NGOs during the military regime.[158] Women's NGOs, however, are choosing to stay open to the possibility of developing links with the state, in part because of their precarious financial circumstances but also in order to enhance their influence.[159] The absence of a working relationship between the women's NGOs and the state, according to Arteaga, reflects and perpetuates the continued marginalization of women and women's issues, and the failure of the women's movement to take an aggressive role in setting the agenda for the state.

Clearly, one of the key problems that has emerged in the role of the women's movement in the Chilean transition to democracy is the development of a strategy that would lock in the state's accountability to women. Although the women's movement during the period of dictatorship did successfully establish that women are important social and political actors, this has not been successfully translated into national political decisionmaking.

Conclusion

It remains to be seen whether the inclusionary aspects of democratization are likely to occur in the process of regime change in Latin America.[160] The Brazilian case, at least, indicates a measure of qualified success in the institutionalization of mechanisms of state access that have permitted women to articulate and act on their concerns. In Chile, the military dictatorship itself produced the conditions that gave rise to what became a strong and independent women's movement and helped create a feminism that was grounded both theoretically and in practice in opposition to authoritarianism, a characteristic deeply embedded in Chilean culture. Despite the military's attempts to eliminate a public role for women, women nevertheless mobilized in the face of political and economic crisis to oppose military rule. The question that remains, however, is whether this crisis mobilization has been transformative.

During the military period, women began to view themselves as equal partners in the political process with the right to occupy and define for themselves what constitutes political space. By empowering themselves as individuals, they challenged the state's right to define their political identities. A concern with women's rights and gender issues became increasingly more legitimate as a vehicle for political activity, and public awareness obligated the opposition to reexamine its own values—often only too consistent with Pinochet's own political project for women. In the later part of the 1980s, women's groups successfully took their agenda into the realm of national politics, first in the opposition coalitions such as the Asamblea de la Civilidad and later in the election campaigns. The tremendous success of the Concertación Nacional de Mujeres por la Democracia as an interlocutor for the Concertación de Partidos por la Democracia reflects the extent to which the women's movement had acquired legitimacy, visibility, and strength as an important social and political actor.

The challenges that faced the Chilean women's movement of the 1980s included building a mass movement, developing cross-class alliances, and coordinating the mobilization of the women's opposition, *and,* importantly, maintaining autonomy to ensure that social movements would not be marginalized by political parties in the transition. In 1987 I was optimistic that the Chilean political landscape and culture had been significantly transformed by the emergence of such a dynamic women's movement. Intense repression and economic hardship had fostered courageous resistance, and women saw themselves as writing a new chapter in their collective history. But this new historical chapter is going to take a bit longer to write. It appears that major cross-class alliances have not been formed, there is not a mass movement that can be mobilized for its own goals, and the women's movement continues to be marginalized by political parties.

But the women's movement itself is in transition. It emerged as an oppositional force, working collectively with other oppositional movements. With the return to democracy and with many members of the opposition now part of the state apparatus, the oppositional identity of the women's movement remains unchanged. What is different is the nature of the state it confronts.[161] Pinochet is no longer the enemy, and the women's movement must redefine its relationship to the state. New social and political actors have (re)emerged to which the women's movement must be responsive, including local and regional governments, trade unions, and SERNAM.[162]

Although the women's movement may be struggling with responses to some of these issues, its accomplishments are significant. Despite its shortcomings,

SERNAM *does* represent an important achievement of the women's movement and it *does* put a public, state-legitimized face on the struggle to end discrimination against women. And although the number of women, let alone feminists, in decisionmaking positions is limited, women like Laura Rodríguez, Adriana Muñoz, and María Antonieta Saa *are* making a difference. As members of Parliament, Rodríguez and Muñoz put so-called private issues like divorce, abortion, and domestic violence firmly on the agenda of public and political debate. Saa, during her two-year term as mayor of Conchalí, hosted a conference on domestic violence organized by five women's organizations and organized a series of women's rights workshops. In July 1990 she facilitated the opening of the Women's Community House (Casa Comunal de la Mujer) by the Instituto de la Mujer, which works with victims of domestic violence and has successfully offered workshops to police officers. New generations of women are forming their own feminist organizations, such as the Feminist Initiative (Iniciativa Feminista), a socially heterogeneous organization formed by women energized by the Latin American and Caribbean Feminist Encounter held in Argentina in 1990. In 1991 over 500 women participated in the first national *feminist* conference in Chile, the second of which took place in January 1993. And "feminism" as a word, as a concept, and as a political project has entered the realm of public discourse.[163]

At this early stage in the Chilean transition to democracy, there are still many unanswered questions. What are the implications of the transformation of so many movement organizations into NGOs? Will partisan-based feminism replace or marginalize the autonomous movement? Will SERNAM simply co-opt the feminist agenda? The answers to these questions will determine the prospects for an increased role for women in Chilean democracy.

Notes

1. These percentages are based on figures from María Eugenia Hirmas and Enrique Gomariz, "La situación de la mujer chilena, en cifras" (Santiago: Departamento de Comunicaciones, Servico Nacional de la Mujer, June 1990), 21–22.

2. For a discussion of the Chilean transition to democracy and its incumbent difficulties, see Alan Angell and Benny Pollack, "The Chilean Elections of 1989 and the Politics of the Transition to Democracy," *Bulletin of Latin American Research* 9, 1 (1990): 1–23; Brian Loveman, "Government and Regime Succession in Chile," *Third World Quarterly* 10, 1 (January 1988): 260–280; Alan Angell, "Why Is the Transition to Democracy Proving So Difficult in Chile?" *Bulletin of Latin American Research* 5, 1 (1986); Augusto Varas, *Crisis de legitimidad del autoritarismo y transición democrática en Chile*, FLACSO, Working Document, no. 415, Santiago, 1989; and Guillermo Campero and Rene Cortazár, "Actores sociales y la transición a la democracia en Chile," CIEPLAN Studies Collection, no. 25, December 1988.

3. I am adapting here a distinction made by Douglas Chalmers and Craig Robinson between democratization and liberalization. They suggest that "[democratization] embraces both a process of inclusion in the political process and the establishment of an open, com-

petitive relationship among those who are already participating. We use 'liberalization' to denote only the second aspect of democracy, that which concerns contestation, competitiveness, openness." "Why Power Contenders Choose Liberalization," *International Studies Quarterly* 16, 1 (March 1982): 12.

4. Historically, political parties have dominated social movement formation in Chile.

5. See Guillermo Campero, "Luchas y movilizaciones sociales en la crisis: Se constituen movimientos sociales en Chiles?," in Fernando Calderón, ed., *Los movimientos sociales ante la crisis* (Buenos Aires: CLASCO-Consejo Latino-americano de Ciencas Sociales, 1986); Manuel Antonio Garretón, "Political Processes in an Authoritarian Regime: The Dynamics of Institutionalization and Opposition in Chile, 1973–1980," in J. Samuel Valenzuela and Arturo Valenzuela, eds., *Military Rule in Chile: Dictatorship and Opposition* (Baltimore: Johns Hopkins University Press, 1986); Adriana Muñoz, *El movimiento de mujeres en Chile: Una realidad deseada,* Instituto para el Nuevo Chile, Working Document, Santiago, 1986; and J. Samuel Valenzuela and Arturo Valenzuela, "Party Oppositions Under the Chilean Authoritarian Regime," in Valenzuela and Valenzuela, *Military Rule in Chile.*

6. For a discussion of the earlier period in the history of the Chilean women's movement, see Julieta Kirkwood, "Feminismo y participación politicá en Chile," in Eduardo Ortiz, ed., *Temas socialistas* (Santiago: Vector, Centro do Estudios Económicos y Sociales, 1983); and Patricia Chuchryk, "Protest, Politics and Personal Life: The Emergence of Feminism in a Military Dictatorship, Chile 1973–1983," Ph.D. dissertation, York University, Toronto Canada, 1984 (especially chap. 5).

7. *La Epoca,* July 1, 1988.

8. This campaign involved over 1,300 women from the popular sectors in and around Santiago participating in 40-day-long workshops over a period of three months on the issue of gender discrimination and women's rights. Teresa Valdés, "Soy mujer … tengo derechos," *Mujer/Fempress* 98 (December 1989).

9. See Sandra Palestro, *Mujeres en movimiento, 1973–1989,* FLACSO, Working Document, Social Studies Series, no. 14, Santiago, September 1991; Natacha Molina, "Propuestas políticas y orientaciones de cambio en la situación de la mujer," in Manuel Antonio Garretón, ed., *Propuestas Políticas y Demandas Sociales,* vol. 3 (Santiago: FLACSO, 1989); and Adriana Santa Cruz, "Con los pies en la tierra y la cabeza en la estrellas," *Mujer/ Fempress* 90 (April 1989).

10. The focus of the present analysis is on the period of military dictatorship. At the end of 1992, the Chilean state was still in a process of democratic transition after barely two years of civilian rule. Municipal elections were held in 1992, and political parties then geared up for the 1993 presidential and parliamentary elections. With such a short tenure, it is difficult to accurately assess the role of the women's movement in the process of constructing the new democracy.

11. Most of the data on which this chapter is based were collected during 1982–1983 for my doctoral dissertation, "Protest, Politics and Personal Life." Return field trips in 1985 and 1987 provided valuable additional material. I would like to thank the Social Sciences and Humanities Research Council of Canada for funding the initial research, and the University of Lethbridge Faculty Research Fund for making a return trip in 1987 possible. I would also like to thank Alicia Frohmann for making materials related to the Concertación Nacional de Mujeres por la Democracia available to me from her private collection and my Chilean research assistants, Rita Valencia and María Elena Boisier Pons, for their tireless efforts in quickly gathering the materials necessary to update this chapter.

12. For example, see Robert Carty and the Latin America Working Group, "Chile: Miracle or Mirage?" *LAWG LETTER*, special issue 7, 5–6 (May-August 1982); Alejandro Foxley, "The Neoconservative Economic Experiment in Chile," in Valenzuela and Valenzuela, *Military Rule in Chile*; and Jorge Leiva, "Evolución de la crisis económica," *Coyuntura Económica* 10 (1984).

13. Phil O'Brien and Jackie Roddick suggest that "Chile ... failed to attract very much attention from foreign investors. Any investment that did come into the country from foreign companies went almost entirely into minerals. The size of the local market was too small to offer any real incentive to the manufacturing multinationals, who could in any case export directly to Chile's unprotected markets. As for its cheap labor, they had the choice of a dozen better-situated countries with equally cheap wages throughout the world for their export platforms." *Chile: The Pinochet Decade* (London: Latin American Bureau, 1983), 69.

14. Stephen Volk, "The Lessons and Legacy of a Dark Decade," *NACLA Report on the Americas* 17, 5 (1983): 8.

15. For a discussion of the economy under military rule, see Foxley, "The Neoconservative Experiment"; Volk, "Lessons and Legacy"; O'Brien and Roddick, *Chile*; Leiva, "Evolución"; and Humberto Vega and Jaime Ruiz-Tagle, *Capitalismo autoritario y desarrollo económico: Chile, 1973–1981* (Santiago: Programa de Económía del Trabajo, 1982). *Apsi Economía*, April 1987, cited in the *New Internationalist* 174 (August 1987): 16.

16. In 1975, the government initiated the Program of Minimum Employment (Programa de Empleo Mínimo, PEM) and in 1982, added the Program for Heads of Households (Programa Jefes de Hogar, POJH), both of which pay well below subsistence wages, in 1987, $23 per month for POJH and $14 per month for PEM (*Apsi Economía*, April 1987, cited in the *New Internationalist* 174 [1987]: 16). In the first quarter of 1983, there were 374,100 workers in PEM and 123,700 in POJH. See Berta Teitelboim, *Indicadores económicos y sociales: Serie anuales, 1960–1982* (Santiago: Programa de Economía del Trabajo, 1984), 22. In 1987, there were only 150,000 of these workers: *Apsi Economía*, April 1987, cited in the *New Internationalist* (1987): 16, not because more real jobs had been created but rather because the government, since the latter part of 1983, had been systematically dismantling the programs.

17. O'Brien and Roddick, *Chile*, 63, 91.

18. Foxley, "The Neoconservative Experiment," 48.

19. O'Brien and Roddick, *Chile*, 80.

20. John Dinges, "The Rise of the Opposition," *NACLA Report on the Americas* 17, 5 (September-October 1983): 23.

21. *Apsi Economía*, April 1987, cited in the *New Internationalist* (1987): 16.

22. Carty, "Miracle or Mirage?" 24.

23. Leiva, "Evolución," 61.

24. Ximena Díaz and Eugenia Hola, *Modos de inserción de la mujer de los sectores populares en el trabajo informal urbano* (Santiago: Centro de Estudios de la Mujer, 1985). See also Ximena Díaz and Eugenia Hola, "La mujer en el trabajo informal urbano," in *Mundo de mujer: continuidad y cambio* (Santiago: Centro de Estudios de la Mujer, 1988).

25. Alicia Leiva, "Las desigualdades en el trabajo de hombres y mujeres," *Coyuntura Económica* 14 (1987): 180; Teresa Valdés and Enrique Gomariz, *Mujeres Latinoamericanas en cifras: Chile* (Santiago: Instituto de la Mujer, Ministerio de Asuntos Sociales de España y FLACSO, 1992), 38.

26. Ibid., 187.

27. Valdés and Gomariz, *Mujeres en cifras*, 38.

28. Leiva, "Las desigualdades," 172.

29. Ibid., 183. See also Berta Teitelboim, *Tercera encuesta de empleo en el gran Santiago: Empleo formal, desempleo y pobreza*, PET, Working Document, no. 189, Santiago, March 1992.

30. Ibid., 189. For a full discussion of women's labor force participation during the period of military rule, see Adriana Muñoz, "Fuerza de trabajo femenina: Evolución y tendencias," in *Mundo de mujer*.

31. Personal communication.

32. Luis Razetto, Arno Klenner, Apolonia Ramírez, and Robert Urmaneta, *Las organizaciones económicas populares* (Santiago: Academia de Humanismo a Cristiano, 1983). See also their updated research, *Las organizaciones económicas populares, 1973–1990* (Santiago: Programa de Economía del Trabajo, 1990).

33. Literally, *olla común* means common pot. This has often been translated as "soup kitchen," but given that a soup kitchen generally involves charity work, it is an inaccurate translation. *Ollas comunes* are run by the people and for the people, so to speak.

34. Clotilde Silva, "Movimiento social," paper presented at the International Conference on Women's Political Participation in the Southern Cone, Montevideo, June 26–29, 1986.

35. Razetto et al., 1983, *Las organizaciones*.

36. Muñoz, "El movimiento de mujeres."

37. Ibid., 6, citing a study by Clarisa Hardy, *Estregias organizadas de subsistencia: Los sectores frente a sus necessidas en Chile* (Santiago: Documento de Trabajo, Programa de Economía del Trabajo, 1985).

38. Horacio Walker Larraín, "The Transformation of Practices in Grassroots Organizations: A Case Study in Chile," unpublished Ph.D. dissertation, University of Toronto, 1986, 65.

39. See Muñoz, "El movimiento de mujeres," who makes a similar point.

40. Walker Larraín, *Transformation of Practices*, 65.

41. Walker Larraín indicated that the source of this conceptual distinction is Berta Suárez, another Chilean popular educator. No further information is given.

42. Walker Larraín, *Transformation of Practices*, 55.

43. Ibid., 95.

44. Vega and Ruiz-Tagle, *Capitalismo autoritario*, 4.

45. Harry Diaz, *Forestry Labour, Neo-liberalism and the Authoritarian State: Chile 1973–1981*, Ph.D. dissertation, York University, Toronto, Canada, 1983, 58. In a recent article, Brian Loveman points out that "in general terms the [1980] Constitution institutionalized the concept of 'authoritarian democracy,' reaffirmed traditionally Hispanic values and practices, and emphasized the role of the patriarchal family as the basic cell in a body politic organized as a hierarchical organic entity" (Loveman, "Government and Regime Succession," 268).

46. Indeed, these offenses were made punishable by loss of enfranchisement and legal right to hold public office.

47. See Jinny Arrancibia, Marcelo Charlin, and Peter Landstreet, "One Decade of State Repression in Chile," in Arch Ritter, ed., *Latin America and the Caribbean: Geopolitics, Development and Culture. Conference Proceedings* (Ottawa: Canadian Association for Latin American and Caribbean Studies, 1984); Jon Barnes, "Appendix: Human Rights and the

Pinochet Decade," in O'Brien and Roddick, *Chile*; Dinges, "The Rise of the Opposition"; as well as recent Amnesty International reports.

48. Barnes, "Appendix," 111.

49. See Sonia E. Alvarez, "Women's Movements and Gender Politics in the Brazilian Translation," in the first edition of this book, *The Women's Movement in Latin America: Feminism and the Transition to Democracy* (Winchester, Mass.: Unwin Hyman, 1989), 18–71. She points out (p. 26) that "the institutionalized separation between the public and the private may have, in an ironic historic twist, helped propel women to the forefront of the opposition in Brazil." A similar argument could be made for the Chilean case. Indeed, Alvarez's work clearly underlines the remarkable parallels between the emergence of the Brazilian and the Chilean women's movements, at least for the period up to the transition. See also her comprehensive and stimulating analysis in *Engendering Democracy in Brazil: Women's Movements in Transition Politics* (Princeton, N.J.: Princeton University Press, 1990).

50. Solidarity work can involve any number of activities: for example, visiting political prisoners, giving emotional support to them and their families, soliciting funds to buy cigarettes for them, providing food, acting as a liaison between legal advisers, bringing a warm sweater, acting as a political lobby (when and where possible), and mobilizing community support.

51. This changed in the late 1980s. There is evidence to suggest that women's organizations were added to the list of those targeted for military repression.

52. Information obtained from a group interview I conducted in 1983.

53. For a detailed discussion of the Agrupacíon de Mujeres Democráticas, and for an analysis of why I call participants in these groups "subversive mothers," see Patricia Chuchryk, "Subversive Mothers: The Women's Opposition to the Military Regime in Chile," in S. Charlton, J. Everett, and K. Staudt, eds., *Women, Development and the State* (Albany, N.Y.: State University of New York Press, 1989).

54. "Mujeres en Lucha," *Madres de la Plaza de Mayo*, 4, 37 (December 1987), cited in Sonia Alvarez, "Women's Participation in the 'People's Church': A Critical Appraisal," paper presented at the Fourteenth International Congress of the Latin American Studies Association, New Orleans, Louisiana, March 17–19, 1988, 21. Although these words are those of a leader of the Madres of the Plaza de Mayo in Argentina, nevertheless they are equally relevant to women's groups throughout Latin America. See also Chuchryk, "Subversive Mothers."

55. For greater discussion of EPF, see María de los Angeles Crummett, "El Poder Femenino: The Mobilization of Women Against Socialism in Chile," *Latin American Perspectives* 4, 4 (Fall 1977): 103–113. Michelle Mattelart, "La mujer y la linea de masa de la burguesía: El caso de Chile," in María del Carmen Elú de Leñero, ed., *La mujer en América Latina*; and Chuchryk, "Protest, Politics and Personal Life," 220–226.

56. Norbert Lechner and Susana Levy, *Notas sobre la vida cotidiana III: El discipinamiento de la mujer*, FLACSO, Discussion Material, no. 57, Santiago, 1984, 56.

57. Ibid., 7.

58. For an excellent discussion of what Pinochet means by "political," see Giselle Munizaga, *La mujer el vecino y el deportista en los micomedios de gobierno: Un estudio sobre construccíon de sujetos políticos a través del discurso oficial* (Santiago: Centro de Indagacíon y Expresíon Cultural y Artistica [CENECA], 1983). See also Giselle Munizaga and Lilian Letelier, "Mujer y Regimen Militar," in *Mundo de mujer*.

59. For a discussion of both of these organizations and the role they played in Chilean society, see Cristina Larraín, *Catastro de organizaciones femeninas del gobierno* (Santiago: Instituto Chileno de Estudios Humanistas, 1982); Munizaga, *La mujer, el vecino y el deportista*"; Lechner and Levy, "Notas sobre la vida cotidinana"; and Chuchryk, "Protest, Politics and Personal Life," 233–240.

60. It is necessary to point out that the military did not invent this very traditionally and very conservative ideological image of women. It is an image of long historical duration not only in Chile but also in the rest of Latin America.

61. This is not entirely accurate. Probably the first women to experience the contradictions were the mothers, wives, and pregnant women who were imprisoned, tortured, or "disappeared." Their status as "reproducers" offered them little protection from repression, as Ximena Bunster-Burotto so poignantly points out. See her "Surviving Beyond Fear: Women and Torture in Latin America," in June Nash and Helen Safa, eds., *Women and Change in Latin America* (South Hadley, Mass.: Bergin & Garvey, 1985).

62. Volk, "Lessons and Legacy," 1983, 4.

63. Ibid., p. 14.

64. Leiva, "Las desigualdades," 172.

65. Julieta Kirkwood, *El feminismo como negacíon del autoritarianismo*, FLACSO, Materia de Discusíon, no. 52, Santiago, 1983.

66. See Alvarez, in this volume, who makes a similar point.

67. Josefina Rosetti, "La mujer y el feminismo" (Santiago: Cuadernos del Círculo, Círculo de Estudios de la Mujer, May 1983), 24.

68. Kirkwood, *El feminismo como negación*, 82.

69. Such as the Agrarian Research Group. These centers emerged as a result of the militarization of the university system. Many were protected by a church umbrella group called the Academy of Christian Humanism.

70. Fanny Tabak, "Women and Authoritarian Regimes," in Judith Hicks Stihm, ed., *Women's Views of the Political World of Men* (Dobbs Ferry, N.Y.: Transnational Press, 1982), 114.

71. Paul Singer, "O feminino e o femenismo," in P. Singer and V. C. Brant, eds., *São Paulo: O povo em movimento* (Petrópolis: Vôzes, 1980), 116–117, cited in Nancy Sternbach, Marysa Navarro, Patricia Chuchryk, and Sonia Alvarez, "Feminisms in Latin America: From Bogotá to San Bernardo," *Signs: A Journal of Women in Culture and Society* 7, 2 (Winter 1992): 393–434. See also Alvarez, *Engendering Democracy in Brazil*, who distinguishes between feminine and feminist groups in her analysis.

72. For a detailed discussion of these and many other Chilean women's groups, see Chuchryk, "Protest, Politics and Personal Life."

73. Some groups have since disappeared or dissolved into other groups. New groups have emerged since 1989. She believed that young women needed to become feminists to effectively participate in other organizations like political parties and trade unions.

74. Julieta Kirkwood, truly one of Latin America's most visionary feminists, died on April 8, 1985. She left behind a rich legacy of feminist theoretical writings, some of which will be briefly discussed here. See *La Formacíon 7* (1980); *Chile: La mujer en la formatíon política*, FLACSO, Documento de Trabajo, no. 109, Santiago, 1981; *Ser política en Chile: Las feministas y los partidos*, FLACSO, Documento de Trabajo, no. 183, Santiago, 1982; "Feminismo y participacíon política en Chile," in Ortiz, *Temas Socialistas; El feminismo como negacíon; Ser política en Chile: Las feministas y los partidos* (Santiago: Facultad

Latinoamericana de Ciencias Sociales, 1986); *Feminarios* (Santiago: Ediciones Documentos, 1987); and Patricia Crispi, *Tejiendo rebeldias: Escritos feminists de Julieta Kirkwood* (Santiago: Centro de la Mujer and La Morada, 1987).

75. In June 1987, the Movement of Women for Socialism organized an extremely well-attended forum on the issue of free elections. For greater discussion of MMS, see Adriano Sepúlveda, "Movimiento de mujeres por el socialsimo," paper presented at the International Conference on Women's Political Participation in the Southern Cone, Montevideo, June 26–29, 1986; and "Mujeres por el socialismo," in M. Angélica Meza, *La otra mitad de Chile* (Santiago: Instituto para el Nueva Chile, 1986).

76. It appears that the 1988 celebration was not nearly as successful, complicated by sectarian battles revolving around the 1989 elections. See Verónica Neumann, "Movilicacíon de mujeres: Una historia de largo aliento," *Apsi* 242 (March 7–13, 1988): The following year, however, 20,000 women participated in International Women's Day celebrations.

77. See Muñoz, "El movimiento de mujeres."

78. Kirkwood, "Feminismo y participacíon," 82.

79. "Democracy in the country and in the home" became the political slogan that identified and distinguished the feminist opposition in the early to mid-1980s as a result of efforts to mobilize a feminist participation in the 1983 Days of Protest. Later it became the rallying cry for the women's movement generally. By 1989, however, it had entered the discourse of the more formal political realm when then presidential candidate Patricio Aylwin used it in his address on the occasion of the endorsement of his candidacy by women of the Concertación de Mujeres. See the "Discurso de Don Patricio Aylwin," Teatro Caupolicán, August 20, 1989. 4.

80. Kirkwood, *Chile: La mujer en la formulacíon política*, 16–17.

81. Many of her writings are mentioned in note 71.

82. For a more complete discussion of Kirkwood's work, see Chuchryk, "Protest, Politics, and Personal Life," 330–337. It is important to point out, too, that she was one of the first scholars to undertake the enormous responsibility of reclaiming for Chilean women their long and rich history.

83. Kirkwood, *Ser política*, 1982, 135–136.

84. Ibid., 16.

85. Kirkwood, *Feminismo como negacíon*, 4–5.

86. Ibid., 9.

87. Ibid., 12.

88. Ibid., 12; *Ser política*, 1982, 9.

89. Kirkwood, *Feminismo como negacíon*, 14.

90. Ibid., 6.

91. Kirkwood, *Chile: La mujer en la formulacíon política*, 5.

92. Julieta Kirkwood, "La política de feminismo," 22, in "El fundamento militar de la dominación patriarcal en Chile," paper presented at the Second Chilean Sociology Conference, 1986. María Elena Valenzuela argues that the Chilean military state is the quintessential expression of patriarchy. She draws similarities between the military's control over civil society to male domination over women. These are not uncommon themes in the Chilean women's movement. See also María Elena Valenzuela, *Todos ibamos a ser reinas: La mujer en Chile militar* (Santiago: Ediciones Chile y América, 1987).

93. Kirkwood, "La política de feminismo," 5.

94. Kirkwood, *Chile: La mujer en la formulacíon política*, 14–15.

95. Kirkwood, *Ser política*, 1982, 7–8.

96. In *Feminismo como negación,* Kirkwood uses the concept of negation as it was formulated by George Lukács in *Historia y concencia de clase* (Mexico: Grijalbo, 1981), which essentially refers to the process of overcoming alienation. Daniel Foss and Ralph Larkin refer to this process as one of "disalienation" in their book *Beyond Revolution: A New Theory of Social Movements* (South Hadley, Mass.: Bergin and Garvey, 1986).

97. Kirkwood, *Feminismo como negacíon,* 15–17.

98. In "Protest, Politics and Personal Life," 316–317, I distinguish between groups with feminist intentions and groups with feminist consequences, that is, that regardless of the objectives around which women mobilize, the activity of working together and sharing often results in the development of an awareness of their disadvantaged situation as women in Chilean society. Contrary to the prevailing conventional wisdom, women who must struggle daily to feed their children are also concerned with their sexuality, reproduction, and the limitations imposed on them by machismo. See Riet Delsing, Andrea Rodó, Pauline Saball, and Betty Walker, *Tipoligía de organizaciones y grupos de mujeres pobladoras,* Studies in Education-Sur, Working Paper, no. 17, Santiago, April 1983; and Eliana Largo, "La paradojal no-participacíon de la mujer," paper presented at the International Conference on Women's Political Participation in the Southern Cone, Montevideo, June 26–29. 1986.

99. Kirkwood, "Feminismo y participacíon," 8–9.

100. Kirkwood, "La política de feminismo," 20–21.

101. Kirkwood, *Feminismo como negación,* 11–12.

102. These include the student-youth, peasant, and workers' movements. It is interesting to note that commentators who address theoretically the issue of social movement formation in Chile tend to ignore the women's movement—a further example of the historical invisibility of women? See Angell, "Why Is the Transition to Democracy Proving So Difficult in Chile?"; Campero, "Luchas y movilizaciones sociales"; and Garretón, "Political Processes in an Authoritarian Regime."

103. Julieta Kirkwood, *La formacíon de la conciencia feminista,* FLACSO, Discussion Paper, no. 7, Santiago, 1980; *Ser política;* and *El feminismo como negacíon;* see also Muñoz, *El movimiento de mujeres.*

104. Muñoz, *El movimiento de mujeres.*

105. See, for example, Alicia Olivia, "Elecciones en Colegio de Profesores: Las mujeres a la palestra," *Análisis* (June 1–7, 1987). She interviewed several female candidates for election to the teachers' federation (Colegio de Profesores), all of whom raise gender concerns.

106. Neumann, "Movilizacíon de mujeres."

107. The original article was written in 1987. This section has been added in 1992 and is based on field research currently in progress.

108. Palestro, *Mujeres en movimiento;* and Molina, "Propuestas políticas."

109. These documents are reproduced in *Mujer/Fempress,* special issue, "Demandas de las Mujeres" (1987).

110. *La Epoca,* July 1, 1988.

111. In aggregate terms, not controlling for region or social class, more men than women voted no. Of all votes cast, 51.2 percent of the women voting and 58.5 percent of the men voting rejected Pinochet. Natacha Molina, "La mujer: Un voto conservador?" *Mujer/ Fempress* 99 (January 1990); and Valdés and Gomariz, *Mujeres en cifras.* It is beyond the scope of the present work to suggest an explanation for what appears to be a greater tendency toward conservatism among women.

112. The Concertación de Partidos por la Democracia was formed by political parties of the Center and Left not only to organize for the no vote but also to present a single presidential candidate. It included the Liberal, Radical, Social Democratic, Christian Democratic, Christian Left, Humanist, Green, Socialist and For Democracy Parties. The Communist Party and the Movement of the Revolutionary Left were not members of the coalition.

113. Josefina Rossetti and Sonia Montecino, eds., *Tramas para un nuevo destino: Propuestas de la Concertación de Mujeres por la Democracia* (Santiago: n.p., 1990).

114. The political parties represented in the Concertación de Mujeres por la Democracia were the same as those in the Concertación de Partidos por la Democracia. As a result, there were some women's groups that chose not to participate in the women's coalition, for example, Mujeres por la Vida, because some of its members are also members of the Communist Party.

115. Rossetti and Montecino, *Tramas para un nuevo destino,* summarizes the work of all 11 commissions, including the proposals for reform and change. It is worth pointing out that many of the women involved in the various commissions of the Concertación de Mujeres eventually went on to take up important government posts. For example, the coordinator of the commission on education was María de la Luz Silva, who was later appointed adviser on women's issues to the minister of education. Delia de Gatto coordinated the commission on the National Women's Office and later became director of regional development for SERNAM. María Antonieta Saa, one of the original 10 women who called for the formulation of the Concertación de Mujeres, was later appointed mayor of Conchalí by President Aylwin.

116. The Concertación de Mujeres por la Democracia presented to the Concertación de Partidos a nomination list of 100 potential women candidates ("La Concertación de Mujeres entregó nómina de candidatas," *La Epoca,* April 29, 1989). As it turned out, only 7 percent of all candidates were women (Adriana Santa Cruz, "Nace la Concertación Nacional de Mujeres," *Mujer/Fempress* 88 [January 1989]).

117. Clearly, the document published by feminists in *La Epoca* laid the groundwork for the demands presented by the Concertación de Mujeres por la Democracia.

118. See also Lucy Davila, "Aylwin anunció medidas para favorecer a la mujer," *La Epoca,* December 4, 1989. This newspaper article summarizes some of the points Aylwin made in a speech at the close of his campaign in Concepción. It is interesting to note that the next day, it was reported in the press that Pinochet had ratified the UN Convention Against All Forms of Discrimination Against Women.

119. Santa Cruz, "Nace la Concertación de Mujeres."

120. Molina ("Propuestas políticas," 81–130) provides one of the very few comparative analyses of political party positions on women.

121. Ibid., 81.

122. Valdés and Gomariz, *Mujeres en cifras,* 105. Interestingly, the PRN at 13.3 percent has greater female representation in executive positions than the PDC at 12.5 percent. There are no data on some parties, for example, the Communist Party.

123. Deputy Laura Rodríguez of the Humanist-Green Party died in August 1992. She and PS deputy Adriana Muñoz have been the feminist members of Parliament who have led the way in proposing legislation to improve the lives of women and put an end to discrimination.

124. For greater discussion, see Chuchryk, "Protest, Politics and Personal Life."

125. For example, the Federation of Socialist Women (FMS), a feminist pressure group within the PS, is largely responsible for many of the changes in the party. According to one informant, this group dissolved when the party was restructured.

126. See Valdés and Gomariz, *Mujeres en cifras,* 102–104, which provides very good figures on the numbers of women in various state agencies.

127. The passage of this law did not occur without considerable public and parliamentary debate. The Right viewed SERNAM as a threat to the family and to the traditional roles of women that have been defined by Western Christianity and to which, they argued, the majority of Chileans subscribed. This debate is summarized in Cecilia Alamos, "Definiendo el papel de la mujer," *El Mercurio,* May 20, 1990, D12, and Ana María Portugal, "Debatiendo en democracia," *Mujer/Fempress* 105 (July 1990): 5–6. For an analysis of the way in which SERNAM was "constructed" by the press, see Giselle Munizaga, "La mujer y la agenda pública: La creación del SERNAM en la prensa de Santiago" (Santiago: CENECA, n.d.).

128. "Qué es el SERNAM?" (Santiago: SERNAM, July 1990), 7–9. This latter point referring to the UN convention is interesting. One of the key recommendations of the UN convention is that the state establish a national women's office. It is worth recalling that it was Pinochet who ratified the UN convention only days before the December 14, 1989, elections.

129. "Información sobre el Servicio Nacional de la Mujer" (Santiago: SERNAM, March 1992), 1.

130. For example, "Ley pareja para la pareja" (Santiago: SERNAM, n.d.); "No más violencia contra la mujer" (Santiago: SERNAM, n.d.); "Trabajadora de casa particular: Conoce y defiende tus derechos" (Santiago: SERNAM, n.d.); *Perfil de la mujer: Argumentos par un cambio* (Santiago: SERNAM and UNICEF, 1992); Gloria Guerra, "Muestreo sobre violencia doméstica en postas y comisarias de la comuna de Santiago" (Santiago: SERNAM, December 1990); Mónica Muñoz and Carmen Reyes, "La familia en Sudamérica" (Santiago: SERNAM, January 1992); "Programas de atención educativos: recreativos para hijos de mujeres temporeras" (Santiago: SERNAM, September 1991); and Carmen Luz Campusano and M. Luz Lagarrigue, *La relación mujer: Trabajo en las funcionarias de la administración pública,* SERNAM, Documento de Trabajo, no. 15, Santiago, April 1992.

131. SERNAM has signed two agreements, one with the Ministry of Housing and Planning to incorporate women, especially heads of households, into the analysis of housing requirements; and the other with the National Consumer Service (Servicio Nacional del Consumidor, SERNAC) to educate women with regard to consumer rights and to educate SERNAC with regard to the situation of women.

132. SERNAM has presented to Parliament, through the minister of labor, a proposal for legislative reform regarding the parental rights of workers (including maternity leave and a modest proposal for paternity leave).

133. This new 12-member commission on domestic violence, the Comisión Interministerial de Violencia Intrafamiliar, includes representatives from seven government ministries, including health, education, external relations, justice and SERNAM, as well as from the police, the National Youth Institute, the General Secretary of the Government, and the Chilean Domestic and Sexual Violence Network. It was formed in June 1992 under the auspices of SERNAM and is coordinated by SERNAM.

134. Raquel Olea, "La redemocratización: Mujer, feminismo y política," *Revista Cultural de Crítica* 3, 5 (July 1992): 31. See also Ana María Portugal, "Con fuersa de mujer," *Mujer/ Fempress* 112–113 (February-March 1991): 13–14.

135. Natacha Molina, "El estado y las mujeres: Una relació difícil," in *Transiciones: Mujeres en los procesos democráticos,* Isis Internacional, Women's Publications, no. 13, Santiago, 1990, 85. See also note 128.

136. Claudio Serrano, "Entre la autonomía y la integración," in *Transiciones: Mujeres en los procesos democráticos,* 103–104.

137. Recently this credibility has been further eroded. Owing to what have been described publicly as ideological differences between Soledad Alvear (PDC), the director of SERNAM, and Soledad Larraín (PS), the vice director, the latter was asked to resign at the end of October 1992. Larraín, who has a long history of activism in the Chilean women's movement and the Socialist Party, was one of the few feminist women in SERNAM with a high degree of credibility in the women's movement. She was replaced by María Teresa Chadwick, who inflamed feminists in her first press interview when she declared that she was opposed to abortion and in favor of life. Chadwick also sidestepped the divorce issue by saying she was personally in favor but that the issue is not on the agenda of the Concertación de Mujeres. See Amelia Miranda, "Confirmada renuncia de Soledad Larraín a SERNAM," *La Nación,* October 29, 1992; "Confirmada la renuncia de Soledad Larraín: María Teresa Chadwick subdirectora del SERNAM," *El Mercurio,* October 30, 1992; and the SERNAM press release published in *La Segunda,* October 30, 1992.

138. "No más violencia contra la mujer" (SERNAM, n.d., n.p.).

139. Most of these have been presented by Rodríguez and Muñoz and supported by other deputies. See note 123.

140. In 1990, for example, there were 7,581 civil and 80 religious annulments. Instituto Nacional de Estadísticas, cited in José Carlos Pérez, "Hasta que la muerte nos una," *Los Tiempos* 1, 2 (October 12–25, 1992): 60.

141. See "No más violencia," the SERNAM educational pamphlet that points out that domestic violence is currently prosecuted (*when* it is prosecuted) using an article of the political constitution, which guarantees to all persons the protection of their physical and psychological integrity. Sentences are limited to up to 100 days in jail, none of which need to be served, or up to six times the state-defined minimum wage, which currently consists of 33,000 pesos, or approximately US$90, per month. The new domestic violence legislation was approved in April 1993.

142. See "El re-cuentro legal," a table in "A paso lento, las mujeres en al transición," *Marea Alta,* December 1991, 6–7, which summarizes various aspects of discriminatory legislation and the proposals for change. The issue of legislative reform has been a key focus during the past few years, in part because the transition to democracy makes change conceivable. One of the groups that has been elaborating proposals for legal reform for several years is the multiparty Subcommission on Women and Legislation of the Study Group on the Constitution. See Wilna Saavedra (and 12 others), *Subcomisión de legislación de la mujer,* Documento de Trabajo, April 1990. Significantly, changes in the provisions of *patria potestad* were approved by Pinochet in 1989. A women married under joint property (*sociedad conyugal*) had been legally defined as similar to a minor; her husband was her legal representative and had dominion over all her goods and could legally forbid her from working outside the home. The new legislation provides that women married under joint property have all the rights that other women have, including the right to dispose of their

own property. This legislation also replaces a woman's obligation to live where her husband chooses and to obey her husband, with a provision for mutual respect and partnership in decisionmaking. See *Nueva ley de la mujer* (Santiago: Ediciones Publiley, 1992). See also María Elena Valenzuela ("The Evolving Roles of Women Under Military Rule," in Paul W. Drake and Iván Jaksić, eds., *The Struggle for Democracy in Chile 1982–1990* [Lincoln: University of Nebraska Press, 1991]), who argues that this and other changes, including the ratification of the UN convention, occurred as a consequence of pressure by women from the right-wing political parties.

143. A table in Valdés and Gomariz (*Mujeres en cifras*, 118) shows 159 NGOs that work with women, 38 of which are specialized and deal exclusively with women, 121 of which have some sort of women's program. See also Ana María Arteaga, Riet Delsing, Lorena Fries, and Catalina Arteaga, *Directorio Nacional de Servicios y Recursos para la Mujer*, 2 vols. (Santiago: Centro de Estudios para el Desarrollo de la Mujer, 1992), which lists no fewer than 138 organizations in metropolitan Santiago alone that work with women (and this does not include those organizations that are mainly research organizations).

144. José Antonio Abalos K. and Rodrigo Egaña B., "La cooperación internacional al desarrollo frente a los cambios políticos en Chile," in *Una puerta que se abre: Los organismos no gubernamentales en la cooperación al desarrollo* (Santiago: Taller de Cooperación al Desarrollo, 1989), 30. In recent years, this discourse has become quite popular. For example, Ana María Arteaga and Eliana Largo, "Los ONG en al area de la mujer y la cooperación al desarrollo," in *Una puerta que se abre: Los oranismos no gubernamentales en la cooperación al desarrollo* (Santiago: Taller de Cooperación al Desarrollo, 1989), 355; Ana María Arteaga, "El difícil camino entre el desencanto y el pragmatismo," *Cooperación International al Desarrollo* 9 (1992): 17–21; and María Elena Boisier Pons, "La mujer en los organismos no gubernamentales y las organizaciones en Chile: Una approximación" (Santiago: CEPAL, 1990).

145. The information in this paragraph comes from interviews conducted in September and October 1992.

146. The decision to operate within the parameters defining NGOs seems to be a very conscious one. MEMCH, for example, decided to cease its coordinating activities to become an NGO and seek external financing. The decision was based on its view that because of diminishing funding resources, an NGO would have greater opportunity to foster movement development. MOMUPO decided that in spite of its funding difficulties, it would not become an NGO precisely because it wanted to maintain its identity as a social movement organization (interview data).

147. Interview data. Also Ana María Arteaga, "Politización de lo privado y subversión del cotidiano," in *Mundo de mujer*; Arteaga and Largo, "Los ONG en el area de la mujer"; and Argeaga, "Las ONG."

148. Fernando Leiva and James Petras, "Chile's Poor in the Struggle for Democracy," *Latin American Perspectives* 13, 4 (Fall 1986): 5–25.

149. In "La paradojal no-participación de la mujer," Largo argues that the way in which Chilean political culture defines political participation excludes women. Kirkwood also suggests this point in *Feminismo como negación* and *Ser política*. Lourdes Arizpe argues that the women's movement in Latin America represents "a new conception of what is political" ("Foreword: Democracy for a Small Two-Gender Planet," in Elizabeth Jelín, ed., *Women and Social Change in Latin America*, London: Zed Books, 1990).

150. Arteaga, "Politización," 565.

151. Serrano, "Entre la autonomía, 103.

152. Ibid.

153. Adriana Muñoz, *Fuera feminista y democracia: Utopía a realizar,* 2nd. ed. (Santiago: Ediciones Documentas Instituto de la Mujer and VECTOR, Centro de Estudios Económicos y Sociales, 1988), 127.

154. Teresa Valdés, "Mujeres latinoamericas: Todo cambia?" *Conosur* 11, 5 (October 1992): 18–23; Regina Rodriguez, "Dos feministas en la administración pública Chilena," *Mujer/Fempress* 102 (April 1990): 5–6; Molina, "El estado y las mujeres"; and Arteaga, "Las ONG."

155. Molina, "El estado y las mujeres," 90.

156. Ibid., 87.

157. The 1992 *Agenda de la Mujer* was the center of a great scandal that played itself out in the media, Parliament, SERNAM, and even the Church. The *Agenda de la Mujer* is one of those daily appointment calendars popular in the feminist community. The 1992 edition, not unlike other editions, carried a number of photographs, commentaries, and short articles all related to the situation of women. One of the short articles was written by Soledad Larraín, in which she attempted to deal honestly with the issue of sexuality. This, in addition to one photograph in particular, enraged the Church and the Right such that the issue was even raised in the Chamber of Deputies. The problem, it was suggested, was that SERNAM, in the representation of its vice director, was inciting a moral crisis. The reaction of the director of SERNAM was to disassociate herself and the state agency from the *Agenda,* indicating that she was unaware of the nature of the publication and would obviously never publish SERNAM material in it again. See "Crisis moral en Chile?" *Mujer/Fempress* 122 (December 1991): 24–25, which republished a collection of newspaper clippings about this event. See also note 137 on the issue of the relationship between SERNAM and the feminist movement.

158. Arteaga, "Las ONG."

159. Ibid.

160. Chalmers and Robinson, "Why Power Contenders Choose Liberalization," 12.

161. I would like to thank Dutch social scientist Frans Schuurman for this insight.

162. Arteaga ("Las ONG") makes these same arguments in her analysis of why the women's movement is in stasis.

163. For example, television interviewers have hosted programs on feminism designed to disabuse viewers of their stereotypes about feminists, and interviewers regularly include questions on gender where appropriate.

FOUR

Women and Democracy in Argentina

MARÍA DEL CARMEN FEIJOÓ
WITH MARCELA MARÍA ALEJANDRA NARI

> Women have enormous social power based on the immediacy of the affection, but they adapt poorly to the institutionalization of politics, which is founded on the masculine logic of power. Their political participation only takes place in moments of extreme tension; their long history of oppression has made brilliant conservatives or ardent anarchists out of women, but never administrators of civilian peace.
> —Rossana Rosanda

Raúl Alfonsín was elected president of a democratic Argentina in 1983; women had played a central role in bringing about the transition to a democracy. But after the election, the day-to-day politics of democracy relegated them to traditional roles and limited their political participation despite their substantial contributions to the process of restoring democracy. The Argentine experience may confirm the generalization that women mobilize to meet the demands of a crisis but that this mobilization is fragile and women often return home when the crisis is past.

The recent history of women's mobilization in Argentina raises two issues: (1) does the Argentine democratic system itself discriminate against women's participation? and (2) to what extent is women's demobilization a consequence of the women's own political discourse? One hypothesis I will explore here is that the political discourse about women that was constructed by Argentine women themselves may have led to the depoliticization of women.

What are the future prospects for women and democracy in Argentina? Politically, the years of democracy since 1983 represent an overall success. Yet the future of democratic development cannot be projected without attention to the role of women; nor can it be assumed that democracy will guarantee the successful articulation of women's interests. The reduction of the number of women deputies elected in 1985 and 1987 is a symptom of the decline in the limited power women attained in 1983.[1] During the civil-military crisis of April 1987, in a moment of extreme tension, women again briefly assumed a leading political role.[2]

As the democratic context matures, women must adapt to the new situation or risk reproducing the very conditions that originally marginalized them. Women could easily become the victims of an obsolete discourse and the victims of a regime that cannot be counted on to share power just because it is "democratic." Argentine experience shows that even when women are a significant factor in the process of democratic transition,[3] the democratic government does not respond by sharing power with them. For their part, women are still using the confrontational discourse developed when they were part of the opposition to dictatorship; they are not adapting to the ordinary requirements of democratic politics, which call for negotiation and bargaining but not (as some feminists have argued) for abandoning their ideals and principles.

The entire period of transition and consolidation of democracy has occurred during a time of international economic crisis. The external debt has imposed severe restraints on growth, affecting women in households and conditioning the multiple choices of daily life. The debt has caused women to increase their efforts to satisfy basic needs. Yet by sending women to the streets to satisfy basic necessities, which displaces them from the traditional private sphere to the public realm, the crisis has the potential for positive effects and may convert the invisibility of women's work into an unavoidable political and public fact.

Although women have been instrumental in the transition and consolidation of democracy and essential to the daily survival of the majority of Argentine homes, they have received very few of the benefits of democracy, whether material or symbolic. Why is this so?

Women and the Military Dictatorship

The struggles of women against the dictatorship have been understood as a novel phenomenon, but they are part of a historical tradition of women's struggles that can be traced back to the latter part of the nineteenth century.[4] Battles forgotten by official historians but remembered by women were resumed in 1981 and 1982, when the women's movement was reawakened. The new politics of women were not a mechanistic return to earlier patterns of political behavior, however, but a new phenomenon which can be understood only in the context of Argentina's Peronist government (1973–1976).

In 1973, women's participation reached new levels in comparison with past political and social mobilization and with past levels of women's political representation. Despite this, the Peronists followed an erratic policy. After Juan Perón's death in 1974, as the Peronist right wing struggled to control the government of his wife, Isabel Perón, antifeminist measures were adopted. The free use of contraceptives was prohibited, and a reform of parental rights, which would have replaced the traditional Roman-inspired law of *patria potestad,* was vetoed by the executive.

But such decisions, though unfavorable to women, did not engage the public's attention, much less speak to the needs of a population that was suffering from political polarization, guerrilla warfare, right-wing terrorism, severe economic crisis, and the ever-present threat of a military coup. In March 1976, a military junta took power. It found society and women organizationally disarmed and unable to respond. Many Argentines were heartened by the possibility of a "reasonable" military regime, but these illusions were dashed when the junta rapidly implemented a set of neoliberal economic policies and imposed a repressive social order. The result was a policy of state terrorism.

It quickly became clear that the socioeconomic process developed by the junta was directed against the popular sectors, who suffered a sharp decline in their net income. Social services, which workers and their families had formerly received from the state, were drastically curtailed; free health services were terminated; and educational opportunities were reduced. As a consequence of these measures, the standard of living of the popular sectors declined abruptly. The household became a buffer for the crisis and its only relief. Women were the double victims of these policies. They were "naturally" responsible for the reproductive role, and thus responsible in the last instance for family welfare, yet they belonged to the least-favored economic class and thus could not compete for good jobs or work for decent wages.[5]

From the psychosocial perspective, the military's conservative project included the privatization of social and interpersonal relations. Women were to be privileged guarantors of this transformation. The military's ideal was that the family should not be just "society's basic cell," as conservatives described it, but society's only cell, after all other types of solidarity-based organizations were destroyed. In this period, an Argentine version of Germany's *Kinder, Kuche, and Kirche* emerged as the only legitimate goal for women, who were suffering hunger, injustice, fear, and repression.

Paradoxically, the fact that the military planned a long-term period of social restructuring—in their words, a process with "no timetables, only goals"—actually favored the mobilization of women. It directly provoked the formation of a new group, the Madres of the Plaza de Mayo, who began meeting in April 1977 to publicize and resist the disappearances of their sons and daughters. The conservative formula of the three Ks led to an unexpected outcome: an organization based on nonviolence and on ethical principles.

The fact that women motivated by "private" emotions of loss were the first to awaken a dormant nation is itself remarkable. But it must be understood within the context of the gravity of the situation. Between 1976 and 1982, according to human rights organizations, 30,000 Argentines disappeared. In 1982, the messianic General Leopoldo Galtieri and his followers dragged the country into the Falklands-Malvinas War. In both cases, politics marked by the most perverse forms of repression made the defense of life an ethical principle and drew more people into political opposition. Women—especially the Madres, but also other groups—were the only ones who could take charge, who could act against all calculations of personal risk or political expediency. It was women who erected the principle of life against a government that dismissed the value of human life. It was women who aroused a society that had become a silent accomplice in the face of these horrors.

Women's responses to the military dictatorship were of two types: One response was to try to overcome the lethargy that had dominated the institutions created before the dictatorship; the second was to create new responses and organizations with new bases of mass support. These women did not try to draw up political party accords, as conventional practice dictated, but called for a new social consensus on themes that united women of different political sectors and social classes.

Women joined three kinds of groups in their struggle for life. First, there were the women in the human rights movement. The Madres were the best known, but also included were the Abuelas (Grandmothers) of the Plaza de Mayo and other mixed human rights organizations such as the Permanent Assembly for Human Rights (Asamblea Permanente para los Derechos Humanos, or APDH), Families of the Detained and Disappeared (Las Familias los Detenidos y Desaparecidos), the Ecumenical Movement for Human Rights (Movimento Ecuménico para los Derechos Humanos, or MEDH), and the Service of Peace and Justice (El Servicio de Paz y Justicia). A second and very different mobilization involved women who were struggling to guarantee the minimum resources necessary for their families to survive, for example, housewives in defense of the standard of living. The groups that formed to fight for women's interests from a feminist perspective constituted a third element of women's mobilization during the late 1970s and early 1980s. All these groups participated in the opposition to the dictatorship, creating and helping shape the transition to democracy after Argentina's military defeat.

The Madres

Much has been written and published about the Madres. The original group was made up of some 14 women between the ages of 40 and 62 who crossed paths in their endless, frustrating search for their sons and daughters. They decided to make a public issue of their pain and demanded that their "disappeared" children be produced—alive—by the junta.[6] Since the creation of their group in 1977, the Madres have had a public role in Argentina's political crises. They have consistently shown their concern for the return of those who disappeared. After the election of a democratic president, they demanded that those responsible for state terrorism be punished. The Madres have demonstrated against various attempts to forget and bury the past (such as the Final Point Law and the Law of Due Obedience), which have removed most of the threat that the military might have to face criminal trials for its participation in the "dirty war" (1976–1983), a time of state terror.[7] The Madres have shown a great capacity to respond to a series of challenges, adapting their proposals to each concrete situation without sacrificing the ethical foundations of their demands. They have maintained an autonomous organizational identity, separate from party politics.

The Madres are notable in that they are strictly a women's movement. This has often been explained as an extension of the sexual division of labor in Argentina, which gives mothers the responsibility of defending and protecting their sons and daughters. Because of the cultural and ideological conceptions of motherhood, which is the basis of Argentine feminine identity, motherhood might be expected to offer more security as a basis for political action than alternative roles. Although subsequent events proved that the notion that women as mothers would be safe from repression was only a myth, the legitimacy of the maternal appeal allowed at least a symbolic refuge.

The Madres' success depended on a symbolic politics based on respect for the traditional role of women. Because women are thought to be altruistic and vicarious, it was possible for women to reject a conventional political model of participation based on the rational calculation of costs and benefits and to substitute another based on sacrifice. Despite its sex role conventionality, traditionalism was used as the basis for a daring gesture that indicted traditionalism's original meaning of passivity and submission. In practice, the Madres became another movement of women who, without trying to change patriarchal ideology or abandon their femininity, produced a transformation of the traditional feminine self-awareness and its political role. As a result, a practical redefinition of the content of the private and public realms has emerged. The task of defending life itself was forced out of the private sphere of the household and into the autonomous space of public and political expression. The Madres' ability to unite and fight for peace, and to make this theme an active weapon in their struggle, was a significant departure from the conventional content of politics.

The Madres showed a capacity for innovation in the cultural dimension of "doing" politics. Their originality was evident in their development of new forms of mobilization, such as the walk (*ronda*) around the plaza; the assignment of new meanings to old symbols (e.g., the white handkerchiefs); and their capacity to resignify a public space (the plaza); and their capability of sustaining a political agenda outside the realm of the political parties. The paradigm of the Madres' politics was based on the all-out defense of the most basic principles—the defense of life and of the right to love. It unintentionally became a new feminist paradigm, sustaining the need for a feminine perspective in the world of patriarchal and masculine politics and suggesting a broader vision capable of destroying the traditional rules of the political game.

This model of politics has been reconstructed after the fact; it was never used by the Madres as a rationalization for their actions, nor was it derived from theoretical premises. Despite its potential, the Madres' approach also imposed some limits that became much clearer once democratic institutions were again in place. The Madres were institutionally weak; they relied heavily on strong personal leadership and were held together by gender solidarity, not organizational sophistication. This has historically been the case with women's organizations and with other social movements, but these characteristics mean that the Madres were more prepared to respond to a crisis than to institutionalize a durable model of participation.

The Housewives' Organization

Between October and December 1982, surprisingly strong urban protests spread through greater Buenos Aires, set off by an increase in the cost of living. These protests, known as *vecinazos,* involved a high level of feminine participation: Housewives' committees called for or joined the protests that took place in the different municipalities surrounding Buenos Aires and took the lead in negotiating with local government authorities.

Although they became visible during the *vecinazos,* housewives had protested before. In the months preceding the neighborhood demonstrations, women had boycotted products and participated in demonstrations against the poor quality of life throughout the country. In July 1982, the national movement of housewives was born in a middle-class neighborhood in the district of San Martín (part of greater Buenos Aires). Women, who had mobilized spontaneously against price hikes by launching the Don't Buy on Thursdays campaign, rapidly generated unprecedented hopes among the public.

Little research has been done on social organizations at the neighborhood level in Argentina, much less on the struggles over consumption and other issues related to the reproduction of the family. Despite the lack of knowledge, we can clearly see some new characteristics. In the past, protests headed by women were linked to political parties, to the Church, or to certain sectors of the Right who tried to improve women's lives through charity. The movement of the housewives that emerged during the Argentine transition brought together women who had worked in neighborhood organizations but who had little experience with broader political currents. The National Movement of Housewives, a new political actor in the fight against poverty, began by distancing itself from both politics and the traditional activities of women: "Our movement is not one of women who have extra time for charitable activities."

As in the case of the Madres of the Plaza de Mayo, the housewives insisted on making it clear that the movement did not follow a particular political agenda or ideological approach. The housewives' movement supported other causes, such as the expression of solidarity with Nobel Peace laureate Adolfo Pérez Esquivel and the Madres and Abuelas of the Plaza de Mayo. Despite this capacity to innovate, they remained faithful to a vicarious definition of women's participation and justified their actions as consistent with their roles as wives and mothers. Their slogan, "Our policy is that of our husbands' wallets," clearly subordinated gender.

The Feminists

The majority of the feminist groups that had emerged in the early 1970s were dissolved after the military coup of 1976.[8] The Argentine Feminist Union (Unión Feminista de Argentina), the Feminist Liberation Movement (Movimiento para la Liberación Feminista), and the Association for the Liberation of Argentine Women (Asociación para la Liberación de la Mujer Argentina) ceased their activities at that point, as did (temporarily) the Front for Women's Rights (Movimiento para Liberación Feminina, or MLF), an umbrella organization of feminist groups and women from the political parties that had formed in 1975. Others continued to exist. CESMA (Center for the Social Study of Argentine Women, or Centro de Estudios de la Mujer Argentina) was created in 1974 by a group of women members of FIP (Popular Leftist Front, or Frente de la Izquierda Popular), who began to meet outside the party to discuss their situation as women in the party ranks. Although most of them left the party in 1976, CESMA remained active. Most of its members believed in "double militancy," that parallel work in parties and in the feminist movement is possible. Their goal was to contribute to the formation of a great national feminist movement, deeply rooted in their people, which would encompass the majority of the women in Argentina and strive for women's dignity, freedom, and justice.

Women from the National Current of FIP and women without political affiliations created the Association of Argentine Women (Asociación de Mujeres Argentinas, or AMA) in 1977 to read and discuss material on discrimination and to exchange personal experiences. They soon connected with other groups and changed their name to the Alfonsina Storni Women's Association (Asosiación de Mujeres Alfonsina Storni, or AMAS). This group expressed its goals in its platform, approved in 1978: to unify women to improve their status, to increase all feminine participation in economic development, and to preserve peace. Toward these goals AMAS issued a newsletter, organized conferences, and showed films.

In Cordoba, a very active group, the Juana Manso Association (Asociación Juana Manso), was organized in 1978 and sponsored numerous outreach and debate activities. The Union of Socialist Women (Unión de Mujeres Socialistas), more closely related to mainstream politics, formed in 1979. It was linked to the Argentine Socialist Confederation (Confederación Socialista de Argentina). Its president, Alicia Moreau de Justo, took the bold step of calling for the restoration of judicial rights in Argentina. In 1981, the MLF was reorganized under the leadership of veteran feminist María Elena Oddone and called itself the Argentine Feminist Organization (Organización Feminista Argentina, or OFA). Once the political opening occurred, the OFA set out to lobby political parties to ensure that party platforms incorporated women's demands. Earlier, several feminists had constituted a committee to reform custody rights under the law of *patria potestad*.

In April 1982, the ATEM November 25 (Asociación para el Trabajo y el Estudio de la Mujer November 25, Association for the Work and Study of Women) emerged as an autonomous movement with the goal of "contributing to the creation of a democratic society, a world of equals, where the differences among human beings do not become an excuse for oppression, but a basis for the respect for the plurality of life." It was made up of "women of different ages, educational levels, and economic backgrounds." Among its specific goals were the organization of campaigns, seminars, and presentations to achieve Argentine compliance with the 1980 UN Convention on the Elimination of All Forms of Discrimination Against Women (CEDAW).

In August 1983, the Women's Place (Lugar de la Mujer) opened its doors in Buenos Aires. Lacking ideological consensus, the women of Lugar de la Mujer defined it as a civil association "with feminist orientation." Lugar de la Mujer offers a space for activities centered around feminist themes (roundtables, workshops, study groups) and offers legal, sexual, and psychological advice to women.

Two months later, a Tribunal of Violence Against Women was constituted on the initiative of the three Argentine feminist organizations. The entity, whose stated goal was to alert the population to the violence exercised against women, organized a demonstration asking for justice in a rape case that had recently shocked the public.

The Transition

These separate yet converging efforts helped create a climate of opinion that showed, perhaps for the first time in Argentine history, the inescapable need to incorporate women into the process of democratization. Sensitive to the potential voting power of women, each of the parties rushed to constitute its own women's front. This produced the first modern women's sectors within the party structures, following the much earlier lead of the Peronists who had created the Feminine Peronist Party (Partido Feminista) as an autonomous section within the party in the late 1940s. Public recognition of the demands of women occurred at different institutional levels. At the party level, the positive response to feminist issues was not a disinterested act of long overdue justice but an effort to win the women's vote in a close electoral race. This was visible in the parties' appropriation of the most important slogans of the women's movement. "We are life," which the Madres had used, became the leitmotiv of the Unión Cívica Radical when Raúl Alfonsín campaigned against the Peronists and the Right in 1983.

Women candidates were often put on the presidential ticket of the smaller parties, though care was taken to ensure that these women would be one level below the men. For example, Elisa Colombo was the vice-presidential candidate for the Popular Leftist Front, and Catalina Guagnini occupied the same position in the Worker's Party (Partido Obrero) ticket, as did Irene Rodríguez for the Communist Party.

The Argentine political consensus seems to be that the term "feminism" turns voters off, but little by little the feminist agenda is having an impact on political party platforms and on the mass media. This is less surprising than it might seem. In greater Buenos Aires, if not in the more depressed rural areas of Argentina, women have been consistently active in the educational system and in the economy. They are predisposed to change their attitudes and behavior.[9] Feminist activists at first only speculated that women's issues would gain support. This was later verified by electoral results.

Later, Alfonsín's striking success in winning women's votes would prove the success of an electoral strategy based on the expectations and hopes of the feminine electorate. His intelligent and daring message not only raised heretofore dormant demands but also used women-sensitive language to the point that his closing campaign speech openly criticized machismo. When men name these themes, women's issues are pulled out of the shadows of women's groups and placed in the strong light of the public arena. Issues such as divorce, shared *patria potestad,* and the defense of peace were repeatedly raised by the two most prominent candidates being elected. This gained new visibility for women's issues and enhanced women's citizenship.

In part because of their party's *machista* traditions, the political leaders did not follow through after the election. Politicians cannot move easily beyond rhetoric; they do not understand women except in their role as voters. When the time comes for proposals, all candidates recycle old ideas. They want to "improve women's condition," which translated into the protectionist models of the past, models that would reinforce the traditional role of women in Argentine society. Supporting the participation of women as true protagonists of political life creates competition inside the parties. It requires redesigning Argentina's social map. These are radical goals and so far they have found little practical space.

Throughout this process of politicization, women's groups have added new interests to the old rather than differentiating among them. This consensus-building strategy is symbolized politically by the approach of the Women's Multisectorial (El Multisectorial de Mujeres). Five decades of alternating between civilian and military government had paralyzed the capacity for exchange among different social groups. But the patterns of participation during the transition showed that the conditions exist to represent women's interests in diverse mediums including the trade unions, traditionally the domain of men, and in the fields of scientific investigation and the arts, where women became active and visible at levels unheard of in the past.

The Women's Multisectorial was organized on March 8, 1984, the day when International Women's Day was celebrated for the first time in Argentina. It laid out an ambitious program of demands, confident that women could be mobilized for political action. The transition began with a series of promising signals, including the cooperation among women's organizations and human rights groups. In the summer of 1984, it seemed that a substantial transformation could take place if the advances already obtained were sustained and expanded, relying on the blend of the old and new elements. Women had achieved new levels of organization, and they were galvanized by the role of the Madres, who had revived one of the oldest myths of Western culture: Antigone's rebellion against the overwhelming power of the state.

But any forecast of success was based on an important assumption: that the women's movement would be sufficiently flexible to adapt to the changing politics brought about by the new democratic rules of the game. The new regime created new and difficult challenges for all social movements: How could they come out from the microspaces of resistance to become effective in the executive branch, the Parliament, the independent judicial branch, and the political parties? How could they move from unified confrontation against a single opponent to the much more complex process of recognizing different opponents with alternative projects? How could they avoid being relegated to the status of a special interest group rather than being seen as representing the interests of the whole? In sum, how were they to go from the rules of the game of opposition to the rules of the game of constructing a civilian peace?

In this context, it was just as necessary to continue to learn, to allow for a departure in practice from what was already known, to find the new forms that the new context made necessary. If feminists could not constitute a mass movement, they could choose to become a lobby in the traditional sense of the word. But their recent history made this alternative appear to be a betrayal of their commitment rather than an appropriate adaptation to the new context. Feminists had experienced a change in the scale as well as the context of their actions. Accustomed to working in groups of self-reflection and consciousness-raising and to identifying with politics as individuals, not as groups united by gender, and fractured by their ideological differences, feminists needed to find an authentic voice. At the same time, they needed to listen to the political concert of the traditional parties, which were run by men and ruled by male discourse.

Women who had organized for peace and against war, acting in the realm of reason but reason rooted in feelings of emotional rejection, had to negotiate with powerful institutions that complicated the straightforward relationship between their ethical responses and their political actions. To be effective, women had to master the armed forces' budget, convince the Committee of Defense in the legislature of their demands, and analyze the potential effects of any hurried move on the political chessboard. To be effective in this new environment required more than principled commitment; it required political acumen and technical know-how. Women were not yet accepted as political authorities in their own right; they needed validation in this role, and only masculine voices were heard. Could women in the human rights movement continue their intransigent struggle and find a place for this struggle within the rules of democratic behavior? Or would they be isolated as an ethical yet solitary voice?

Adapting to Democracy

In this new phase of the dynamic and heterogeneous reality of women's groups, power was transmitted from the de facto president Reynaldo Bignone to President-Elect Alfonsín. All the political groups and social movements that had mobilized during the transition presented problems for the government. However, women's demands presented the stiffest challenge. Feminist groups expected that Alfonsín's campaign promises (including the passage of a law of shared *patria potestad,* the ratification of the UN Convention Against Discrimination, and the cancellation of the decree that banned free access to contraceptives) would be fulfilled. The housewives' organizations expected a just redistribution of income and wanted price controls that would allow them to meet their family's needs. The human rights women, faithful to their principles, demanded that their loved ones be returned alive and that the guilty be punished.

The Radical Party's ethical basis and political commitment were expressed in its 1983 campaign slogan of the human rights movement. The use of the language of human rights underscored the nonnegotiability of the platform while generating confidence in the potential of democracy to face this problem. Later, the failure of the Alfonsín government to meet the Madres' expectations caused the Madres to reinforce the ethical component of their struggle and make their demands more intransigent. Ethics and politics, which had complemented each other during the transition, became locked in a mortal conflict.

To meet its preelection promise, the government created a parliamentary committee, CONADEP (National Committee on Disappeared Persons, or Comité Nacional para los Desaparecidos), in December 1983. With one exception (Graciela Fernández Meijide), the Madres refused to take part in this committee. Although its members had considerable prestige, CONADEP's makeup and function made it difficult for it to generate solutions. What impact it had was due to the compilation and the publication of information on state terrorism. This constituted a formidable moral sanction against such actions by the state but fell far short of the retribution demanded by the Madres.

Meanwhile, the well-publicized trial of the junta became a showcase for the way in which repression had become routine. The mass media transmitted the testimonies of witnesses as if it were doing sportscasts. The only concrete results of the trial were sanctions against a few top junta leaders, but no action was taken against the lower-level military officers responsible for carrying out policies of torture and kidnapping. The torture was declared abhorrent, but those responsible for implementing it went free. This allowed repressors (such as Lieutenant Astiz, an active navy officer whom the Madres hold responsible for the kidnapping of Azucena Villaflor, the first mother of the group who disappeared, in 1977) to escape prosecution. Not even the repeated claims made by the Swedish Crown in relation to the disappearance of a young Swedish woman, Dagmar Hagelin, could prevail on the government or the judiciary to punish Astiz.

The Madres' rejection of the different solutions presented by the government was their response to the possibility that their group might fade into political oblivion, thus ensuring a de facto amnesty for the military. However, their intransigence met with hostility from the Alfonsín government, which began to dismiss them and to create a climate of confrontation that would have been difficult to imagine during the days when the Madres were seen as heroines. Meanwhile, the Madres' critics gained a public hearing, and steps toward an undeclared amnesty were initiated. The difficulty of putting those responsible for tortures and deaths in jail, the promotion of military officers in accordance with the normal rules internal to the armed forces (whether or not they played a role in the "dirty war"), and the military's virtual dictation of the Final Point Law and the Law of Obedience to halt legal actions against individual officers all showed that the Alfonsín government was moving toward a pardon and encouraging Argentines to forget what had happened.

Despite the difficulties encountered in this democratic period, the Madres have continued their efforts, creating new and imaginative ways to sensitize a public that would be content to bury the past. They were present at the junta trial, with handkerchiefs on their heads and carrying silhouettes with the names of the "disappeared"; they organized a "chains of hands" campaign to search for those who had disappeared and to prevent the repressors from passing through. During the dictatorship, the Madres were able to transform politics merely by their presence. In the long process of transition and the consolidation of democracy, their actions are creating a new political culture by incorporating novel practices that require a high level of direct participation by their followers.

This process is of great interest, not only to understand the problems of the transition and the political reconstruction of Argentina but also from the point of view of feminist theory. From the political standpoint, the role of women in defense of life, political behavior rooted in affections and emotions, and a high level of confrontation against the fixed yet morally brittle power of the authoritarian state are very effective in times of crisis. But they are insufficient during the consolidation, a phase in which the role of the "daughters of Antigone" is not enough to ensure women's participation in the democratic political game. It is true that the human rights movement never consciously decided to "make politics" (*hacer la política*), but even without that decision, the Madres' goal of staying above politics could not be realized effectively once the political rules changed.

From a feminist standpoint, *haciendo la política* emphasizes behaviors based on emotions as opposed to rational calculations of self-interest. But there is a tendency to fall into the trap of creating a new system of legitimacy that is then easily displaced. In Argentina, the weakness of this approach meant an appeal to women based on the most conservative aspects of feminine identity. Perhaps no other outcome was possible.

The movement of the Madres of the Plaza de Mayo is obviously related to the mobilization of women's human rights movements in other countries of the region, such as Chile, Honduras, or Guatemala. Studying those movements might provide a more optimistic prognosis. But analytically, a defense of human rights based on women's reproductive roles reinforces the conventional sexual division of labor. Linking the possibility of change to feminine emotionality constitutes a paradoxical vicious circle. Politics based on emotions (which can be praised for breaking the artificial division of the private and public realms and for transcending a vision of politics based on rational cost-benefit calculations) ends up making altruism sacred. The Argentine case, showing the explosion of women as mothers onto the public scene, carries with it great potential for change. But for this potential to be transformed into new concrete realities for women as a whole, it is necessary to balance the concept of motherhood that breaks away from tradition and those elements that reinforce old behaviors.

There are signals that it is not easy to develop such an equilibrium. Although the term should be used very carefully, it could be argued that a new *marianismo* has arisen that could stimulate greater isolation.[10] The *marianismo* of the Madres, the solitary carriers of the ethical demands of a society and the recipients of its critical conscience, was bestowed on them by a dictatorship that labeled them "crazies" (*locas*). Their success brought us back, unexpectedly, to the traditional worship of the Mary-mother characteristic of the most conservative sectors of Argentine society. The vicious circle is completed by the fact that women are still largely absent from conventional politics. But the circle closes in a new way because the discrimination against women in the public realm can now rely on a secular, not merely a religious, rationale.

In this discourse, even women who are not members are credited with behavior inherent in motherhood; they are "impregnated" with "natural" maternal instincts that are held to be present in all women. "The men who conduct this nation need the feeling of protection that only you know how to provide," an audience of women was told by the Radical Party candidate for governor of the province of Buenos Aires during a campaign speech. "We are life" can become a trap for women as the forces of change are stymied by the weakness of women's discourse and as the most traditional aspects of that discourse are appropriated by a political class dominated by men.

Although the high point of women's role in the transition was very brief, the gains were substantial. But they are part of a slow process that is made slower by the lack of political will on the part of the government. In the absence of a women's movement capable of mobilizing public opinion effectively, the promised legislation was delayed and then weakened by endless bureaucratic wrangling.

The Alfonsín government responded to women's demands in a variety of ways. It constructed a women's sphere within the state itself by creating a National Women's Agency in the Ministry of Social Action, which has created a Women's Health and Development Program, Women Today, and several women's agencies and undersecretariats were formed in the provincial governments. Women's issues now have a place in the state structure. Faced with government initiatives, feminist groups have often reacted negatively, but they have not offered their own alternatives. Feminist mistrust is similar to that held by many groups in civil society who feel that the state is only interested in co-opting social actors and in preempting their demands.

In spite of these difficulties, democratic government continues to make room for a new feminist agenda that takes problems out of the private realm and places them in the public sphere. Women's rights to control their own bodies and to make reproductive decisions, as yet unmentioned in political discourse, are becoming less of a taboo. The data on the number of abortions performed annually in Argentina (about 300,000) and on the number of deaths stemming from postabortion complications are considered indirect indicators of the fact that women lack both the right to control their own bodies and the information to make informed decisions about reproduction. At the end of 1986, a decree was passed that canceled the restrictions on the distribution and use of contraceptives. The goal was to allow the population "the exercise of their human right to make responsible decisions regarding their reproduction." In a country like Argentina, where the state has historically supported prolife positions while the society has followed the opposite pattern, the recognition of the need to adjust the law to reflect social reality was a promising sign.

Another theme that has moved from the private to the public sphere is violence against women. Domestic violence has finally been recognized as a social problem, not an individual one, and as a crime that must be denounced. Self-help groups initiated by the feminist movement have been complemented by several institutional actions, both state and private, in the form of health services, legal counseling, and police-training programs.

During the consolidation phase, autonomous women's groups formed in the trade unions. Some women, especially those who came in contact with feminism while in exile, have tried to change traditional treatment of the "woman question" in the unions, treatment that generally confined them to the secretariats of social welfare and family. These groups, which remain small, faced a huge task. Union negotiations were barred for a decade, but suddenly women had to be prepared to discuss the changes in employee roles, debate salaries, and offer effective means of participation for working women. A different vision of women in trade unions would mean raising new issues, not only working conditions but also maternity benefits, social security, special allowances for working mothers, and child care programs. The issue of child care requires rethinking under the new egalitarian perspective outlined in the UN Convention Against All Forms of Discrimination Against Women, which Argentina has signed and ratified.

As women in trade unions revise assumptions traditionally held by the labor movement vis-à-vis the working mother, women human rights advocates must take advantage of the experience gained in the confrontation against the dictatorship and extend it to other themes that are incorporated in the very concept of human rights, such as the pursuit of a dignified standard of living, access to housing, health, and education, and reproductive choice. These issues should be pursued in spite of the fact that the economic crisis, the debt, and the continuation of austerity programs will no doubt inhibit efforts to expand the agenda.

For their part, the women in the barrios face problems shared by all women who must enter the realm of daily life at the household level and at the level of neighborhood organizations. Little by little, a new consciousness is being created that changes women's role from the invisible one of performing tasks recognized as "naturally" feminine to the active one of ensuring family survival in conditions of severe economic stress. Information gathered from different barrios in greater Buenos Aires confirms this progressive transformation: Women are mobilized in the struggle for better housing conditions, for water, and for basic services. They have constituted small groups focusing on gender issues—sometimes within the context of state programs such as the National Food Program and the National Literacy Campaign. These activities prove the potential for change that can arise out of performing traditional tasks.[11] Other groups have organized in new ways around churches, political parties, and nongovernment organizations. Still, in Argentina, the level of organizational development derived from these experiences is far lower than levels of action and organization reached by other women's groups in the region.

Women's Participation
in the Menem Era

Since 1988, Argentina has experienced significant political and economic changes. During 1989, Argentina experienced its first democratic change of government. After five years and mixed political results, Alfonsín's radical party was defeated by the controversial Peronist candidate, Carlos Menem, elected with 47 percent of the votes. At the same time, growing inflation had exploded into hyperinflation, followed by food riots that had never before occurred in Argentina. Alfonsín's government ended abruptly in July 1989, when he left office five months before his constitutional term was over. President Menem's first efforts were to stop the inflationary process by calling for an alliance among the political parties.

Since he took office, Menem has faced serious political problems, especially with the military. His "final solution" for the members of the military juntas who were found guilty of the kidnapping, torture, and murder of 30,000 people was an amnesty (Decree 2741-90), granted in December 1990. The amnesty, together with the repression of the last in a series of dramatic military rebellions, was intended to provide a future for democratic politics in Argentina. Many citizens were strongly opposed to the amnesty. Human rights organizations called for a mobilization against the decree in many parts of the country, but Menem sustained the policy and continued to work to reform the economic situation and reduce the historically high inflation rates.

Freedom for the assassins of the "dirty war" (1976–1983) solved the immediate problem of military unrest, and some signs of renewed economic growth gave new political support to the Peronist government, now allied with its traditional enemies on the right. Political stability and the possibility of sustained economic growth put the more radical redistributional agenda long associated with Peronism on hold. The political stage was set for substantial changes in women's economic and political situation.

The posttransition period was characterized by the affirmation of democracy, but in conditions of economic crisis that were having a strong impact on women. During the dictatorship, women had risen to defend the simple right to life with all its connotations, fighting against state terrorism, claiming the "disappeared," and confronting the military dictatorship. Women's political action had two purposes: to call for democracy and the investigation of state crimes and to demand better living conditions.

The "lost decade" of the 1980s meant a sharp deterioration of the standard of living among the low-income population, a decline so severe that it endangered this sector's historical reproductive capacity. In 1988, the inflation rate reached 388 percent, and in 1989 it surpassed all barriers to nearly 5,000 percent annually. By May 1989, hyperinflation had generated a social process without precedent in the country, visible, for example, in the *saqueos,* the looting of food markets. Women, who have the leading role in the daily fight for survival, were the victims of the so-called invisible adjustment, but they lacked the power to voice their demands or to influence public opinion.

Because the democratization process occurred within the framework of neoliberal economic adjustments, government spending on social services was reduced. To meet the crisis, lower-class women increased their labor force participation, often taking temporary jobs without social benefits and working longer hours. The effects on the middle class were even more striking. Female participation in the labor force increased among middle-aged and married women; there was a sharp decline in male income and employment. Between 1974 and 1987, middle-class women increased their participation by 33 percent; that of poor women increased by 11 percent. For married middle-class women, the increase was 53 percent, and the comparable figure for poor women was only 33 percent. Women who were too poor or too burdened with family responsibilities to enter the labor force engaged instead in survival activities. Food centers or neighborhood food programs, microenterprises, and different kinds of neighborhood jobs concentrated women's social energies in response to the challenge of survival.

The economic crisis, in addition to making the extreme poverty politically visible, created a laboratory for women who were changing and redefining the boundaries of what was historically considered public and private, collective and individual, social and state. The crisis provided a dramatic stage for the discussion of women's roles in democratic consolidation. Solutions that had worked before, such as women's demonstrations in defense of the standard of living, proved insufficient. The concept of the right to life, which had been part of the Madres' discourse, was now placed in a new economic context. Paradoxically, this strengthening and empowering of women in the public sphere was the direct result of their increasing exploitation and sacrifice in the private sphere.

Human rights had been the focal point of the democratic opposition to the military. In the consolidation phase, the human rights movement faced political difficulties as the economic crisis replaced state terror as the most disturbing daily issue to be confronted. In April 1986, the Madres' movement split over the issue of whether the bodies of those who had disappeared and been buried illegally could be exhumed. One group called itself the Mothers of the Plaza de Mayo—The Founders, and the other became the Mothers of the Plaza de Mayo Association. The latter, following the leadership of Hebe de Bonafini, opposed the exhumations on the grounds that accepting the deaths of their children would be a form of acceptance of what the military had done and would close the book on the dirty war. The two groups avoided a confrontation but differed on possible strategies.

Some see the changes in both groups as a sign that they are moving into ordinary politics and that they are doing so because the legal and political changes needed to meet their goals have not been implemented. Others argue that the groups' unwillingness to work with political parties is evidence that the Madres have not contributed to democratic reconstruction.

For many feminists, the case of the Madres is exemplary because the Madres redefined the arbitrary division between private and public. The feminists focus on the innovative possibilities within their way of "doing" politics, which starts from the position culturally assigned to women, rather than denying that women's experiences as women are politically relevant.[12]

In my view the Madres' potential for democratic political innovation is less clear despite their proven capacity to remain the conscience of Argentine society. Relative to the expectations generated during the transition, the results are disappointing. The Madres' approach has been vindicated by their success in locating the children who were taken from their "disappeared" parents and adopted by families with connections to the military. Since 1977, Abuelas of the Plaza de Mayo have searched for more than 200 children and have found 51. Their historical role now centers on the idea of keeping alive the memory of genocide: "We will not forget, we will not forgive."

One important trend in the women's human rights groups is their progressive approach to incorporating women's issues into their permanent fight for justice and their participation in feminist forums. The Madres' strategy, beginning from the place culturally assigned to women in the sexual division of labor, has been successfully extended to new issues. In 1991, wives of steel workers led a demonstration to defend their husbands' jobs. During the same year, wives and children of coal mine workers barricaded a local highway in the South while their husbands and fathers went to Buenos Aires to protest against the closure of the mine. In response, Argentine feminists have increasingly structured their arguments in human rights terms.

Since 1989, women's organizations, feminist groups, and women in political parties and trade unions have continued the ties begun during the transition, networking with other regional and global organizations. In addition to sharing a feeling of commonality with women in other regions of the world, they have learned new ways to solve their problems. One example is the women's police precincts, adapted from the *delegacias da mujer,* which were pioneered in Brazil to respond to violence against women. A number of *comisarias de la mujer* were established under the Women's Council of the Province of Buenos Aires. Other networks are more academically oriented, such as the Women's Studies Association in Higher Education. Institutional and personal relations have increased as women participate in forums such as the Fifth Latin American and Caribbean Feminist Meeting held in 1990 in San Bernardo, Argentina, and the successive National Encounters of Women. The 1991 *encuentro* attracted 6,000 participants. In addition, some of the militant trade union women have been able to consolidate their position; among their initiatives is a training and research forum for trade unionist women.

On the negative side, as democratic consolidation proceeded, the number of women elected to the Chamber of Deputies declined. In 1991, women deputies were only 3.8 percent of the total number, down from 5.9 percent in 1989. The most striking debate during this period was the fight over the "quota law," an attempt to mandate that 30 percent of the electoral candidates had to be women. The law was finally approved in November 1991, but it has never been enforced. The debate produced serious discussion between politicians and feminists and established the principle of quotas. More important, the experience of passing the law developed a feeling of sisterhood among political party women and the feminists, many of whom were critical of the law.

The democratic state supported change by opening new institutional spaces to deal with women's issues, following the example of the Brazilian posttransition state. The Alfonsín administration had taken the lead by creating the post of undersecretary for women, which the Menem government continued to support. In 1991, the National Council of Public Policies was created. Its accomplishments include a law (23179-85) against discrimination against women. At the provincial and municipal levels, different "women's areas" were created that developed initiatives on a broad range of issues, including violence against women, family income generation, health, housing, training and education programs. In addition, the women's areas have supported women in extreme poverty through activities that, although admittedly welfarist, are essential.

Conclusions

Whatever the institutional sphere in which women act, they face the difficulty of reconciling their immediate interests with those of other social actors, and they must balance strategic and specific gender interests.

The struggle to pursue tactical interests, for example, by representing the interests of other social groups (such as children), makes us question the efficacy of a feminist strategy that is devoted to improving conditions for others. This places women among the underprivileged whose general position must be improved.[13] An adequate analysis would distinguish the problems inherent to women from broader social concerns, even when women are given the responsibility for meeting those concerns. Women are assigned social responsibility for child health care, for maintaining the household, for providing children's schooling, and for defending the lives of their sons and daughters under conditions of state terror. Just listing these themes argues against the view that reproduction and the struggle for a democratic society are gendered specialized tasks. We must make room for a women's agenda that is not a matter of human rights or of "asking for more" (more maternity leave, for example) or of helping others and substitute one that recasts typically feminine tasks so they are no longer only women's responsibilities.

Although they are rooted in civilian society, the still embryonic forms of women's grassroots organizations depend closely on the state for further growth and consolidation. The state can choose (through the implementation of its social welfare programs) to ignore these grassroots organizations or to work with them. Receptive attitudes at all levels—national, provincial, or municipal—would make a substantial difference to their survival and effectiveness.

At the same time, the state itself would become more efficient and effective if its policies were more closely geared to women's needs and energies. This logic of articulation between civil society and the state deserves much more attention, especially because of the impact of structural adjustment programs that hit the poor hardest but that have also lowered living standards for the majority. Today the government can barely respond to the demands of grassroots organizations. Restructuring the organizational branches of civilian society, especially women's organizations, could bring together several groups lacking political power and create new resources for cooperation.

Perhaps the most interesting trends of the 1990s are the different strategies that women are trying to create in order to make a place for themselves in the social, political, and economic spheres of the country. In reinventing the classical debates—autonomy versus involvement, feminist versus feminine, number versus quality—women opened different social spaces in which to participate. The advantage of this strategy is that gender consciousness can be found everywhere; the disadvantage is that this kind of involvement is centered in groups that are rarely sufficiently articulated or empowered to make these strategies effective. The whole social structure is strengthened when women are included, but the feminist movement itself is weakened, becoming merely an intellectual reference point. As Temma Kaplan argues skeptically, feminine mobilization does not question women's place in society, and it does not raise the level of feminist consciousness. An optimistic argument would be that feminists with different levels of consciousness crisscross the social structure, reflecting every woman's class position and the different spheres in which women perform their activities.

We must recognize the existence of a double challenge: what democracy demands of women and what women will demand of democracy. The challenge to democracy is to raise women to the category of a legitimate social group in the public sphere and to connect them effectively with political institutions: to make women full citizens. Democracy challenges women to demand and obtain more participation, to define women's issues, and to empower themselves. Women must create the collective mechanisms that are necessary for such participation. With this potential for convergence, women and the political regime must seek effective channels of communication through which women must simultaneously educate their listeners while voicing demands that express the problem of women as persons, not as the vicarious vehicles for the needs of others.

Notes

1. In the national general elections of 1983, of approximately 250 deputies elected to the Congress, only 9 were women. This proportion was maintained in the elections of 1985 and 1987.

2. Information on the Holy Week crisis may be found in *Nueva Sociedad* (Caracas) 90 (1987) and in *Unidos* (Buenos Aires) 4, 15 (August 1987).

3. The rest of this section draws extensively on an article written with Monica Gogna. The empirical data and analysis on mothers and housewives are almost entirely hers. The text was published in Spanish in Elizabeth Jelín, ed., *Los nuevos movimientos sociales,* 2 vols. (Buenos Aires: CEAL, 1986). In the original version, footnotes provide empirical information that has been summarized in this article.

4. A historical long-term approach to women's struggles in Argentina can be found, among others, in María del Carmen Feijoó, *Las feministas: La historia de nuestro pueblo,* 9 (Buenos Aires: CEAL, 1982). See also *Todo es historia,* 183 (August 1982).

5. A similar result for women's role and position within the household, in this case related to the social cost of external debt in Third World economies, is described in UNICEF, *The Invisible Adjustment* (Santiago: UNICEF, 1987).

6. The first narrative of this movement can be found in Jean Pierre Bousquet, *Las locas de la Plaza de Mayo* (Buenos Aires: El Cid, 1983). See also Monica Gogna, "La ronda de las madres" (Buenos Aires, 1986), mimeograph. Since then many different materials have been produced, either written or in video and cinema. Especially important is *Todo es ausencia,* a video production with a screenplay written by the well-known historian Osvaldo Bayer. The official version was produced by CONADEP (National Commission on Disappeared Persons) in the report published as the book *Nunca más* (Buenos Aires: Eudeba, 1985). The

number of missing persons reported to the CONADEP is 10,000; human rights organizations give the more commonly accepted figure of 30,000.

7. For a full account on governmental performance in human rights, see the excellent article by human rights Argentine leader Emilio Mignone, "The Military: What Is to Be Done?" *NACLA Report on the Americas* 21, 4 (July-August 1987).

8. Little has been written on post-1960s feminist organizations. For an overview of this process, see Cano Ines in *Todo es historia,* 183 (Buenos Aires: CEAL, 1982).

9. Data from censuses and the permanent Household Survey show the slow increase in women's participation in the labor force. The number of women entering the University of Buenos Aires has begun to exceed the number of men. See Zulma Recchini de Lattes, *Dinámica de la fuerza de trabajo feminino en la Argentina* (Paris: UNESCO, 1983).

10. See Elsa Chaney, *Supermadre: La mujer en la política en América Latina* (Mexico City: Fondo de Cultura Económica, 1983). The fact that *"supermadre,"* like "machismo," reflects current stereotypes on masculine and feminine behavior in Latin America may explain its success. But as has often happened with other successful terms, it may help to conceal the phenomenon it is trying to explain rather than shed light on it.

11. Maxine Molyneaux, "Mobilization Without Emancipation? Women's Interest, the State, and Revolution in Nicaragua," *Feminist Studies* 11, 2 (Summer 1985): 227–254.

12. Jean Bethke Elshtain, *Power Trips and Other Journeys* (Madison: University of Wisconsin Press, 1990).

13. Discussion on this topic may be found in the proceedings of the seminar held at the Universidad Federal de Rio Grande do Sul (Brasil) on women and the transition to democracy, held by CLASCO's group on Women's Condition and the university, published in *Revista de Ciencias Sociais* (Porto Alegre) 1, 2 (1987).

FIVE

The Uses of Conservatism: Women's Democratic Politics in Uruguay

CARINA PERELLI

In the Uruguayan calendar, 1985 constitutes a very special year. The dictatorship ended and democracy was reborn—the country "returned to the sources." In a sense, we Uruguayans have reshaped this most conservative of symbols in order to bring about the restoration of something that seemed dead and buried: the old Uruguay of voters and ballots, civilism and education, shared memories, faith, hope, prosperity, and employment—the Uruguay of milk and honey.

After the rule of naked fear and of Uruguayans' "fear to fear,"[1] they were thirsty for this partly mythical country of *la douceur de vivre*,"[2] comfortable, secure, and mediocre. It was the very same country we had helped destroy in the past with our ambition, our dreams and our pride, our immobilism, our lack of imagination, and our greed. Democracy, crystallized in this date-symbol 1985, came to mean all this and something more: Uruguayans' willingness to exchange the will for power for the will to remain and survive, built on the acceptance that "the worst is always the worse."[3]

A regime built on nostalgia for the past could only be "hyperstable" and conservative. Security born of the rule of law became the most marketable of commodities, the symbolic good most appreciated. Once upon a time, before 12 years of military rule gave flesh to the wildest and most dreadful of our intellectual speculations, the rule of law had not been in great demand. At the time, we had courted freedom, justice, equality and socialism. We wanted *les lendemains qui chantent*" (tomorrows that sing),[4] in a sense more of the same: the "Uruguay of the fat cows," the "Switzerland of America,"[5] the "model country."[6]

Our revolutions have always been conservative, even the most radical ones. Each epoch has constructed its own social reality, defined its terms of reference, its modalities of socially acceptable discourse, its areas of visibility and invisibility, its memories, and its stereotypes (although as good descendants of the ancient Romans, we excel at syncretism). In their wake, the waves of change have re-shaped the ways of defining self and other, male and female, good and bad, desir-able and unacceptable, and heroic and cowardly. They have given salience to cer-tain facts; darkened, erased, or outlined others. Some facts have been forgotten.

What happened under the 12 years of military rule is perhaps the best example of this continual reshaping of an impressionistic memory.[7] The role of certain ac-tors has been so obscured for political and psychological reasons as to remain for-gotten. To my knowledge, no one has spoken in real (and not apologetic and gen-eral) terms of the role of women in the most conservative of resistances, the one that prepared and colored the whole transition to democracy. This female partici-pation was so unheroic in classical terms as to be deemed nonpolitical by the more professional actors. It was so traditional as to be best forgotten by feminists. It was so conservative that it was revolutionary. It was so unorthodox, so unex-pected, as to be impossible to defeat. The ancient Greeks would have made a trag-edy out of it; in this chapter I will try to give a plausible account of what hap-pened.

The Social and Historical Context:
From Paradise to Breakdown

Uruguay is a small country,[8] something of a dwarf in a continent of countries that are larger and richer in natural resources. It is also an anomalous nation, so anomalous that foreign scholars have termed it a "lab" or a "model country."[9] As a country that used to boast (as a good daughter of the Enlightenment) of the proverbial stability of its democracy, the tolerance of its inhabitants, the probity of its justice, and the advanced character of its social legislation, Uruguay lacked many of the social and political problems that affected its neighbors. Its all-white population was—and still is—highly educated,[10] urban,[11] and mesocratic.[12]

Social legislation before the dictatorship was actually very advanced, as an en-lightened ruling class and a particularly combative political elite, aided by the economic bonus of two world wars, had developed an anticipatory style of gov-ernment that contributed to a great extent to the stability of the political system.[13] Schooling, even at the university level, was then and is now free of cost, as educa-tion was used as an important tool of integration and indoctrination in Uruguay's ways. The labor unions worked without any political restriction and were among the strongest of the continent.[14] Health coverage, without ever reaching levels of excellence, was adequate, especially as compared with the other Latin American countries. Many special laws gave members of the middle classes the chance to own their own houses, whereas the lower classes tended to be protected by contin-ual freezes in rent enacted by legislators interested in gaining votes. The state made liberal use of subsidies and legal protections in order to secure public welfare—and political peace.

For women in everyday life, this anticipatory style meant the early passage of divorce laws that clearly favored them,[15] legal gender equality, equal parental rights, maternal leave of absence, equal opportunities to study and work,[16] as well as a sense of equality and freedom. Female participation in the workforce had always been high; many were professionals or, at least, qualified workers. Their political participation, albeit less than that of their male counterparts, was also high: Women had voted since 1933 and were integrated into the internal life of the parties (especially those on the Left) and into the trade unions. A minority held office and could be considered professional politicians. This participation was coupled, however, with conservative private values, a strong separation of the public and the private realms, and the archetypical middle-class dream of "and then they married and lived happily ever after."

Inexpensive and generally well-trained domestic help, in combination with a more traditional extended family structure (with grandmothers, aunts, and sisters in abundance, ready to alleviate the burden of child care), provided the necessary bridge between public and private "virtues," which was necessary to liberate middle- and upper-class women from many pressures and guilt pangs. For the popular sectors, networks of family members and neighbors alleviated at least some of the most urgent problems of child rearing, thus enabling women to get outside work. Amid the legal rights conceded by the state in the first decades of the century and the human resources provided by the society of an underdeveloped country, the feminist message had little chance of being heard.

Our brand of paradise, however, had a strong caveat. Despite the advancement of its legislation, the stability of its political regime, the integration of its polity, and the modernity of its society, Uruguay was a poor country dependent on its capacity to export goods. But the First World began to need less and less from Uruguay after World War II. By the 1950s, a nation that had grown accustomed to affluence was faced with the painful process of learning how to live with poverty. Money was no longer at hand to continue new programs of redistribution and reform, or even to maintain the existing ones. The state lost its capacity of shaping and serving the aspirations of the population, instead having to content itself with the more modest role of administrator of the crises of a stagnant economy and a paralyzed society. The long decline had begun, a decline particularly painful for the pampered middle classes, who were accustomed to looking upward to the steps of the social scale they were soon to occupy if they studied more, worked hard, and were good. The projected country of progress of the "liberal trotskyites"[17] had failed for lack of money. The era of conservatism, from the Right and from the Left, had begun.

To the Right, conservatism meant literally that it was necessary to conserve what existed, even if it was bad, even if it meant bowing to stagnation and accepting the defeat of the model of the past in order not to lose any more ground to the chasm that had developed. The art of governing was thus reduced to the art of "freezing":[18] of salaries, of prices. Had the government been able (and it might have been had it not been democratic and representative, which meant elections and electorates that had to be seduced and conquered) it would have frozen our hopes and our hearts in its vain attempt to slow down *kairos* (time as process).[19]

To the Left, conservatism meant projecting, recuperating, and continuing with the flow of reform toward the horizon of infinite progress that had marked Uruguayan history in the twentieth century. If "freeze" epitomizes the rightist conservatism, "more" and "now" epitomize the leftist conservatism of those times. It was *more* justice, *more* money, *more* education, *more* jobs, *more* hopes, *more* dreams, until we learned to speak in absolutes, of "utopia now." The guerrilla was born.

Until the mid-1960s and according to liberal orthodoxy, democracy had been viewed as a means to an end: the common good. To embrace the ultimate end, the utopia of peace, equality, justice, and plenty for all, was to consider all means equally valid, including the destruction of the previous means. Torn between both groups of nostalgics, amid the scarcity of economic stagnation, a bewildered country was about to learn a new political vocabulary. By 1967, the guerrillas were to popularize first and foremost their own name, the Tupamaros,[20] with a series of daring actions and communiqués that taught us that a "foco"[21] was not only a phenomenon pertaining to electricity. A powerful mythology began to develop. We consumed it with greed, especially those of us who had been born in an already disenchanted world.

It was a time of fire; it was a time of ice. It was the most exciting of times; it was the least creative of times. Iron and blood mingled with poetry and love, as the guerrillas killed people to save their souls in the name of human brotherhood. Some of the killers were women.

To the astonishment of the older generations, the 1960s introduced a new role model for women: the *guerrillera*. And I still remember, from a childhood punctuated by official communiqués and harsh repressive measures, songs to the "new Man" and violent demonstrations, the mute admiration many of us felt for those mythical older sisters who braved the bullets to bring about a new order. They incarnated a new way of being a woman; they were not bound by the limits of a household with husband, children, family obligations, or by the routine of schooling, a job, and bills. They seemed so free to us, we who were searching, probing, adjusting, in a milieu that had become so stagnant as to asphyxiate us!

But were they really so free, so equal, so new? Time and distance, those great tamers of dreams, have shown that in order to be a woman revolutionary, the revolutionary had to negate the woman. It was not only a matter of clothes (after all, we all dressed alike, having discovered the freedom of sameness in our jeans and our absence of make-up), and not only a matter of violating a few legal and "moral" conventions by living together without marrying or by bedding a few fellow revolutionaries. The *guerrillera* had to prove, time and time again, to herself and to the rest of the world, that she was as good as, if not better than, any man. She had to show more resilience, more harshness, less compassion, no squeamishness. Her femaleness was biological: No femininity could be allowed lest others (or, still worse, herself) doubt her revolutionary fervor. As she abandoned more—her role models, her sense of normalcy, her family, her children, and her body—she had to doubt less lest she ask herself, Is it worth it?

Other women participated in politics. They were the rank and file of the more-established leftist groups and parties. Their involvement, though intense, was of a more traditional kind. Many would have to pay dearly for it, side by side with the *guerrilleras*. For their devotion to a tomorrow that was never to be, however, the latter earned the dubious privilege of becoming the first female political prisoners in the whole country of Uruguay.

Women in Hard Times: Twelve Years of Military Dictatorship in Uruguay

On June 27, 1973, we awakened to the sounds of a military march announcing the end of an era. It had taken time, but the military was finally in power.[22] Nobody had really wanted to believe in the possibility of a military coup, although many had toyed with the idea of having the armed forces intervene in politics in their favor. The majority of the citizens held an almost childish belief in the resilience of the battered institutions of our republic[23] and in the potential for survival of a democratic regime that had become our favorite plaything in the last years before the takeover. The coup caught us unprepared, unaware, naked. Now we would have to learn how to survive under the rule of fear.

Contrary to what happened in Chile, the first aim of the new government was not the construction of a new order but the total control, through terror, of the population. Any kind of political participation, and even of participation *tout court*, became illegal by definition. In fact, the whole country was transformed into a big prison, one in which the "good" and "acceptable" external conduct and appearance of the citizens were strictly demarcated and defined, and one in which the sanctions for deviating were swift and without appeal. The citizens were controlled from the top by the shadow of the two political prisons for dissenters (Punta Rieles for women and Libertad—Freedom Prison—for men) and by the prospect of long sessions of torture that belonging to these exclusive clubs entailed.[24]

The military government's task was rendered easier by the fact that we had always been a society with a strong state presence in our midst. The vast majority of the workers were registered, many of them being public employees. Thus, it was relatively simple to establish repressive measures: Either people conformed to the norm or they lost their jobs. Many were fired only as a precaution, being guilty of the youthful sin of having signed a declaration in favor of Cuba in the 1960s or of having participated in the trade union movement. Private employers were sent lists of people it would not be "convenient" to hire. Those who did not comply were so harassed by state audits and controls as to convince everybody that the lists were to be taken seriously. Unemployment and the menace of unemployment (in both public and private sectors) were transformed into one of the most effective tools of control.[25]

The regime did not require people to support it actively; the name of the game was compliance. By 19175, it had attained its goal. The will of the Uruguayans to openly express their disconformity had been utterly broken. There were not many opportunities left to do so, either. Fear exterminated all social life in the public realm. No one spoke in the streets for fear of being heard. No one protested in lines for fear of being reported to the police. One tried not to make new friends for fear of being held responsible for their unknown pasts. One suspected immediately those who were more open or were less afraid of being agents provocateurs of the intelligence service. Rumors about tortures, arrests, and mistreatments were so magnified by our own terror as to take on epic proportions. Many cafés closed their doors for lack of patrons; the rest vegetated in the dullness of a clientele rendered morose by its self-imposed mutism. The fear of accountability loomed larger than life, over every single activity in the public realm.[26]

Even the enchanted inner circle of home and family was not entirely free of external pressures. At first, the *allanamientos*,[27] followed by the fear of more *allanamientos,* provided a glimpse of what the eruption of public control into the private realm could mean. Then a more subtle form of control prevailed: self-censorship. The reign of the "just in case" began. One burned the books presumed to be dangerous, just in case another *allanamiento* could take place. One did not visit friends known for their political dissent, just in case they were under surveillance. One did not speak too openly against the new authorities in front of children, just in case they might innocently repeat in front of that dangerous "other" at school or in the street what they had heard at home.

Despite the strains—or perhaps because of them—the family retained and even reinforced its capacity as shock absorber. It was, after all, the last bastion of warmth and security in a world turned dangerous and hostile. Home meant a stronghold where one could set aside the persona and, for a few hours, become once again a person. Home meant a fortification of secure ties, tested through many years of acquaintance and love. Home meant the very possibility of maintaining significant relationships with others, of exchanging senses of true identity, of bringing down the barriers and really communicating once again with other people. Inside its protective cocoon, one could remember and be remembered as the old self of yesteryear.

Never had the gulf separating the public realm and the private sphere been so profound, so apparent, so felt, as in those times when the public became out of control and out of reach of normal citizens. If the private world had always been guided by the principles of interiority and rationality of feelings, as opposed to the exteriority and "rationality of reason" of the public arena,[28] this separation now transformed the home into a militant ghetto of affective warmth and security and the "world" into a big theater of masks and impersonations.

But the normal separation between public and private also tends to demarcate gender universes under "normal" circumstances. It is commonly believed that the public arena is defined in terms of maleness—intelligence, exteriorized through public eloquence; power, exercised as organizational command; and efficacy, understood instrumentally. The private realm is perceived as essentially feminine, a "sphere of nonpublic intimacy" organized on the basis of a community of effects in which women play an axial role.[29] It is precisely the existence of this perception of "reigns divided," of "natural habitats," that helps to explain why men and women reacted differently to the abnormal situation of those years.

The foreclosure of public spaces by the new regime (as well as the many sacrifices in terms of freedom, self-respect, and a sense of self-worth that the previous dwellers had to make in order to propitiate those in command) drove a vast majority of the former "natural" inhabitants of the public sphere—men—to take refuge in the private realm. For many, it was not even a matter of choice, as they were unemployed and classified as second-rank citizens.[30] They even had to face the final humiliation of losing their status as breadwinners and become as dependent as the children on the earning capacity of their spouses. Their sense of despondency increased with each day, and a great number of them adopted attitudes that can be labeled as "socially autistic."[31]

Their autism did not mean only closing the doors to the external world. It was a much more complex and profound attitude, as they slowly turned into social and political "musulmans."[32] Vanquished, they lacked the force of adopting the *taquiya*[33] as a procedure of survival, perhaps because the monstrosity of what was happening to the country forced them to recognize their own contribution to the debacle. Doubt and self-doubt, as well as a terrible sense of partial responsibility for the disaster, predominated in the group of former militants who escaped the punishment of formal prison. In fact, the regime had condemned them to a prison of their own making, to the torture of their guilt and shame.

Even men in less extreme circumstances showed signs of this fatigue and paralysis as they dealt day after day with the uncertainties and dangers of the public arena. They were much more conscious than women of the traumas of living in a world turned unrecognizable, as all their socially defined interests, obligations, and sense of identity were associated with the outside world. They exercised a greater measure of caution in what they did and what they said, and this had a strong bearing on the way they tried to socialize their offspring.

As for women, their attitudes varied, depending in part on their involvement and degree of contact with the external world. Those who depended strongly on the public arena for their investment in their jobs or political participation were as shell-shocked as men. Their numbers were few, however, for the mainstream pattern in Uruguay had been either to combine a job or profession with a strong commitment to family life or to be a homemaker fully dedicated to child rearing.

Even the incorporation of women into the labor market during the dictatorship tended to reinforce those patterns, as the economy's demand for workers fit to occupy "women's jobs" (seamstresses, knitters, leather workers, etc.)—often inserted in a "putting out" system of production—did not provide the new wage earners many opportunities to rub shoulders with the realities of the external world.

The majority of women, then, were able to continue living in the limbo of the household, more concerned with the cost of living, the quality of their children's formal education, and the strategies for survival than with the change of regime. Even though they could regret the old times, their immediate concerns were not defined by the nature of the legitimacy of those in power. Paradoxically, they were less aware and less afraid of the dangers in the outside world and of the consequences of deviant conduct under the rule of fear.

It is precisely in defense of those everyday life issues that women came to constitute the most formidable, if largely ignored, opponents of the new masters. Theirs was an antlike resistance, made of patience, words, gestures, and especially marked by the absence of silence. Women talked, women criticized, women protested, as they had always done, as they still do. Invoking rights long dead, they claimed better teachers for their children, better school buildings, and better textbooks. They were harsh and outspoken in their criticisms of the quality of the education offered and they did not hesitate to criticize in front of the children. And they were not afraid to recall the past. They spoke of a time when teachers knew the subject they taught, and of when Uruguayans were proud of being Uruguayans because the country was known internationally for the high level of education of its citizens. In a land of make-believe created by their own inability to process the new situation, they established patterns of past normalcy and took them to be the present rules of the game.

At a time when silence was ordered, they spoke. They spoke in markets and supermarkets, protesting the cost of living, the poor quality of the products, the members of the armed forces who could get "free milk, free meat, free medical care, and God knows how many other privileges, while we. ..." At a time when those who wore uniforms had become untouchable, when one could go to prison for attacking the honor of the armed forces, they talked about so-and-so, who was the lover of a colonel and who "has been placed by him as a teacher without even having finished secondary school, just imagine!" They spoke of the son of their neighbor, "a good-for-nothing who has entered the army and now has bought a house." And of "the daughter of doña María,[34] who is divorced from a lieutenant colonel and receives such a huge alimony that she need not work. ... Can you imagine how much his salary must be?" Each time they had to pay the medical bills, they reminded each other that the military had free medical coverage. When paying the rent, they spoke in enraged tones of "their" housing plans that "allow a lot of useless soldiers to own their roofs while hard-working people are condemned to pay and pay!"

In their criticisms, women were often joined by old people; neither group had much to lose, and both enjoyed a seemingly ineffectual chat that was profoundly conservative. In fact, before finding fault with the military, they had used the very same arguments against politicians. Anyone in power is by definition corrupt and immoral, seen from that angle. The difference lies in the fact that the power of the Uruguayan dictatorship rested on its capacity to impose a monologue, whereas the very essence of a democratic regime is dialogue and open social communication. With their conservative and often moralistic gossip, women created an undercurrent of irrepressible criticism. As Monsieur Jourdan spoke in prose without being aware of it,[35] women broke the authoritarian order of discourse without knowing it.

Nowhere was their irreverent attitude more marked than in the household. In charge of the children, they nurtured them with tales of the past, rendering alive a country they had not had the chance to know. As the storytellers of traditional societies, they transmitted many values deeply ingrained in the older generations to the new ones; they created a fund of shared concepts, myths, and symbols that helped perpetuate the Uruguay of old in the memories of the young. For their so-very-special audiences, they re-created a world where one dared to answer back.

Nobody has ever seriously evaluated the role played by those narratives in the configuration of anti-authoritarian attitudes in younger Uruguayans raised under the rule of fear. Such a study surpasses the scope of this chapter. However, the very fact that the narratives existed and that many teenagers recall them as important in their personal development[36] seems to indicate that we cannot lightly dismiss them.

At the beginning of the new democratic era, many adolescents who participated in groups resisting the regime were highly critical of the "gods of their fathers." They considered that their parents had failed because they "just talked," but they recognized that, at a time when books, conferences, and meetings were forbidden, they had been able to reconstruct not only the facts of a lost past but also the feeling of it through the stories of their parents, and more particularly of their mothers.

Certain women did not just talk; they acted. The sharp decline in salaries pushed many middle-class women to commit the ultimate sin in a dictatorship: They united. In the last years of the de facto government, to defend their meager cooperatives, they opened soup kitchens for the unemployed *(ollas populares)*. Those who had family members imprisoned by the regime grouped themselves in organizations with limited aims (food packets or certain modest tasks of advocacy). Those who had children in public secondary schools often had to come together to defend their children's rights, to protest against unjust sanctions, and to speak with the head of the school against an especially obnoxious teacher.

All of those women's groups had sets of characteristics in common. First, they were limited in their scope and in their life span. They were directed toward a particular goal, and once it was attained, they disintegrated. They could not and would not evolve toward a more complex and stable kind of organization, especially as they shared a second characteristic: They were very loosely structured, with fluctuating memberships and an amazing lack of medium- and long-term plans. The latter can be explained by the absence of a political intent that would have guided their actions; the groups were formed to solve particular problems without any reference to the global context. If a certain number of mothers of students of a secondary school discovered they shared a common problem (i.e., the students of a certain grade were sanctioned because of what the authorities considered a misbehavior, such as teenagers wearing blue jeans instead of their required uniforms), they might form a loose group in order to petition the headmaster to remove the sanction. They could even go further, presenting their problem to the media or making higher authorities intervene. But once the problem disappeared, the group was dissolved because the particular issue that had motivated their action was not associated to a larger context.

Seen from that angle, the groups were appallingly "feminine." The personal was political, but as always happens when the personal and only the personal becomes political, they never saw the forest because of the trees. The way women acted to fight certain damaging aspects of the de facto government was no different from the way they acted in their "natural habitat," the private realm: atomistically, individualistically, and oriented to perpetuating the family in the best possible way. The principles that guided their actions were conservative and very traditional: devoted defense of home and family at any personal cost. There was nothing feminist in their formulation; motherhood and housewifery propelled them to act. There was nothing very political in their actions, at least in party politics terms; they were set to modify their own situations, not to change the world or overthrow the regime. But more by the fact that they existed than by what they did, those women's organizations contributed to erode the monologue imposed from the top. They helped show that something could be done; they forced the "other" in command to enter into a dialogue, however authoritarian its terms of reference. And the impact they had on those silent observers, their children, must not be dismissed.

In later years, many have tried to capitalize on what these women did, distorting the sense of their action, of their gossip, of their lack of cooperation with the authorities. Political parties, trade unions, feminist groups, and political activists who saw in the social movements a platform to propel their own political careers have tried to color their resistance with all the existent shades of the doctrinal palette. The danger for women, and for the whole of the Uruguayan people, is to believe those one-sided tales of what did not happen and to lose sight of how effectively women helped create the climate of the transition.

From Housewives, Mothers, and Spouses to Housewives, Mothers, and Spouses: The Unconscious Resistance in Perspective

The way Uruguayan women fought the military dictatorship poses unusual problems for a political scientist because their resistance lacked even the consciousness of being resistant. There was no Pasionaria[37] in our midst, no Celia Sánchez,[38] no Clara Zetkin,[39] no Rosa Luxemburg,[40] no Inés Armand,[41] no Eva Perón,[42] not even a Hebe Bonafini.[43] The times, and our own national culture of mediocrity, were not ripe for great feats of heroism.

The single most important path of resistance undertaken by Uruguayan women was in the most traditional of the roles, and it was followed in the most traditional of ways. In the intimacy of the private realm, mothers, aunts, and older sisters took charge of the rearing of the younger generation and transmitted to it the powerful antiregime, "subversive" democratic values that helped keep the flame of hope alive. By keeping the Uruguay of the past alive through tales and through their acts, they prevented the grim, authoritarian present of the dictatorship from becoming their children's reality.

Their conservatism implied, at the time, the preservation of the old values in even the most radical ways. Today, this conservatism is still alive and well. In the streets and in the markets, women continue to gossip against the corruption of those in power, to protest against the prices, and to talk against the injustices of life in this world. Their discourse has not changed because they have not changed. They are traditional women in traditional roles, seeking their traditional share of traditional happiness on earth. What has changed are the political circumstances. Their discourse is ineffective and anodyne in a regime based on freedom of association and speech.

But in an authoritarian regime, the impact of women's discourse takes the form of dissent. Their resistance was not in the form of raised consciousness of actions in areas other than the properly domestic. Women in general did not resist because they wanted to change the society they knew, with all its gender and class inequalities; on the contrary, they wanted to restore the good old Uruguay with which they had been comfortable. What kind of activism do you engage in once you recover what you have lost?

Paradoxically, their resistance was so effective because it was so feminine, so traditional, so unexpected. The armed forces, a male organization par excellence, were ready to cope with Tania.[44] They could have dealt with Clara Zetkin. They could have killed Rosa Luxemburg. They could have exiled La Pasionaria. But they did not know how to repress women who were just devoted mothers, good housewives, and dedicated spouses. Uruguayan women fought from precisely those trenches. They fought as spouses by visiting their husbands in prison, by giving them strength and hope, by "keeping their act together" even at the worst of times. How can you punish a woman for being faithful? Women fought as spouses by making ends meet, by inventing hundreds of ways of keeping a sound budget, by seeking paid labor when their mates were unemployed—or had been dismissed from their jobs for political reasons. How can you punish a woman for being a sound housewife? Women fought as housewives by seeking the best prices, by creating consumer goods, by protesting against raises and abuses. How can you punish a woman for being thrifty? Women fought as mothers by defending their children's rights to education and fair treatment, by caring for their needs at school or in prison, by not abandoning them to their fate in the public realm. How can you punish a woman for being a devoted mother?

The political ideology of the military was, in a sense, their best ally. This military ideology, with its paternalistic overtones, could not find fault with what Uruguayan women were doing because women were doing what they were supposed to do according to the military definition of gender roles: They were acting as mothers, wives, and housewives. Thus, the military could not identify this very peculiar form of dissent as a political threat to be taken into account in the everyday struggle for power. They could not see that by speaking freely, by not acknowledging that the rules of interaction were different and that power had changed hands, and by ignoring the possible reprisals, women were challenging the very bases of the rule of fear the military was trying to impose on the country.

Unfortunately, the return of democracy to these latitudes has not helped to clarify these simple facts. Our kind of collective blindness affects not only women's issues but the whole series of issues connected with the past. Instead of reviving the strands of our collective and individual memories, of recomposing the richness of the many voices military rule unwillingly helped unearth, political organizations continue fighting, trying to impose a hegemonic narrative of our past.

The Return to Democracy

After more than a decade of military rule, the first years of democratic government were perceived as a second honeymoon by the population at large. The Sanguinetti administration thus benefitted from the restraint of its political adversaries, the moderation of the trade unions, and the general goodwill of the population. On the one hand, with the menacing presence of the military still looming large at the horizon, nobody wanted to endanger what was still viewed as a fragile democracy. On the other, the restoration of democracy was perceived as a return to normalcy after the "accident" of military dictatorship. Thus, the spirit of Fray Luis de Léon with his "As we were saying yesterday"[45] permeated society while we still sometimes looked fearfully over our shoulders. Nowhere was this spirit more present than in the family, where after years of defensiveness, the shutters—and I am speaking both of the physical covers that protect windows and of the masks worn to shield intimacy from prying eyes—could be removed. The change took time, as we felt naked in our newfound freedom and loath to show ourselves unarmed.

The process involved settling accounts with the past,[46] dealing with the pain and shame of being the subjects and objects of the culture of fear that had paralyzed the country and us for so many years.[47] We had to arrive at some sort of basic agreement on the matter of retribution for past suffering in the case of victims, past misdeeds in the case of victimizers. How to close the past was an obsessive issue discussed through and through, at all levels of society. Politicians unsuccessfully negotiated several solutions; projects went back and forth that dealt with the pressing matter of how to settle accounts with blood memory. It took two years for politicians and the military to reach some kind of compromise that, without fully satisfying any of the negotiators, could be perceived as a settlement. This agreement was translated into law, the Ley de Caducidad de la Pretención Punitiva del Estado (Amnesty Law). The state renounced its right to prosecute members of the police and the armed forces for human rights abuses during the years of military dictatorship and allowed victims to claim financial retribution in civil courts.

The matter seemed settled, at least from a rational point of view, as everybody gained at least something from the negotiation: The security and armed forces got an amnesty that was not labeled as such;[48] politicians, an institutional and legal response to an unsolvable problem that did not fully alienate the military and endanger the precarious stability; victims, the possibility of at least claiming financial reparation for their suffering and loss. It was an imperfect and unsatisfactory solution from many points of view, but it represented the maximum degree of compromise—and concession—the actors involved could grant at the time.

Many sectors of society did not judge the outcome as fair. All had suffered great losses. Many had been imprisoned, tortured, exiled, or exiled within the country. As a society, we had been divested of that sense of inviolability of rights only the security of a state that operates under the rule of law can provide to its citizens. Resentment over the losses as well as a genuine belief that compromise was inappropriate in a matter as serious as human rights abuses pushed many Uruguayans to challenge the law of amnesty by means of a referendum.[49] Many women participated in the daily tasks of the movement; they intended to be less tolerant than their male counterparts regarding any possibility of compromise on the issue.

A committee was formed to promote a revision of the law. Not surprisingly, the joint presidency of the committee was occupied by women who had personally suffered great losses and who lacked previous political experience. Even though many worked on the Committee in Favor of the Referendum, the best known faces of the movement were Matilde Rodríguez de Gutiérrez Ruiz, widow of a Blanco legislator assassinated in Buenos Aires by the *cuerpos de tareas* (task forces); Elisa Deila Piano de Micheline, widow of a Colorado legislator assassinated in the same episode; and María Esther Gatti de Islas, grandmother of Marian Zafforoni Islas, a "disappeared" child whose photograph came to symbolize the plight of all the children of Uruguay kidnapped by the security and armed forces in Argentina.

Paradoxically, even though the referendum campaign deeply shook renascent Uruguayan politics, many of its participants did not consider it a political movement.[50] Moreover, many of its members rejected the essential tools of the political craft: negotiating, reaching compromises, acknowledging the existence of boundaries. In a sense, the proreferendum movement was a movement of absolutes, an ethical crusade disguised as a legal and political battle, the struggle between moral values and *raison d'état.*

Although the movement lost the vote, the tensions it represented have deepened in Uruguayan society and politics since then. This has been especially evident in those movements headed either by women or by retired people:[51] The logic of the private sphere becomes and sometimes overcomes the logic of politics; the general good is compromised in the name of the interests not only of particular groups but of the individual members of those groups; morality is elevated to the role of a general standard of politics.

This conservative privatization of politics has resulted in a personalization of political practice. Leaders are followed because of their charisma and not because of their ideas, and a strong rhetoric that gives primacy to the inalienable right to individual felicity precludes any invocation of the public interest. The definition of politics as the pondered art of attaining what is possible is being abandoned for a vague concept of politics-as-spectacle where no member of the audience must be left without his or her share of individual satisfaction. The autistic retrenchment from public space and the atomization of discourse that had been forced upon us by repressive practices during the years of military dictatorship have given way to the shattering of the concept of the general good and its substitution by the maximalist summing of private interests and agendas.

In this frame of reference, some events that had women as their chief protagonists have come to epitomize this deeply conservative trend. After years of a moving search and a bitter struggle to recover Mariana Zaffaroni, the Uruguayan "disappeared" child who had been adopted by a noted member of the Argentine repressive apparatus, Mariana, now a young woman in her late teens, refused to return to her biological family. She also addressed a public letter to the Argentine president, Carlos Menem, begging him to pardon the man who had helped torment and kill her biological mother and kidnap a child from a center of torture, arguing that she considered this man her real father and that the couple who had denied her her identity and contributed to the disappearance of her parents had been good to her.

This episode could be dismissed as a simple curiosity, a footnote in the brutal history of military rule in the River Plate, or even as the inner crisis of a youngster torn between two conflicting sorts of love and moral obligation. However, what was indicative of the new trend was the lack of public discussion, the absence of further deliberation on a political process and a political issue where public and private interests necessarily intermingled. The search for the lost children of those who had disappeared had in itself been a process where these planes had often been confused, where the private angst of bereaved parents and grandparents had become a political banner; where public issues such as what the boundaries of repression and terror are in the civilized society and how violent dissent must be dealt with interfered with private sorrow and mourning and in some cases impeded effective action to achieve a settlement in the best interests of the children. In that sense, the action of Mariana Zaffaroni was a cruel corollary of its process and a painful reminder that some distance must be maintained between the moral and political planes and their corresponding logic if society and politics are to function at a level that is not merely defensive.

In 1992, an episode shook Uruguay that was led by a woman; women as wives, women as mothers, and women as homemakers took the limelight: A national strike of the members of the police force culminated in a march of policemen and -women and their families into Montevideo to press for better wages. Had we forgotten, this incident would have reminded us of the power of conservative resistance and would also have reminded us to think about the effects of blurring the boundary between public and private spheres.

The spark that ignited this quasi-insurrectional movement originated in a distribution of spoiled foodstuffs.[52] Policemen's wives in the provinces then mobilized, and as an act of protest, they deposited the rotten food in the street in front of a police precinct. As a result of this action, several of their husbands were transferred to other postings, a sanction that meant that they would be likely to lose their other jobs or be separated from their families. Having assessed this as an attack by the state on their families—as Sandra Dodero, the leader-to-be of the movement, put it[53]—the women marched through Montevideo and organized a hunger strike. Little by little, all sectors of the police force joined their protest, and the movement became national. Negotiations between the government and the strikers began with the police wives, led by Sandra Dodero as spokesperson, because "who will be a better spokesperson for a policeman than his own wife and his children? Who will defend him better than his family? Certainly not two or three gentlemen with political aspirations, who have acquired compromises with the government and who never risked their careers for the police force when they should have done so!"[54]

During the whole strike, Sandra Dodero refused to acknowledge the need for concessions and opposed the logic of the general good with her own brand of "the private is political." Using the media, she brandished the right of a policeman's child to have the same consumer goods as other children in the country as if it were self-evident justification for an increase in police salaries. The well-being of the family was used to counter any discussion of why a police force should not go on strike and paralyze the country. Instead of discussing if and when public servants endowed by the state with the legitimate use of violence could make use of that violence against government and state, we ended up entangled in a debate over the right of children to eat yoghurt and the entitlement of housewives to decide how to spend the national budget because they are the ones that go to the supermarket. A great communicator, Sandra Dodero made us accept not only her own terms of discourse (terms that the opposition had used during the long years of military rule) but also the very premises of that discourse: to wit, that in the new fragmented reality that has resulted from the retreat of the state, each individual and each circumstantial grouping of individuals is entitled to further his or her personal, private interests at all costs, regardless of the price others have to pay. In the framework of a world recession, with a state forced for economic and ideological reasons to pull back from its role as arbiter and regulator, Sandra Dodero's position may well herald the form and content of future social and political conflicts in Uruguay.

As a nation, we are torn between the need to conserve what is best in the heritage a bountiful state provided in the past and the need to change, to overcome our stagnation and energize our country. We won't be able to accomplish those tasks as long as we deepen existing conflicts by assuming maximalist positions. In the 1960s and early 1970s, only *raison d'état* and the common good were recognized as legitimate triggers of political action. In the 1970s and early 1980s, we were forced to endure massive doses of *raison d'état* and common good by way of military repression. This process resulted in a revalorization of family and private space, of morality and individual freedom. We have now reached a point where we seem to value only individual need and interest as political motivation and to prefer closed communities and fragmented realities over a universal, open society. This could be a short-lived trend, but it could also be a sign that the nation-state, the basis for democratic politics, is disappearing.

Notes

1. Expression used by Juan Rial in C. Perelli and J. Rial, *De mitos y memorias politicas: La represión, el miedo y después* (Montevideo: EBO, 1986).

2. From the maxim of Talleyrand: *"Qui n'a pas connu l'ancien regime ne sait pas ce qu'est la douceur de vivre."*

3. The expression was used by Mario Benedetti, one of the apologists of the leftist brand of conservatism, in one of his journalistic mea culpa during his exile in Spain.

4. From a poem of the communist resistance leader Gabriel Peri, dead at the hand of the Nazis during the German occupation.

5. Expressions used to describe the country in its period of splendor.

6. Title given by Milton Vanger to his book on the second presidency of Don José Batile y Ordoñez. It is taken from a discourse of Batile. See Milton Vanger, *Model Country: Jose Batile y Ordoñez of Uruguay 1907–15* (Hanover, N.H.: University Press of New England, 1980).

7. See Perelli and Rial, *De mitos.*

8. Uruguay has approximately 187,000 square kilometers and 2.9 million inhabitants.

9. Expression used by George Pendle in his book *Uruguay, South America's First Welfare State* (London, 1952; Spanish version, Montevideo: Arca, 1961).

10. To give but one indicator, in 1972, of a total population of 2.8 million inhabitants, 145,000 attended secondary schools. In the same year, the registration at the university level was 35,000 students. The literacy rate was approximately 97 percent of the population.

11. Eighty-two percent of the population lives in urban centers of more than 5,000 inhabitants. More than half of the population lives in the capital.

12. Measured by social stratification indicators, the proportion of the middle class could reach 40 percent of the population. However, surveys show that 50–60 percent of Uruguayans see themselves as middle class.

13. See J. Rial, *Partidos políticos, democracia y autoritarismo* (Montevideo: EBO, 1984).

14. See J. L. Lanzaro, *Sindicatos y sistema político* (Montevideo: FCU, 1986).

15. The divorce law was promulgated in 1907 and perfected in 1912. Among the modalities of divorce it establishes, one clearly favors women: Divorce requires only the woman's decision.

16. The bill called De Derechos Civiles de la Mujer was promulgated in 1933.

17. Expression used by Carlos Real de Azúa to characterize the *battilista* reform movement.

18. The expression was officially used to name economic policies to combat the inflation rate.

19. Term used by the Greeks (particularly Aristotle) to describe time as process, distinguished from chronological time *(Chronos)*.

20. The Movimiento de Liberación Nacional (Movement of National Liberation). Tupamaros (founded in 1962) took its name from the Indian chief Tupac Amaru, who headed a Peruvian revolt against the Spanish Empire. The works on the Tupamaros are all in an apologetic vein. No serious academic effort has been made to better comprehend this political movement.

21. The theory of the revolutionary *foco* was developed from Ché Guevara, *La guerra de guerrillas* (Havana: Casa de las Americas, 1960); and from the later work of Regis Debray, *Revolutión en la revolución* (Montevideo: Sandino Libros, 1965).

22. The Uruguayan coup of 1973 has been called "the long coup," as it formally spans from February 9, 1973, to June 27, 1973. The whole process that led to the coup really began in 1968; the governmental repressive measures increased thereafter.

23. Perhaps the best example of such a constellation of Panglossian beliefs and attitudes is given by the Tupamaros, who when arrested for trying to overthrow the constitutional arrangements of the country invoked in their legal defenses the very same constitution they sought to destroy.

24. See the work on political prisons and the hierarchy of terror by Juan Rial in Perelli and Rial, *De mitos*. Testimonials of political prisoners also abound in the press of 1985; they give a vivid account of those years.

25. The number of people who lost their jobs for political reasons is calculated to be around 12,000. Once the military left power, 6,000 of its members initiated the legal process to be reinstated in the positions they had previously occupied.

26. See Perelli and Rial, *De mitos*.

27. The *allanamientos* were procedures officially aimed at searching the houses of a neighborhood in order to combat the guerrillas. They really served to initiate the population into the psychological dynamics of fear. They were carried out at unexpected times by

armed servicemen in fatigues who made meticulous searches of books and papers in each house, confiscated books and photographs, and paralyzed a whole street or neighborhood to put the fear of God in the heart of even the most innocent and uninvolved of bystanders.

28. See José Joaquin Brunner, *La mujer y lo privado en la communicación social,* FLACSO, Material de discusión, no. 51, Santiago, 1982.

29. Ibid.

30. Citizens were classified into three categories according to their ideological "purity." These categories, labeled A, B, and C, delineated groups of citizens with differential rights. The A citizens could be employed by the state as well as by the private sector. They could travel freely and had at their disposal the scarce and limited freedoms such a regime offers. The B citizens could be hired in the private sector but not by the public administration. They could get a passport limited to certain countries and had to request it every time they traveled; they were also more likely to be harassed by the police and by the intelligence services. The C citizens were considered the "scum of the earth," as the category was reserved especially (but not exclusively) for political prisoners who had been liberated or for political dissenters. The C citizens had no rights whatsoever. One could be changed from one category to another without any explanation, and this uncertainty was another way of inspiring fear.

31. For a broader utilization of this concept of Bruno Bettelheim's to the Uruguayan context, see Perelli and Rial, *De mitos.*

32. Term used by the prisoners of the Nazi concentration camps to designate those inmates who had lost all interest in what happened around them and had lost the will to live. For a description of the state of "musulman," see Bruno Bettelheim, *Surviving and Other Essays* (New York: Vintage Books, 1980).

33. *Taquiya* refers to the practice of the Muslim religion that allows its followers to deny being Muslims under extreme conditions and to fake conversion to save their lives, as long as in their hearts they continue to be "true believers."

34. Doña María is the generic name given to the matrons of the popular sectors in Latin America.

35. Molière, *Le Bourgeois Gentilhomme.*

36. Data drawn from interviews with secondary school students who belonged to the organization of resistance inside the high schools, the FES (Federation of Secondary School Students, Federación de Estudiantes Secundarios). See the study on that movement in Perelli and Rial, *De mitos.*

37. La Pasionaria (Dolores Ibarruri), communist agitator and fighter on the side of the Spanish Republicans during the Spanish civil war.

38. Celia Sánchez, one of the most important female leaders of the movement "26 de Julio" during the Cuban Revolution. I could also have named Vilma Espin de Castro and Haydee Santamaria, coleaders of the same movement.

39. Clara Zetkin, the first important Marxist feminist during the Second International.

40. Rosa Luxemburg, the most brilliant Marxist theoretician in open opposition to Lenin.

41. Inés Armand, lover of Lenin and organizer of the first stage of the Soviet Revolution.

42. Eva Perón, first lover and then official wife of Juan Domingo Perón of Argentina. She was a populist leader herself and was reputed to be the éminence grise of her husband's government. She has become a sacred figure for the popular sectors in her country.

43. Hebe Bonafini, second leader of the movement of Madres of the Plaza de Mayo in Argentina.

44. Tania, German guerrilla who fought and died with Ché Guevara in Bolivia.

45. After being imprisoned under charges of heresy by the Spanish Inquisition for many years, upon his reinstatement as a professor at the University of Salamanca, the poet and teacher Fray Luis de Léon began his first class with the words, "As we were saying yesterday."

46. I have dealt with this matter on the subject of Argentina in "Settling Accounts with Blood Memory: The case of Argentina," *Social Research* 59, 2 (Summer 91): 415–451.

47. On the concept of "culture of fear" see Juan E. Corradi, Patricia Fagen-Weiss, and Manuel Antonio Garréton, eds., *Fear at the Edge: State, Terror and Resistance in Latin America* (Berkeley: University of California Press, 1992); Saúl Sosnowski and Louise Popkin, eds., *Repression, Exile and Democracy: Uruguayan Culture* (Durham, N.C.: Duke University Press, 1992).

48. The military were especially insistent on the solution not being called an amnesty, as they considered that no crime had been committed in this just war against subversion. At the very most, they admitted that some officers could have committed abuses but that no criminal intention had presided over the institutionalization of repression during the state of internal commotion and civil war that had existed in the country.

49. See IIDH-CAPEL, *El referéndum uruguayo del 16 de abril 1989* (San José: IIDH, 1989).

50. Thus, the committee dissolved itself after its motion to revise the law was defeated.

51. In the 1989 national election, a motion to regulate the increases in the retirement pensions in a way that would clearly generate more inflation was put to a vote. Although everybody knew that the measure would harm the economy—and thus went against the general interest—the pressure of the retired people was such, in a country with 600,000 retirees, that the political parties felt forced to support it.

52. Until then, provisions were normally supplied as a complement of the meager wages earned by members of the police force.

53. This and the following excerpts are all quotes from an extensive narrative by Sandra Dodero that led to the police strike: "Estas son mis verdades" (These Are My Truths), *Análisas y Desafíos* (Montevideo) 2, 14 (January 1993): 19–25.

54. Dodero, "Estas son mis verdades," 23.

SIX

The Difficult Equilibrium Between Bread and Roses: Women's Organizations and Democracy in Peru

MARUJA BARRIG

The end of the 1970s was a period of intense mobilization in Peru. The feminist movement emerged as part of the regionwide wave that followed the UN International Women's Year Meeting in 1975 in Mexico City; the second Latin American *encuentro* was held in Lima in 1983. Its emergence coincided with a period of democratic renewal: The military government called for a constitutional assembly in 1978, and a civilian president was elected in 1980. The severe economic crisis, which began earlier in Peru than in the rest of Latin America, mobilized urban women to create new strategies of subsistence through the establishment of communal kitchens, the Glass of Milk (Vaso de Leche) program, and other neighborhood-based initiatives.

This chapter begins with a description of the transition from military rule in Peru, followed by an analysis of the popular and feminist strands of the women's movement and their changing strategies from the transition through the decade of the 1980s. I argue that the feminists' strategies of political autonomy and the primacy given to strategic gender issues may have unnecessarily isolated feminists from the popular women's movements, and that the grassroots women's movements also made strategic choices that weakened them in the broader political arena. The chapter then turns to the rise of urban terrorism in the 1990s as the Maoist Sendero Luminoso (Shining Path) extended its campaign to the cities and to the impact of Sendero's strategy of threatening and assassinating popular leaders of the women's movements in Peru.

The Transition from Military Rule

The categories most commonly used to analyze military governments and the transitions to democracy in Latin America are not readily applied to Peru. Contrary to modernization theory, which would have predicted military coups in the least-developed countries, it was in the most-industrialized countries of South America—Argentina, Brazil, Uruguay, and Chile—that the military installed dictatorships to neutralize the social conflicts arising from the processes of industrialization and urbanization. These regimes also sought to integrate their economies more fully into the international economic system.[1]

Although the military dictatorship in Peru did not conform to the model of a bureaucratic authoritarian regime, the methods used to contain the opposition were similar in that there were repression and restriction of the freedoms of leftist parties, enforced paralysis of democratic institutions, and denial of certain basic liberties. Because the traditional spaces of politics, such as unions and political parties, were denied their usual functions, new social actors emerged: women, young people, and a revitalized Church. Their role in the transition was quite significant, and they brought new perspectives and called for changes in areas formerly seen as outside the realm of politics.[2] The traumatic experience with military governments in Latin America changed the focus of intellectual debate from the issue of revolution to the theme of democracy, but democracy in a much broader sense than the formal mechanisms that guarantee democratic rights. There was an equal concern with expression of democratic values and practices in everyday life.

Social movements are the expression of oppressed or dominated groups in society. They organize in a spontaneous and often discontinuous way, and their demands are immediate rather than ideological. The political actions of these groups are often marginalized from mainstream political institutions such as the state and political parties. Within social movements, political action provides the environment for creating group identity through democratic participation. The fact that these political groups are new and that they are drawn from the least-privileged sectors of society offers a challenge at the sociocultural level. Their political actions represent new ways of "doing politics," yet their appeal to political power often seems weak, if not entirely absent.

Social movements develop broad agendas and seek to modify norms as well as institutions. Many argue that there is a more radical exercise of democracy within social movements than can be found in conventional political institutions, even during times of full and open democracy. The return of democratic governments in South America focused attention on these heterodox forms of political activity and raised questions about their viability and their effectiveness in expressing new interests.

There are important differences among the countries undergoing the process of democratic transition and consolidation in the region. Peru is not only one of the poorest countries in the region, but it has a very limited system of political representation that has traditionally excluded the majority of the population through ethnic, cultural, and social discrimination. The military government established by Juan Velasco Alvarado in 1968 was a reaction against the dominant class, whom the military opposed, and not against the popular classes as was the case elsewhere. The armed forces acted in a context of political immobilism and extreme maldistribution of economic and political power. The Velasco regime initiated a program of economic reform and radical social ideology that had no counterpart elsewhere in the region. The Velasco reforms opened new channels of representation for those who could potentially benefit from its policies. Although they were under close government tutelage, agrarian cooperatives and worker-managed firms provided new spaces for political participation and created expanded expectations of citizens' rights.

To delegitimize the traditional political parties, which had been powerful during the previous decades, the military closed off their exclusive arenas of action, such as Parliament, and strengthened alternative forces such as the Communist Party, which supported the Velasco government. The New Left, which was critical of Velasco but which benefited from the reforms, discovered a fertile terrain for developing its ideas and expanding its base of support among leaders of the unions, the shantytowns, and the universities.[3] In 1983, the United Left Front, the electoral coalition of the New Left, became a major political force in Peru, second only to the traditional populist party, the APRA.

In the late 1970s, when the military government adopted economic austerity policies to deal with what had become a profound economic crisis, the union and shantytown organizations mounted a strong response. Hundreds of thousands of Peruvians from diverse social sectors were mobilized under the slogan "Down with the dictatorship."

These groups did not demand the recovery of democratic rights, which were barely understood as benefits by the popular classes who had fared poorly under past "democratic" governments. They asked for better salaries and improved living conditions.[4] Democratic values have since gained some ground as these new organizations have responded to opportunities for democratic participation, but in the late 1970s, democracy itself was not the main issue.

The fact that the popular classes were active in the antidictatorial demonstrations of the late 1970s argued strongly for their inclusion at the very center of the parties of the Peruvian Left. In the past, the leftist parties had been dogmatic, and internal leadership had been quite authoritarian. Internal party democracy was now called for because of the vital presence of those sectors that had been discriminated against historically, and also because of the practical fact that the massive demonstrations that filled the streets of Peru's cities could take place only because these new popular organizations had emerged.

The leftist parties, however, proved unable to develop a program for the country that could incorporate these new social democratic expressions. The elections for a Constitutional Assembly (Asamblea Constituyente) in 1979, and the subsequent general elections in 1980, were inadequate responses to the complexity and depth of social mobilization in the late 1970s. Elections alone could not meet the demands for self-determination arising from these newly mobilized groups.

The Mobilization of Women

Although they had previously existed in Peru as elsewhere in the region, grassroots women's groups began to organize rapidly beginning in 1979. In that same year, middle-class women's groups were formed, inspired by the spread of feminist ideas. Both types of women's organizations were supported, in part, by funds available through international agencies concerned with community development and by foundations newly concerned with improving the status of women. The moment was propitious: The United Nations had declared 1975 the beginning of the Women's Decade and had called upon member governments to improve the health, employment opportunities, and educational levels of women under the banner of equality, development, and peace.

A hasty analysis might conclude that some sort of biological sisterhood unified the political expressions of the diverse groups of women who emerged on the public scene at the end of the 1970s. However, Peruvian women were brought together by the problems of human reproduction under conditions of poverty, the alarming population growth rate, the economic collapse, and the social crisis it produced.[5] The situation of women is at the heart of analysis of these issues. It is at moments like these when the questioning of the traditional role of women is the most productive, but it is also the time when the concrete demands of diverse social classes rise to the surface and women's issues are often submerged.

Peruvian women participated fully in the street demonstrations against the military dictatorship. Public-sector employees and teachers were called upon by their unions to swell the ranks of the demonstrations for better salaries. The parties of the New Left, notwithstanding their influence among the unions, depended on conventional political practice; they could not broaden their goals or develop ways to guarantee democracy in daily life, and certainly not in the primary arena of the exercise of power: the family.

Something quite similar occurred with the women on the margins of human existence, whose presence in barrio protests in Lima was significant but whose capacity to act seemed limited to creating strategies of family survival. The defense of life—from seeking out those who had been "disappeared" by dictatorships to providing food for the living—continued to be women's mission in Peru as elsewhere. Their condition as women seemed an irreducible identity, but their actions, though clearly gendered, revealed class differences as well.

Among middle-class women, social practice took the form of feminism and, among lower-class women, the creation of community organizations for economic survival, issues that had been marginal to traditional politics. Whether consciously or intuitively, these women tried to democratize human relations in those places that had been bypassed by the grand strategies of politics. The success women had in articulating the content of daily life coexisted with a strong inhibition against extending this vision to the public sphere of politics. In this sense, the limited impact of women's actions, I argue, was self-imposed.

The proposals to democratize society that were generated by the new social movements needed to be consciously linked to political power to have a long-term effect. Conventional political institutions failed to develop proposals to democratize the spaces of daily life *(los espacios cotidianos)*. The communal kitchens and the other new forms of local organization did not succeed in changing the way in which women valued their potential as citizens or as dynamic agents of change in their own communities. Their mobilization did not give them political weight in the exercise of community power, except where they were directly involved. Nor has participation brought about a new awareness of gender identity.

The political demand for the necessities of life arises from women's reproductive role and from women's responsibility for that role; as long as the issues of daily life are reduced to demands for employment or wage increases, the fight for public services in the barrios will be "feminized" and isolated from the demands of the unions and the parties. Lacking consistent links to the public sphere, the political dimension of everyday life remained separate from local and municipal politics, further accentuating false dichotomies: Political power is man's discourse, and the domestic sphere and the quality of life is women's (undervalued) concern.

Feminism in Peru emerged with renewed force at the end of the 1970s and continued into the 1980s. Its political strategy fluctuated between joining other social movements and defining itself as autonomous, both organizationally and ideologically. The unquestionable legitimacy of women's groups, which had formed nuclei of theoretical discussion, personal reflection, and self-help, fell apart when feminists tried to universalize the priorities of gender for all women and from there mount a campaign for political office—in the conventional political space that they themselves had rejected.

The 1980s also brought the rise of Sendero Luminoso, a radical Maoist guerrilla movement that would become a mortal threat to the leadership of urban popular movements by the end of the decade. Although Sendero remained a rural threat, the issues for feminists were (1) their relationship to the political parties, particularly on the Left, and (2) the linkage between the feminists and urban popular movements led by women. A third concern, raised in this chapter, is the degree to which both movements were dependent on international funding and on the international network of NGOs.

From Political Militancy to
Feminist Autonomy

The political parties of the New Left in Peru were born with the enthusiasm of the Cuban Revolution, a Leninist bias, and a strong dose of self-flagellation. The majority of the middle-class university students who made up the New Left were influenced, perhaps in spite of themselves, by Catholicism, especially by liberation theology. They lived their militancy like apostles and tried to be at one with the masses, with whom they identified and whom they tried to represent.

The years at the end of the 1960s and the beginning of the 1970s showed how difficult it was to judge the reforms of the military government by the standards of classical Marxism. Despite its flaws, this period did change people's lives, creating a kind of voluntary exodus from the middle- and upper-class neighborhoods to the shantytowns and a switch from private to public schools. This was the era of the "enlightened vanguard" and of a unidimensional focus on the political; the personal was rejected as exclusive and exclusionary.

Without intending to do so, the parties of the New Left were repeating the path that Peruvian socialists had followed in the early 1930s, a path that did not succeed in incorporating nationalism or the day-to-day culture of the people. The APRA was much more effective than the socialists in mobilizing the popular sectors, and APRA integrated the family into militant party life. Although it was unwilling to fight for women's right to vote, APRA did integrate children, young people, and women under the paternal and protective leadership of the party's leader, Victor Raúl Haya de la Torre, who directed his messages to "Aprista homes." Although the family discourse of Haya was traditional and tended to reinforce internal hierarchy,[6] entire families joined APRA, and identification with the party was passed down to new generations as a kind of political inheritance. Haya's approach to the family facilitated the extension of networks of solidarity and mutual help during the periods when APRA was banned and had to operate clandestinely, that is, for much of the time between the 1930s and the 1960s. By contrast, the leftist parties proved unable to integrate any aspect of everyday life into their militancy.

The inability of the Left to connect the diverse spheres of life has been a weakness in recruiting women. Women who have both domestic responsibilities and low levels of education remain alienated from a discourse that assigns them to the abstract state, and that commits them to class conflict without paying the slightest attention to domination in the domestic sphere, where women live their everyday lives.

For Peruvian women university students, joining leftist parties represented an opportunity to try out new formulas of liberty; for the women of the party cadres, party membership provided salaried work to maintain their households and support their husbands' political work, which they eventually "joined" by typing and cooking for meetings.

These conditions of women's political labor were ripe for rebellion but even before the women rose up, there were signs that other sectors were rejecting the hierarchical and elitist political practice typical of the Peruvian Left. In the Revolutionary Vanguard (Vanguardia Revolucionaria, or VR), one of the most important parties of the new Peruvian Left, there were new questions about how to "do politics." The classical Marxists came under attack for limiting participation:

> The functioning of VR has been such, especially in recent times, that frequently the leadership oppresses the rank-and-file, the comrades who have more knowledge oppress those who have less, those who are "leaders" dominate those who are not, and those with university education lord it over the workers and the campesinos. The Party controls the movement.[7]

These critics neglected to add the oppression of women, either that of their wives or of the women members of the party, to this list of political accusations. That would come later. What was under attack here was a political style that kept those on the margins in line; at stake was the fundamental issue of internal democracy within the party.

In March 1979, four militant women from VR asked the party's central committee to create a women's commission. They pointed out the absence of any theoretical discussion of the issue of women's political participation; they noted that the party's few female militants were mobilized only when the inner group decided they should be involved and that women's organizations were not sufficiently integrated into the party structure.[8]

The attempt to raise these questions was met initially with indifference and later with marginalization. The leaders were not at all disturbed about having a group of self-isolated and inexperienced women set up a women's commission, so the initiative had little impact. However, it was one of the factors that led to a major reform in the party, an effort to replace the party of cadres with a party of the masses.

But for women, as for many other groups within the party, the reform came too late. Many were burned out and chose to find renewal in the spaces of daily life, sometimes in the most puerile ways, as if an overemphasis on the personal could block out the causes of anger. The women's commissions in the parties of the New Left grew in numbers, however, and established new levels of coordination. A leftist front held a Metropolitan Encounter of Women in Lima in 1981, and there was a march against hunger in October of the same year. In the case of the Revolutionary Vanguard, the debate over creating a revolutionary party of the masses led women and a few of the male leaders to begin to think that it was important to reestablish—or create—a personal dimension to political life:

> The family has never commanded the Party's attention, rather, it has been denied in practice, which has caused many homes to be polarized between false contradictions such as the necessity of choosing between the party and the family ... a situation sus-

tained in a party composed of militants and not of people of flesh and bone, in supermen who think that from one minute to another they may be able to take power. ... This concept has not only affected party militance, but also our relation with the masses; there is a divorce between the consciousness of the militants of the left and the daily consciousness of the masses and the people.[9]

Similar debates took place in the other parties of the Left at the end of the 1970s and the beginning of the 1980s. Despite advances, women's commissions of the parties did not connect their issues with other instances of domination within the party, and the leadership continued to ignore the importance of women's issues. This occurred not only because of male resistance but also because of the unwillingness of the members of the women's commissions to participate in debates or in acts of militancy from which they could have advanced their proposals more effectively.

Recognition of the deformities and divisions that the dogmas of youth imposed on the life of the parties of the New Left and the growing awareness of the undervaluation of women inside the very organizations that were promoting change in the name of all the oppressed caused several militant middle-class women to leave the parties. They formed consciousness-raising groups and then organized centers for the study and advancement of women. The most important feminist institutions in Peru date from 1979: The activists of the Manuela Ramos Movement and the Flora Tristan Center were drawn from the talented women of the New Left.

The lack of fit between women's needs and a global revolutionary plan, the tendency to stifle the legitimate exchange of individual differences, and parties that sought to recover the rights of the oppressed but did not take up the issue of women were common phenomena in countries experiencing political mobilization in the late 1970s,[10] those same countries in which feminists were seeking to recover women's voice. The difficulties that these movements encountered and the precariousness of their victories make us realize how fragile these small spaces of cultural resistance are if they do not gain control of larger institutions and gain access to the centers of power.

The Feminist Groups in Peru

Feminism can develop in a reformist direction that sets out to improve the status of women by means of laws and rules designed to improve educational levels, give access to employment and public roles, and enhance the welfare policies of the state. Radical feminism is more ambitious and attempts to resolve the male-female contradiction by focusing on patriarchy as the only source of male power. Radical feminists attempt to improve the social and emotional levels at which women live by means of legal and technical advice and by forming separatist groups that seek to break patriarchal practices of leadership and oppression. Working in small groups, radical feminists attempt to promote a female culture expressed in music, song, and literature; they isolate themselves from the male world, hoping to construct alternative identities with collective support from and for women.

Finally, there are feminists who make the connection between the problems of class and gender. In Peru this was the most important feminist tendency.[11] The label "socialist feminists," which the women of the middle classes initially adopted when they organized in informal groups, or *centros de promoción,* not only retained some hint of their earlier political militancy but recognized Peru's enormous social inequalities. It obliged feminists to align their feminist analysis with broader social transformation. The socialist emphasis was visible in the Flora Tristan Center, the Manuela Ramos Movement, ALIMUPER (Action for the Liberation of Peruvian Women, Acción para la Liberación de la Mujer Peruana), Women in Struggle (Mujeres en Lucha), and the Women's Socialist Front (Frente de Mujeres Socialista), which joined together in a coordinating committee. This committee included some nonmilitant professional women and representatives from the feminist sections of the political parties of the New Left.

The late 1970s were years of intense political activity in Peru. There were national strikes and street demonstrations by middle-class unions (teachers and state employees) with many women in their ranks. This was also a time of centralization in some sectors, particularly the shantytowns, which were seeking a more effective way to mobilize.

There were demonstrations for political rights. About 300 women marched in the streets of Lima against the Somoza dictatorship, then about to fall. In June 1979, the five feminist groups of the Coordinating Committee circulated a "Communication to the Public" to protest sexual harassment against 26 union women. This document affirmed the commitment of the feminists to fight for the rights of poor women:

> We women have fought for social change, which we consider an integral part of our liberation as women, we are committed to fight for the rights of other oppressed groups and, fundamentally, to the women of the popular sectors.

At the end of 1980, although without the support of Manuela Ramos, the Coordinating Committee wrote and circulated a document explaining its intention to develop a socialist feminist analysis and praxis. This statement rejected the "economism" of conventional Marxist analysis and argued for feminist autonomy from the political parties, with autonomy understood as:

> independence from any organization that considers the battle for women's liberation a secondary goal. ... The autonomy of the movement is not autonomy from social reality or from ideologies, but as an indispensable at this moment of social conflict.[12]

These proposals from the feminist groups were recognized, at least publicly, by the women of the party organizations. The argument for autonomy arose out of their concern to save the democratic character of their political action and to avoid the "hegemonic and sectarian" politics of the political parties. Yet they recognized that autonomy could also imply passivity in the face of Peru's social reality and isolation from potential political allies.

The proposal of the feminist *políticas* included the idea of linking with feminist groups that did not have connections with any political party to form an alliance that could push for social reforms. The parties' efforts to control social movements in the name of "giving them direction" was a precedent that contributed to the decision of the feminist groups to protect their autonomy; this would later bring them into conflict with women party militants.

An account written in this period illustrates how difficult it was to maintain autonomy. Although the Coordinating Committee continued to show its solidarity with other women—teachers dismissed for strikes against the government, the female Montoneros assassinated in Argentina, and so forth—"there was no difference between the militant actions of the Coordinating Committee and those carried out by any of the other movements, unions or groups."[13] What made the feminists different were the diverse situations in which they took a combative role and the fact that the women's movement took sexuality and women's reproductive rights as central points of departure. Autonomy sustained the effort to democratize everyday life and to eliminate the relations of power between men and women.

Constructing a system in which power, democracy, and autonomy can work together is a risky process. Celebrating horizontal relations based on qualities culturally attributed to women generates a contradictory sisterhood and can create an environment where a form of female *caudillismo* can arise. Feminist autonomy can also restrict the arenas of power in which democratizing efforts can be pursued. When the standard methodological approaches for the study of women's situation are rejected, as they were by these feminists, there is an increased likelihood that social theory will be superficial and divorced from reality. Finally, when autonomy is achieved, these groups run the risk of being dependent on external financial sources, especially foundations and development assistance agencies.

The construction of a private space for women can only reinforce the very conditions that feminism is trying to change. Feminine space makes us think of, say, the sewing room, which in the past served as a refuge for women—those wealthy enough to afford one, of course. Feminists hoped to build a new identity based on women's "natural" qualities, such as compassion, solidarity, and tenderness. Yet these are precisely the attributes that patriarchal society foisted off on women to make them utterly powerless in the public sphere, which is the private preserve of men. Fighting the battle so as not to repeat the pattern of domination of the oppressors denies the oppressed the means to confront their foes. Nor does feminist sisterhood prevent the establishment of hierarchies between "greater" and "lesser" sisters. The *caudillo* model of leadership contaminates all group relations, independent of their gender composition.

The theory of the cultural impact of feminism emphasizes the slow transformations that modify power relations, bit by bit, from the periphery to the center, in accordance with Michel Foucault's microphysics of power. In this logic, conquering public space—running for office or holding formal power—can seem quite irrelevant. But masculine power can actually be reinforced this way. If feminist power is based on the emotional principles that usually sustain women's power in the domestic sphere, we are back to square one because this form of power cannot easily be used in the public sphere.[14] Manipulation and persuasion, the common forms of women's power in the family and with close friends, are not effective when used to attack the nuclei of public power or to alter the conditions of oppression and domination of women.

Although the isolation of feminist organizations can be understood as a necessary stage to develop and strengthen women as a collectivity, this can also be a cover for the insecurity women feel when they enter the public domain.[15] The feminist approach can become self-inhibiting by not engaging in social transformation in the broadest sense. It can further deepen the gap that separates the social from the political. To paraphrase Fernando Henrique Cardoso, it is as though we go to the university to study, to the church to pray, to the factory to work, and to the feminist group to do feminism. Feminist spaces that encourage the exercise of criticism can develop actions to bring about corrective changes in politics, not simply create a distinct political sphere.[16]

There is a risk of schizophrenia that is always present for feminists in an impoverished country. This becomes paranoia when it comes to confronting the political parties, which are seen as not just influential but highly manipulative:

> The meddling of the parties and political institutions often obscures and acts as a barrier to the important advances of the women's movement. ... It is discouraging to take part in the marches celebrating [Women's Day, March 8], because although it is true that there is an undeniable presence of women from the popular sectors, they do not make their demands as women, but instead present the positions of the parties, converting these marches to a polarization between "feminists" and party "classists."[17]

This quotation also suggests a risk derived from the ideological autonomy of feminism in Peru. Accepting uncritically the need for feminist space produces theory inadequate to our reality—fragmented not only socially but also geographically and ethnically. The sense of certainty on the part of the autonomous feminists has meant a lack of interest in finding ways to better connect their fight against oppression with the national characteristics that this oppression inevitably assumes in each country. Those who rely on feminist space to construct a feminist theory, but whose practice conflates that which is distinctive about each country, and who also accentuate divisions among women by asserting what "is" and "is not" feminism cannot be an effective force. If the construction of feminism in Peru begins from negotiation and exclusion, it will be difficult to convert it into a critical consciousness that will have an impact on the rest of society.

Without trying to minimize the complexity of the Peruvian feminist movement, I would say that another risk, which contradicts the notion of autonomy itself, is the dependency of Peruvian feminist centers on external sources of support. It is difficult to determine whether the centers are operating on the basis of
militancy, that is, as groups of people committed to a set of beliefs and to voluntary action, or on the basis of employment, because the centers provide paid professional work.[18] The effort to attain programmatic autonomy can also be con-
taminated by the interests of the international funding sources from which the
centers derive their support.

Given these relationships, the centers for the study and advancement of women
(all NGOs) have demonstrated firmness and strength in their publication of pamphlets directed to workers and other women of the popular sectors. Their work
has raised interest in a deeper understanding of women's issues, particularly in
the universities. And although they have not always been consistent, the centers'
efforts to assist small groups of poor urban women have made it possible for the
leaders of these groups to meet and share experiences.

Feminism in Peru began with "socialist feminism," which combined class and
gender and suggested a strategy. The process then moved on to radical feminist
autonomy, with its weaknesses and contradictions. In 1985 this latter position was
converted into its opposite when two radical feminists decided to run for political
office as independent candidates with the United Left Front.

Middle-Class Feminism and the
Politics of Autonomy

The basis of autonomous feminism is gender, but the concept fails to distinguish
the diverse and conflictual ways in which the oppression of gender is experienced
on a daily basis by women of distinct social classes. Many of the theoretical prop-
ositions of feminism that are valid in industrialized countries have not proven
useful in understanding the situation of poor urban women. As Carolyn Moser
and Kate Young[19] point out, the private world of the domestic is neither private
nor domestic when poverty obliges women to collectivize their consumption and
to "socialize" their product as housewives through communal kitchens and other
means of sharing labor.

Adherence to socialist feminism compelled the members of these feminist
groups to mobilize in the name of poor women, which made it more difficult for
them to articulate their own demands. They were required to seek the approval of
men, of the Left, and of the urban and rural poor when they marched as women
and held meetings.[20] Virginia Vargas wrote,

> We must overcome our schizophrenic practice of not converting the private into the
> political, of taking on the development of our identity in a closed process, without
> confronting the public, that political space to which we carry our other demands,
> where we submit ourselves to a logic that is not ours, where we demand (for "other"
> women) economic assistance and support in support of general political causes into

which we bring, although with shame, our own issues: control of our bodies, changed relations between the sexes, and an end to the daily violence against women. It was a first step away from the awareness of permanent guilt (for being middle class, for not thinking only about hunger, for thinking about ourselves, for not being sufficiently political) toward a consciousness that all of these attitudes were in fact legitimate and necessary.[21]

Vargas points out that key moments for the development of Peruvian feminism were the Latin American feminist *encuentro* held in Lima in 1983 and demonstrations against the Miss Universe Contest, also held in Lima that year. The infusion of resources and the experience of setting up workshops, conferences, and demonstrations definitively consolidated the space needed for creating a consciousness of gender and projecting that consciousness onto the public sphere.

Although feminists could show clearly that women suffered oppression by reason of their gender, they did not distinguish those demands that could mobilize non-middle-class women. For example, abortions are performed under very different conditions in different social classes. It is true that the cause, undesired pregnancy, is a situation that all fertile women share, independent of class. But lower-class women are in much greater danger of infection, which leaves them no other option but to go to the hospital; there they must face a police investigation so that those who are illegally performing abortions can be found and prosecuted. Or imagine facing the tedious and often anxiety-producing complications of home life without any domestic help and with a work day that is lengthened by having to cope with public assistance agencies in order to guarantee that one's family will be fed.

In the Peruvian case, the limitations of the feminist practice of working from small groups that are insulated from the causes of poverty are evident, just as it is clear that it is counterproductive to make demands in the name of "other" women when they are really the group's demands. Maxine Molyneux's work, which distinguishes practical from strategic gender interests, provides a useful analytical approach.[22]

Strategic gender interests are at the base of women's subjection: The sexual division of labor, sexual violence, control of reproduction, and the domestic, to name only a few, constitute the boundary of women's affairs. Practical gender interests, although defined by the concrete experiences women share, are strongly affected by class. Dealing with those interests will not directly modify the basic causes of women's subordination. Doing so can even reinforce them, as when poor urban women organize and run communal kitchens or set up crèches. The formulation of strategic interests, Molyneux argues, can only be efficacious if feminists take into full account women's diverse practical interests: The politicization of these, and their transformation into strategic interests, is the central purpose of feminist political practice.

The provision of urban services illustrates the point. Under this rubric, citizens—almost exclusively women—provide health, education, and infrastructure for their families, looking to private sources in accordance with their possibilities in the marketplace or trying collective and self-help solutions. The availability and quality of urban services are factors that cannot be separated from the everyday conditions of reproduction of the members of the domestic unit. In Peru, as elsewhere, this responsibility falls largely on women, who work to provide for their own, employing the variety of strategies made necessary by poverty. Making claims on basic services, which are set up to benefit the community as a whole, becomes a practical gender interest.

The social practices that are expressed in popular women's organizations are often viewed with mistrust by feminists because these organizations do not raise the purely feminist flag. In 1985, when the general elections for executive and Parliament were held, the distance between the theoretical proposals of the feminists and the concrete demands of the women of the popular sectors was sharply illuminated.

The United Left expected to win relatively few seats and, after a negotiation between the party leaders and the representatives of nonparty groups, agreed to list two women from the feminist movement among their independent candidates. Even before the campaign started, the strategy was doomed, for it is difficult for a closed group that tenaciously defends its right to autonomy to leap into the public arena. Mounting an electoral campaign meant abruptly abandoning faith in the transformatory power of the personal and the adoption of the opposite assumption—that feminists should take on the public sphere with its norms, styles, and rituals.

The campaign slogan of both candidates, "Women, vote woman!" (*Vota por ti, mujer),* further complicated the issue by positing a kind of biological sisterhood among Peruvian women without incorporating any of the practical concerns of significant groups. The candidates ran solely on strategic gender issues and promised to use the forum and the power of the legislature to bring about change. This slogan lacked concrete meaning, a weakness that was made worse when the candidates decided not to compromise the autonomy of the feminist movement by identifying with the United Left.[23] Not one of the feminist candidates was elected to Parliament even though the mechanism of preferential vote (allowing voters to mark the candidate of their choice no matter where the candidate stood on the party lists) was used for the first time.

What failed as an electoral strategy was effective as a discursive strategy, however. The candidates took the opportunity to discuss and publicize women's demands during the course of the campaign, which was one of the major accomplishments of the women's movement in the 1980s. Nevertheless, the opportunity to provide new perspectives and new language was lost in abstractions and undermined by a unilateral, middle-class approach. The cultural lag between feminist consciousness and the society's ability to absorb feminist ideas made the move from consciousness-raising to electoral politics premature.

Neighborhood Women's Organizations:
The Loaves and the Fishes

In 1986, the municipal Vaso de Leche program distributed milk every day to a million children in metropolitan Lima. It organized nearly 100,000 women to distribute milk in 7,500 neighborhood programs. Although there is no hard data, about 600 communal dining halls were organized by poor women in 1988, with a greater or lesser degree of cohesion and self-management on the part of their members.[24] These two mobilizations, which represent a social phenomenon of substantial size with important repercussions, can be traced directly to the severe decline in the standard of living of the urban population. They are also a spontaneous expression of female organization. Studies of this phenomenon almost invariably conclude that the dining halls represent the popular resistance of women to government hierarchies and to state manipulation.

Research shows that positive benefits accrue to the members of these organizations because of their internal democratic organization and because they have created space for female solidarity. But the euphoria caused by the success of these movements can obscure the origin and profile of these organizations or fail to distinguish different impacts for women and for their communities.

The communal kitchens are subsidized by cooperative buying and by cheap food available through U.S. food aid. The purpose of food aid, according to the U.S. Congress, is to reduce agricultural surpluses in the United States and help "friendly countries." At the end of the 1980s, food aid was greatly increased. Two philanthropic organizations, one Catholic and one Adventist, and a single state agency distribute the food made available.

The second Belaúnde administration (1980–1985) made a political decision to devote more than 50 percent of the government's budget to defense and to payments on Peru's foreign debt. This not only weakened domestic demand for goods and services and created unemployment and economic recession but also reduced investment in public services. Although the Peruvian state reduced urban service provision under Belaúnde, this position changed somewhat under the more clientelistic practices of the APRA government (1985–1990).

In Lima, more than 30 percent of the population lives in squatter settlements. They share common characteristics: lack of basic infrastructure, high rates of infant mortality, and high levels of unemployment and underemployment. A diversified group of service providers is also present. The state is represented by the public schools and government health clinics; private enterprise and cooperatives provide transportation; housing is constructed by the free labor of the poor population. The municipal government organizes local groups, such as Vaso de Leche, and the Church has offered assistance to communal kitchens and health committees. NGOs, including feminist groups, give training to women and girls.

Finally, the political parties are also active, and the APRA has installed mothers' clubs and dining halls that offer daily low-cost meals.[25]

At an earlier stage, efforts to gain land to get the state to provide infrastructure made the squatter settlements politically visible. The *barriada* residents made innumerable efforts to achieve their goals by pressuring government offices and demonstrating at the Cathedral of Lima and in the streets of the city center. Among their ranks, the presence of women was intermittent but significant.

Now, in the early 1990s, the "survival organizations" based on women's participation seem to be making a permanent place for themselves. These "volunteer" efforts compensate for the lack of government services and feed hungry families; they represent different styles of organization from those traditionally found in squatter settlements.[26]

Urban family incomes depend not only on money incomes but also on access to urban services. There is a strong relationship between urban services and the reproductive tasks assigned to women, for the lack of services makes their reproductive tasks more difficult. During the economic crisis, food, a basic necessity, has become a "service" that is provided through the communal kitchens and Vaso de Leche committees. This change creates organizational space for lower-class women and offers opportunities for training.

But these survival strategies can become welfarist despite their self-help orientation. They rely on a set of temporary, though ultimately false, solutions. The immediate problems are dealt with, but the cause of those problems—the inefficient redistributive capacity of the state—is ignored.[27]

To the degree they are not dependent on food donations, some communal kitchens can be considered autonomous. But the majority receive dry stores from outside sources, leaving to the members the responsibility of buying the perishables.[28] In some districts, the communal kitchens coordinate with the municipal government to buy foodstuffs at below-market prices. The connection between food donors and grassroots organizations is easily subject to abuse and offers the opportunity for political manipulation.

There are other issues as well. The NGOs that act as intermediaries are distributing handouts, not increasing the ability of women to feed themselves. Women face difficulties in allying themselves with other community organizations. Relying on women to solve the food crisis accentuates the sexual division of labor.

The demand for urban services has not matured into the ability to question, much less confront, the state's role as economic and political regulator of the conditions of reproduction of the population. For example, in a citywide meeting of communal kitchen organizers in June 1984, the women were faced with a reduction in the food quota. The delegates did not take this opportunity to question the structure of food donations; instead they called a march in support of the Peruvian episcopate to demand that the Agency for International Development (AID) restore the original quota.

The second problem with the role of assistance organizations is the role played by their advisers and *promotoras*. NGO development professionals or the nuns of the parish play a key role in creating these organizations and often consider the women's groups their private fiefdoms. As a result, there are few connections among the various women's organizations, and women are unwilling to respond to neighborhoodwide mobilizations. There is competition among the various groups, which works against the unity of the *barriada* as a whole, not just its women's sector.[29]

A third problem is the issue of who is mobilized and for what. The economic crisis reduced the rate at which the *barriada* population invested in its own infrastructure. In the 1970s women responded to the call of local leaders to attend meetings and marched to demand water pipes and paved streets; they lent their work or contributed from their meager funds to pay the costs. From 1980 to 1985, the state ceased to take primary responsibility and called upon neighborhood women to run health and food distribution programs themselves. The family and the community replaced the state as the source of these services, and survival strategies were co-opted and given official standing.

But the needs for health and food are not met by the community as a whole; they are met by women. The assistance agencies see motherhood as women's most important role. They put women together in groups to solve problems, and they counter poverty by training them in income-generating activities. These are then called antipoverty programs by the international agencies attempting to compensate for the negative effects of economic austerity. But the programs are palliatives hardly likely to achieve an improvement in the conditions of life for the population, much less affect women's gender subordination.[30]

Learning to Speak

Studies that have observed women in self-help or "functional" organizations find that these organizations have beneficial effects on their members. Within such groups, members show a democratic respect for each other's concerns and derive positive psychological benefits from group interactions. For example, women surveyed in self-help groups in four neighborhoods of the *barriada* El Agustino say that the group is important to them because they "have friends," because they are "not so timid," and because they "share their problems." According to Cecilia Barnechea, women make similar comments in the other districts of Lima. In these organizations, women recover the ability to speak, which is very significant because silence is one of the most evident forms of women's oppression.

Sharing personal problems, leaving the isolation of the house, and enjoying each other's company are activities valued by urban poor women even more than by women in other social classes. Because of poor living conditions and fights over economic problems (as well as lack of effective role models from childhood), the relations of the couple living in poverty often lack intimacy and good communication between the partners. The women think that their husbands do not understand them.[31]

The women involved in food programs perceive an improvement in their lives. They say that they worry less because they are sure that their families will have something to eat or that their younger children will at least have a glass of milk each day. They can acquire new skills learning to manage the budgets of the communal kitchens and to share responsibilities, which bring an awareness of solidarity. They learn to speak, to share, to be responsible for others—to "grow."

The point of my analysis is to raise some new issues, to balance the current enthusiasm with a more skeptical look at the impact of these organizations on the individual and on the broader community. Studies do show that economic necessity is the incentive for women to get involved in these programs but that the women stay involved because of the solidarity they come to feel with the other women in the group.

But there are also some very real limitations. Although women have recovered speech, it seems to be useful only for women to communicate with other members of the group, not to project their concerns into the public sphere. In the organizations surveyed in El Agustino, there was no relationship between the Vaso de Leche committees and the mothers' club ("Their functions are very different," say the women); nor was there a connection between a communal kitchen established by the Catholic relief agency and another supported by APRA ("because that is for members of the party"). This was not simply a question of different functions, although such differences are used to rationalize the lack of connection. The underlying reason is that there was competition between these groups that arose out of their relationships with different assistance agencies.

In El Agustino, with the exception of Vaso de Leche, which was coordinated by the municipal government, there was very little communication between women's groups and the municipal government or elected officials. In every case, the political leadership eventually sought the support of the women's organizations for certain actions; for their part, the women waited for the neighborhood committees to act to improve the communal kitchen equipment or to provide more space.

The theory that women first learn to speak among themselves and then are able to project their demands toward the institutions of power seems not to be justified. Some of the facilitators of these women's organizations have even observed that the women fall silent, by their own initiative, in mixed groups and that they respect the decisions of the men when they are invited to the community meetings.[32]

A second limitation of neighborhood organizations is the weak effect that women's actions had on their perception of their situation as women. The work of women's organizations fulfilled a relatively important role in ameliorating the practical and even the emotional necessities of women. But by accentuating the division of labor by sex, it weakened the alternative possibilities for constructing a different self-image. Poor urban women, despite their organization, do not see themselves as subjects of these services, although (or perhaps because) these services allow the women to fulfill their reproductive tasks. That these tasks are women's tasks is not questioned within the family or at the communal level.

Training can reinforce traditional attitudes because it responds to the concrete demands of the female members of society. The women interviewed in El Agustino noted that they wanted instruction, particularly in sewing and handicrafts, in order to get work or to apply their new knowledge at home for their families. This is not to question the content of the training, which met the women's felt needs. But this kind of responsiveness, if not accompanied by materials that broaden the vision of what is socially and politically possible for these women, remains welfare-like.

A third aspect of these neighborhood organizations is that the activities of these groups prolong the working day of these women, who are already quite burdened by the lack of services. It is convenient for governments when women voluntarily provide social services. But the level of essential services to the poor is reduced, and the "profit" of the government is sustained because women work for free.[33] This observation is not made in an attempt to inhibit women's participation in these times of crisis but only to note that this emergency effort should not be interpreted to mean that women have the responsibility to "supply water to someone else's mill" at their own expense. The women themselves recognize that this work is worth some payment. Almost 60 percent of those interviewed in El Agustino felt that the economic return they received from these efforts should correspond to the time and work they had invested.

Self-help has a long history in the *barriadas* of Lima. In the case of El Agustino, self-help construction of houses was carried out because the government wasn't interested. There is a strongly held notion that it is the responsibility of the neighbors or the community leaders rather than the state to attend to the needs of the population. These antecedents and beliefs underlie the practice of these women's organizations and represent a long-term difficulty for those who would seek alternative models of organization and political mobilization.

It is hard to know whether the growth and consolidation of women's organizations brought a group of new leaders to the fore or whether these leaders had a highly developed political sense before the expansion of the women's groups. Of the 143 women enrolled in assistance programs in four neighborhoods in El Agustino, 31 were leaders, predominantly housewives; in a population with a high percentage of illiterates, nearly 50 percent of these women had entered or completed their secondary education; and although the family incomes of these women were average, the majority had been born in the city or province of Lima.

Although the state adopted a low profile in the provision of urban services, the community in its self-help response gave up the opportunity for political confrontation to serve its more immediate needs. A similar choice was made by the autonomous groups that organized with some success around cost-of-living issues but found themselves marginalized from broader political influence.

Politically, self-help mobilization to provide services nearly always involves only women, just as the invisibility and undervaluation of women's work is a constant in economics. The creativity of these social feminine practices and their democratic potential can spill over into broader contexts. But the fear of co-option by political parties and the importance of emotional security as a motive for involvement inhibit more decisive approaches.

Elizabeth Jelin has argued that through their educational experiences and through their ties of solidarity, these groups can eventually create the basis from which to question the system.[34] However, if this is left to chance or to some vague future, there is a risk that the potential energy of women's efforts will be dispersed. Autonomy with respect to the state and to political parties is important, but it is still necessary to create a current of feedback or of mutual support between women's groups and other local organizations. The marginalization of women's organizations from the centers of local decisionmaking can accentuate the inadequate representation of the dimensions of everyday life in local government. Seeing social problems as statistics leads to activism that serves only immediate needs and that is incapable of strategic projection even at the local level.

The Impact of Sendero Luminoso on Women's Movements in the 1990s

In 1980, Sendero Luminoso, one of the few active guerrilla groups in operation in Latin America and a Maoist-oriented communist group, began an internal war that has been responsible for 25,000 deaths and $20 million in damages, an amount almost equal to Peru's external debt. From 1980 to 1985, there were 8,103 deaths; from 1985 to 1990, under APRA president Alan García, the number reached 9,660; and since 1990, when Alberto Fujimori was elected, over 7,000 people have been killed. The Sendero Luminoso was a destabilizing factor in the 1980s, but its spread in urban areas, especially Lima, was not visible until the end of the decade. Government victories in the early 1990s, such as the capture of the elusive Abímael Guzmán and other Senderista leaders, have slowed but not stopped Sendero's campaign to make Peru ungovernable.

Sendero's campaign of destabilization has had two major elements: the destruction of the physical infrastructure and of competing forms of grassroots leadership. The latter strategy, which involves threats against local leaders, especially those with a leftist following, and exemplary assassinations of those who do not get the message, has had a devastating effect on neighborhood women's organizations in Lima as well as on grassroots organizations and municipal governments throughout the country.

The day I received the request to update this chapter, one of the leaders of the Vaso de Leche program in El Agustino was killed. The newscaster gave the details without mentioning the name of the slain woman or her neighborhood. I thought, "My God, I hope it is not Elvira; I hope it is not Victoriana; I hope it is not Zeneida ..." I hoped it was not any of the leaders that I know, my friends and *compañeras* for many years. It was Bernadina. Her bloody body lay on the street. She was 40 years old and had six daughters.

I have in this chapter taken issue with the feminist strategy of autonomy. Feminists in Peru constructed a collectivity and gave specificity to gender through an analysis that grew out of the material conditions of female existence. But in contrast with women's organizations in the *barriadas*, they failed when they made feminist separatism their point of departure. As a result, feminists did not become a powerful force among the social movements in Peru, and their electoral strategy also failed. Although the economic crisis created the conditions for the development of popular women's organizations, which did contribute to the political awareness of urban women and to their recognition of themselves as a collectivity, it did not succeed in giving women access to local power. The APRA government (1985–1990) saw women's organizations—such as the 2,000 mothers' clubs created in Peru under a program headed by Alan García's wife—as a promising arena for co-optive, clientelist politics.

As the feminist strategy of autonomy has reduced women's access to local power structures, so have women's self-help organizations reduced the responsibility of the state to provide basic services. Also, clientelistic forms of organizing women make them vulnerable to manipulation and populist appeals, neither of which is conducive to democracy.

However, the relationship between feminist groups and organizations of lower-class urban women has been a very dynamic process. In her recent book, Virginia Vargas argued that the period of isolation of the feminist movement between 1982 and 1986, with its separatist tendencies and its middle-class issues, was necessary to solidify an idea, a group, an inspiration.[35] She points out that from that period onward, feminists began to reach out across a broad spectrum that successfully reached the labor unions, the neighborhoods, the media, and the professions. Perhaps she is right.

Still, I could argue that postmodern trends in feminist analysis have reinforced my conclusions. Against those who would define what feminism is, there is the now widely accepted view that there is not one single truth or one single way to express and feel gender subordination. This idea, which was just emerging at the beginning of the 1980s, foreshadowed the recognition of Peruvian women's plurality of expression. The complexity of the Peruvian woman's experience constitutes the richness of the movement and not its dispersion.

In summer 1992, when Vargas presented her book, I shared a panel with María Elena Moyano, deputy mayor of the Villa El Salvador district in Lima and a positive force behind the Popular Women's Federation (Federación de Mujeres Populares). She, with the freshness of her youth, joked with the audience about how the "elders" of Peruvian feminism were reconstructing its history with all its complications and disagreements. Some days later she was killed by Sendero, which used five kilos of dynamite to dismember her body.

As feminism created new strategies, the women of the communal kitchens also developed new forms of organization. The leadership was centralized and became the focal point for all private agencies and public officers in charge of assistance programs. The faces of a few women leaders were widely recognized, and they gained political clout that could not be ignored or undermined by those administering the emergency social programs.

At the same time, however, the gap widened between the leaders and the women members of the communal kitchen movement. The former worked to consolidate their roles and their relationships to outside agents and donors, and the latter were responsible for delivering the food—one million rations per day in metropolitan Lima alone. Valuing their autonomy, the communal kitchen leaders also kept their distance from the political parties.

This did not happen with the leaders of Vaso de Leche, which had strong political ties from the beginning. Many women from that program have been elected to municipal offices. But the two groups could not unite, although their work and their motivations were quite similar. This split also contributed to the isolation of the leaders of the communal kitchen movement.

Sendero's urban strategists took full advantage of this gap, accusing the leaders of corruption and mismanagement. The leaders in turn had little local support structure, and they could not afford to hire bodyguards, as do many wealthy residents of Lima. Many succumbed and abandoned their organizations because they and their families were subject to personal threats by Sendero.

As feminists we underestimated Sendero due to our urban bias and our faith in the strength of existing popular organizations. As Sendero Luminoso advanced in the Andes, we denounced its barbarism while criticizing the military for the "dirty war" it had launched against the masses. But we felt the war as a distant problem.

Many of us believed that Sendero Luminoso operated in the margins of the country, that it would not do well where there were strong grassroots movements. We did not count on Sendero's abandonment of the countryside and its infiltration into the cities. We did not anticipate how terrorism and fear would sweep through the streets of Lima, penetrating the houses like the seven plagues of Egypt in the time of Moses. The leaders of the popular women's groups were accused of collaboration with the government and imperialism; their self-help efforts for subsistence were rejected because they ameliorated the economic crisis and lessened despair—and crisis and despair are the open door to Sendero and its violent methods.

The "self-coup" of Alberto Fujimori in 1992 solidified the tendency of the armed forces and the government to come together with the support of the urban mass organizations while further reducing popular support for political institutions. The capture of Abímael Guzmán, leader of *Sendero*, and his sentence to life imprisonment increased Fujimori's popularity further in the polls.

The imprisonment of Guzmán and many of his high-ranking followers reduced the number of terrorist acts in the following months as well as the level of conflict in the urban shantytowns. But fear has left enduring marks, as has the economic decline brought about by structural adjustment. The attempts to reconstitute women's survival groups suggest that their old organizational approaches may be replaced by more pragmatic strategies. The Vaso de Leche and communal kitchen groups may organize small enterprises or income-generating activities with the support of the NGOs and international donor agencies. These organizations, whose leaders and advisers in the past strove to strengthen internal ties of solidarity, avoided an orientation toward production and the market. The economic necessities and the prevalence of market thinking in the 1990s are bringing about a change.

What was learned over the years, and the energy women displayed in constructing their identity in organizations from the communal kitchens to the NGOs, are still collective reference points. Months before the referendum to approve or reject a new constitution (which was drawn up by a progovernment majority), the Committee of Women for an Aware Vote brought together feminists, political activists, and leaders from the women's shantytown organizations. They succeeded in mounting a modest petition drive and publicity campaign to alert voters to the reverses women will experience under the new constitution, which eliminates the prohibition against sex discrimination and calls for the privatization of public services. It is not possible to know how women voted (and they were joined by other groups in opposing the new constitution); the referendum approved the constitutional change by a margin of only 2–3 percent. This narrow victory has given the opposition new strength, but the future for women's groups is uncertain.

Notes

1. This chapter is a revised version of "Emergent Democracy and the Women's Movement," in Edvardo Ballon, ed., *Movimientos sociales y democracia: La fundación de un nuevo orden* (Lima: DESCO, 1986).

2. Fernando Enrique Cardoso, "Transición política en América Latina?" Giorgio Alberti, "Desarrollo y democracia: Algunas reflexiones sobre el caso peruano," in *Los límites de la democracia* (Buenos Aires: CLACSO, 1985).

3. Henry Pease, "Nuevos espacios y tiempos políticos en la experiencia peruana actual," in Norbert Lechner, ed., *Qué significa hacer política?* (Lima: DESCO, 1982); Teresa Tovar, *Velasquismo y movimiento popular: Otra historia prohibida* (Lima: DESCO, 1985).

4. Tovar, *Velasquismo.*

5. Teresita De Barbieri, *Mujeres y vida cotidiana* (Mexico City: Fondo de Cultura Económica, 1984).

6. Kathryn Burns, "Mas allá de ese esencial femenino: El desarrollo feminista en el Perú, 1900–1950," cited by Jane Jaquette, "Female Political Participation in Latin America," in Ruth Ross and Lynne Iglitzin, eds., *Women in the World, 1975–1985* (Santa Barbara: ABC-Clio, 1986).

7. "El emperador está desnudo," Documento de la cédula Artemio Zavala, Vanguardia Revolucionaria, 1978.

8. Vanguardia Revolucionaria, April 1982.

9. "El partido revolucionaria, de masas y la Mujer," Vanguardia Revolucionaria, April 1982.

10. Rudi Pallabazzer, *Salto di Binario: Teoria della crisi e della rivoluzione globale* (Milan: Machina Libri Edizioni, 1980); Adriana Seroni, *La questione femminile in Italia, 1970–1977* (Rome: Editori Riuniti, 1977); Jo Freeman, *The Politics of Women's Liberation* (New York: Vintage, 1980); Juliet Mitchell, *La condizione della donna* (Turin: Giulio Einuadi Editore, 1972).

11. Cornelia B. Flora, *Socialist Feminism in Latin America,* Michigan State University, Women in Development Working Paper, no. 14, November 1982.

12. "Feminismo y política en el Perú: Aportes par una necessaria discusión." La coordinación (Lima, 1980), mimeo.

13. Virginia Vargas, "El movimiento feminista en el Perú: Balance y perspectiva" (Lima, 1982), mimeo.

14. Jane S. Jaquette, "Power as Ideology: A Feminist Analysis," in Judith Stiehm, ed., *Women's Views of the Political World of Men* (New York: Transnational Press, 1984).

15. *Revista Sottosopra* (January 1983).

16. Rosanna Rossanda, *Le altre* (Milan: Casa Editora Bompiani, 1979).

17. Virginia Vargas, "Las mujeres en movimiento (o de como somos políticas las mujeres)," paper presented at the Seminar of the Social Science Research Council and the Centro Flora Tristán, Lima, 1985).

18. Roxanna Carillo, "Centros de mujeres, espacios de mujeres." Introductory text to the *Directory of Women's Centers* (New York: International Women's Tribune Center and Flora Tristán Center, 1986).

19. Caroline Moser and Kate Young, "Mujeres del sector trabajador pobre," 1982, mimeo.

20. Vargas, 1985, "Las mujeres en movimiento."

21. Ibid.

22. Maxine Molyneux, "Mobilization Without Emancipation? Women's Interests, the State and Revolution in Nicaragua," *Feminist Studies* 11, 2 (1985), 227–254.

23. Vargas, "Las mujeres en movimiento."

24. Amelia Fort, "Servicios urbanos para los pobres de Lima: Problemas de genero" (Lima: Grupo de Trabajo SUMBI, 1984), mimeo.

25. Maruja Barrig, *Servicios urbanos y mujeres de bajos ingresos* (Lima: Grupo de Trabajo SUMBI, 1983).

26. Cecilia Blondet, *Muchas vidas construyendo una identidad: Las mujeres pobladoras de un barrio limeño* (Lima: Instituto de Estudio Peruanos, 1986).

27. Gustavo Riofrio and Maruja Barrig, *Los programas de promoción dirigidos a la mujer en los barrios de Carmen de la Legua y El Agustino* (Lima: CENCA, 1982).

28. Violeta Sara-Lafosse, *Comedores comunales: La mujer frente a la crisis* (Lima: Grupo de Trabajo SUMBI, 1982).

29. Cecilia Barnechea, "Organizándose para cambiar la vida (La experiencia de las mujeres pobladoras)," in *Mujer, victima de la opresión, portadora de liberación* (Lima: Lora, Barnechea, y Santisteban, Cuadernos del Instituto Bartolomé de las Casas, 1985).

30. Caroline Moser, "Women's Needs in the Urban System: Training Strategies in Gender-Aware Planning," in Marianne Schmink, Judith Bruce, and Marilyn Kohn, eds., *Learning About Women and Urban Services in Latin America and the Caribbean* (New York: Population Council, 1985).

31. Quotes in the previous paragraph and following observations and statistics are from Dagmar Raczynski and Claudia Serrano, *Vivir la pobreza: Testimonios de mujeres* (Santiago: PISPAL, CIEPLAN, 1985).

32. Barnechea, "Organizándose para cambiar la vida."

33. Jeanine Anderson, "Implicancias de la generación de ingresos en la situación de la mujer en el Perú," in *Mujer y desarrollo* (Lima: Galer, Guzmán y Vega Editoras, Centro de la Mujer Peruana Flora Tristán y DESCO, 1985).

34. Elizabeth Jelín, "Ciudadania e Identidad: Las mujeres en los movimientos sociales latinamericanos," Report prepared for Programa de Participación Popular UNRISD, Buenos Aires, 1985.

35. Virginia Vargas, *Como cambiar el mundo sin perdernos* (Lima: Ediciones Flora Tristán, January 1992).

SEVEN

Feminism, Revolution, and Democratic Transitions in Nicaragua

NORMA STOLTZ CHINCHILLA

Revolutions and Democracy

Revolutionary movements and periods of revolutionary transition are often assumed to be outside the bounds of Western social science discussions of democratic transitions because nonelectoral regime transformations are regarded as inherently undemocratic. But if the definition of democracy is expanded to include what Carole Pateman and others refer to as participatory democracy,[1] then revolutionary movements and periods of revolutionary transition may be as democratic or more democratic than social movements or regimes focusing more narrowly on elections.

Nicaragua, El Salvador, and Guatemala provide important examples of both forms of democracy—formal electoral processes and the expansion of popular participation through revolutionary movements in recent decades.[2] Of these, Nicaragua is a unique case because it includes a long-standing dictatorial regime headed by Anastasio Somoza and overthrown by a revolutionary movement, the FSLN, and two periods of electoral activity, 1984 and 1990. During the struggle against the dictatorship and throughout the time it was in power, the revolutionary Sandinista government encouraged democratic participation through mass mobilization and the creation of organizations for different social sectors and interests. In the first period of electoral activity, international observers concluded that genuine efforts were made by the government to have a wide spectrum of opposition interests represented. These efforts were ultimately undermined with the withdrawal of Arturo Cruz, the U.S.-backed candidate.[3] A wide range of opposition parties participated in the 1990 elections, most of them grouped into the conservative United Opposition Coalition (Unidad Nacional Opositora, or UNO), which unexpectedly won the elections, peacefully replacing the ruling revolutionary party.

Criticisms of particular events or practices notwithstanding, the decade of the Sandinista government was indisputably the most democratic in Nicaraguan history and, by any definition, one of the more democratic in Central American history. Unfortunately, the political advances toward greater democracy were not matched by economic gains or the achievement of lasting security. A deteriorating economy and continuing outbursts of armed resistance have made the democratic transition somewhat unstable. Furthermore, the activation of sectors previously inactive, particularly rural and urban workers and women, meant that these groups were not likely to passively accept structural adjustment programs. Thus, both in the latter part of the Sandinista period and under the new government, popular democracy, that is, democracy based on a broad coalition of democratic progressive forces, has made it difficult for both governments to shift the burden of structural adjustment onto popular sectors as much as they would like, thus creating a great deal of political as well as economic instability.

The case of Nicaragua is important to a discussion of women and democratic transitions because of the unique type of democratic transitions that Nicaragua has undergone and the unprecedented role women have played in them. An examination of this case allows us to explore important issues in the relationship between feminism, political parties, revolution, and democracy.

Revolution, Women's Political Participation, and Feminism

Nicaraguan women played an important role in the overthrow of the Somoza dictatorship, constituting some 20 percent of the armed combatants, with a large proportion of those in neighborhood organizations. Young women participated actively in revolutionary student organizations, Christian youth groups, the Sandinista Front, and guerrilla insurgent units. Older women and young women with children organized under the banner of the Nicaraguan Association of Women Confronting the National Problem (Asociación de Mujeres Confrontando la Problematica Nacional, or AMPRONAC—Nicaragua's first cross-class women's association formed with Sandinista support) and defied the National Guard and police by marching in front of prisons, police stations, and military barracks to demand the release of political prisoners and an end to human rights violations. They organized and coordinated neighborhood participation in the insurrection and provided homemade weapons and food, as well as medicine, communications, and support structures for the FSLN.[4]

In the process, women found a new boldness and confidence in their ability to fight for social justice and national sovereignty, insisting that from then on, no one could question their ability or right to participate in politics on an equal basis. Many men echoed the sentiment that Nicaraguan women's daring and sacrifice in the struggle against the dictatorship guaranteed them the right to be included in decisions about the future of the nation. Nicaraguan women formally received the right to vote in 1955, but it was their participation in the Sandinista-led overthrow of the dictatorship that gave them real citizenship, including the right to speak and act in the public sphere.[5]

After the overthrow, AMPRONAC became AMNLAE (Asociación de Mujeres Louisa Amanda Espinosa, the Louisa Amanda Espinosa Women's Association), the Sandinista-affiliated women's organization. It defined itself as a mass-based, popular (i.e., democratic and progressive) organization parallel in its organizational form, mission, and relationship to the revolutionary party and to other Sandinista-affiliated organizations such as trade unions and peasant organizations. During this period, some core AMNLAE activists saw themselves as feminists but were reluctant to argue the point publicly, since feminism had often been portrayed negatively as antifamily or antimale; feminists had been portrayed as borderline prostitutes by the Latin American mass media during the 1970s.[6] The traditional Latin American Left had attacked feminism as divisive, and many leaders genuinely believed that feminism was bourgeois or a concern in developed countries but not appropriate for women in a poor, backward country like Nicaragua.

Throughout 1980, AMNLAE's membership grew among housewives, market women, and mothers of combatants or Sandinistas killed in the insurrection. It attracted health and education workers who had been drawn in as a result of specific campaigns such as literacy, neighborhood cleanup, and health. But it drew only lukewarm support from Sandinista women professionals, government employees, and members of the party apparatus. Women agricultural and industrial wage workers, young women, and women in the army were noticeably absent from its ranks.[7]

In October 1981, AMNLAE claimed a national membership of 25,000 women,[8] but there was concern about the representativeness of AMNLAE support. It was clear that women were demobilizing as a result of the pressures from family members or, in the case of working women already active in other Sandinista organizations, because of the pressures of a "triple day" of work, family, and political activism.[9]

Sandinista feminists took the position that AMNLAE's lack of dynamism was due to its timid defense of women's specific demands, its failure to articulate an explicit critique of sexism, and its passive dependency on the FSLN hierarchy for its strategy and program. Like the Cuban Women's Federation (Federación de Mujeres Cubanas, or FMC), AMNLAE ratified rather than made decisions. The AMNLAE leadership responded by arguing that the criticisms were too radical and too feminist or out of sync with the needs of women from the popular classes.[10]

The issue was dealt with pragmatically rather than ideologically through a proposed change in AMNLAE's organizing strategy and self-definition. AMNLAE would no longer be a direct-membership organization like other mass organizations in Nicaragua. It would become a "political-ideological social movement," a catalyst for building a broad mass movement to promote a women's agenda and women's leadership in all revolutionary institutions and would continue to mobilize public opinion on behalf of reforms and programs for women.[11]

Democracy, Feminism,
Autonomy, and the War

The devastating seven-year war against the Contras (1982–1989) had contradictory effects on the status of women and the Nicaraguan women's movement. Women were forced to assume a double and triple burden of work as shortages resulted from the U.S.-imposed blockade, internal sabotage, and diversion of resources for the war. Small but significant improvements in social services, such as health care, education, and childcare, from which women had benefited in the early days of revolutionary government began to erode as government spending shifted to the war effort. Many projects and demands that would have specifically addressed the subordinate status of women were put on the back burner. Women bore the brunt of frozen wages, inflation, black-market speculation, shortages, scarce child and maternity care. For poor women, the war meant greater poverty. For all women, the war represented greater sacrifice and the postponement of their hopes and dreams for a better life.[12]

In stark contrast to the struggle against the dictatorship, the armed defense of the nation against the Contras became almost exclusively identified with men. The reinstitution of the draft so soon after the bloodshed of the insurrection was controversial and gave an opening to right-wing politicians and the Church hierarchy. The FSLN felt that adding women to the draft, as the leadership and core activists of AMNLAE demanded, would make it impossible to build a broad base of support for the war. Women trained for the armed defense of neighborhoods in the civilian militia and built a civilian infrastructure in support of the war effort. But the frontal assault on traditional images of gender roles that occurred when women fought alongside men was not sustained in the anti-Contra war. Traditional gender role definitions began to reappear in some sectors of the public and even occasionally in the discourse of some Sandinista leaders.[13]

However, the mobilization of men for the army opened up new roles for women and favored a new public identity for many women. Because women had to assume public-sector roles "for the good of national defense," women activists could raise the issue of the right to leave their homes to occupy public spaces—not just for the purposes of the war, but permanently. They demanded that domestic obstacles to women's equal involvement in politics and work be addressed. Toward the end of the war, men in military units were educated on issues of domestic violence and women's rights. In this way, the second mobilization helped to counteract the postdictatorship demobilization of women. At the same time, it made women increasingly less interested in sacrificing for others without concrete promises of improved lives for themselves as well.

The extent to which these opportunities were exploited depended in part on the desire of AMNLAE and other women's groups to negotiate their agendas in relation to the war effort. In general, AMNLAE leaders were reluctant to challenge the tasks assigned to them by the National Directorate of the FSLN or suggest additional ones as priorities. In 1983, when the FSLN called for all popular organizations to make the defense of the revolution their principal task, AMNLAE leaders interpreted this to mean that any specific women's demands—which were beginning to evolve from public debates on proposed changes in the legal code—regarding the value of women's labor inside and outside the home, familial relations, sexuality, gender-role socialization of children, and abortion had to be postponed. AMNLAE agreed to the FSLN National Directorate's request that it focus its work on support for mothers of combatants and on attempts to win the allegiance of mothers who opposed military conscription of their sons. It organized logistical and material support for the war effort by collecting materials for recycling and mounting campaigns for saving energy and scarce goods.[14]

To their credit, AMNLAE leaders, some of whom were themselves ex-combatants, waged a valiant but ultimately unsuccessful battle against the exclusion of women from the draft, believing that women's claim to more equal representation in political leadership during and after the war would be undermined if women did not serve in the military. Failing that goal, AMNLAE encouraged and publicized women's participation in the volunteer army battalions, the civilian militia, neighborhood defense networks, and strategic areas of production, particularly agriculture.

During the fall 1984 campaign in Nicaragua's first national elections since the revolution, women expressed their discontent to FSLN representatives. Worried that frustration from working double and triple shifts and making economic sacrifices might cause women to transfer their support to the right-wing opposition, withdraw from politics, or refuse to make the voluntary sacrifices needed for the war effort, the FSLN called for a review of the role of AMNLAE and a general reevaluation of its approach to organizing women in the context of the war.[15]

In the debate that followed, AMNLAE leaders were surprised to discover that women activists were critical of agendas imposed from the top down and of AMNLAE's having placed discussions of domestic violence, machismo, rape, contraception, and abortion on the back burner, incorrectly assuming that they were not of interest to working-class women. It was agreed that AMNLAE's diminished base of support was due in large part to the passivity of the leadership, which accepted the FSLN priorities and assumed it knew what poor and working-class women wanted rather than aggressively reaching out to consult them.

AMNLAE and many FSLN leaders' unspoken assumption had been that mobilization for the war and deepening feminist consciousness were inherently contradictory. But the work of Sandinista feminists with men and women in the Agricultural Workers' Union (Asociación de Trabajadores del Campo, or ATC), carried out with the blessing of an all-male leadership, had shown that it was possible to link mobilization for war with consciousness-raising about women's dual roles in production and reproduction. Women could be more effectively mobilized by increasing their access to nontraditional job training, adopting participatory organizational and decisionmaking styles, and struggling against machismo.[16]

AMNLAE announced a new approach whereby its agenda would be derived from groups of women with similar interests meeting together to discuss their problems and proposing concrete actions to the organization as a whole. Toward this end, more than 40,000 women in 600 base assemblies gathered to generate proposals and discuss ideas that were then taken by over 1,000 elected delegates to the Second National AMNLAE Assembly on September 28, 1985. The assembly delegates asked for educational and action campaigns to be developed on the topics of sexuality, workplace discrimination, and domestic violence.

The new priorities requested by the assembly delegates raised concerns about AMNLAE's relation with the FSLN. The FSLN feared that the new focus might mean that political work with mothers of combatants would be abandoned. AMNLAE delegates responded that they would seek to achieve a balance but that the organization needed to broaden its base and sharpen its focus on women's specific interests. Much to the consternation of AMNLAE activists, Comandante Bayardo Arce, representing the FSLN National Directorate, responded that the proposed "concrete demands" would reinforce notions of women as the weaker sex. He questioned the need for an organization such as AMNLAE, implying that other organizations could represent women's needs. Rosario Murillo, poet and wife of President Daniel Ortega, had published an article saying that women's organizations might be needed in societies that had not resolved their "fundamental contradictions" but that separating women and men after the revolution was won reinforced separate male and female identities. To argue that men were incapable of changing implied a sort of "machista feminism."[17] Delegates to the second AMNLAE assembly responded by saying that revolution is an ongoing process of transformation, which continues long after the previous regime is overthrown, and that "nobody can struggle for our demands better than we ourselves."[18]

For the first time it seemed that women constituted a real pressure group capable of making their own demands on the state, the popular movement, and the FSLN. The second AMNLAE assembly, one participant wrote later, signaled "the birth of the Nicaraguan women's liberation movement … its entrance into the political stage of the Sandinista revolution."[19]

The new leadership and popular mandate encouraged AMNLAE to play a more aggressive and visible role in educating Nicaraguan society about workplace discrimination; sexual harassment, rape, and domestic violence; the need for sex education, contraception, and abortion; and the need to institutionalize avenues for women to gain power and influence. One of these new institutions was the Women's Legal Office (Oficina Legal de la Mujer, or OLM), created on March 8, 1983, and strategically located in the president's office so as to have an impact on all stages of national planning. The data collected by this office and the research studies it commissioned proved to be an important catalyst for the discussion of the reality of Nicaraguan women's lives in labor unions, educational institutions, hospitals and clinics, and governmental agencies as well as in national planning. The OLM, together with popular organizations and other government agencies, spearheaded debates about the medical and social consequences of clandestine abortions, domestic violence, and the widespread problem of male abandonment of responsibility for biological children. Like many initiatives that were to follow, the OLM was officially a project of AMNLAE and projected itself as "working in coordination of AMNLAE," but it functioned relatively independently. One observer called the OLM Nicaragua's "first feminist institution."[20]

Other important initiatives during this period included advances in feminist research projects such as those looking at the situation of rural women under the sponsorship of ATC and the Center for Research and Study of the Agrarian Reform (Centro de Investigación y Estudios sobre Reforma Agraria, or CIERA). A women's agenda for constitutional reform was presented to the National Assembly by a group of longtime AMNLAE grassroots activists who were now also part of the professional staffs of other Sandinista popular organizations and state institutions. This surprise proposal was not publicized or widely distributed, but it made governmental bodies and popular organizations aware of women's intentions to expand the boundaries of discussion even in the context of war.

Many formerly taboo topics began to be raised in public discussions: voluntary maternity, reproductive rights, sexual harassment, power relations in the family, official and unofficial tolerance of machismo, the right of peasant women to own land, sexist education, and feminism itself. During the same year, the OLM took on a more active and visible role with the appointment of Ivonne Siú, a well-known Sandinista feminist formerly in charge of international relations for AMNLAE, as director. The explosion of demands from women during the three months of *cabildos abiertos* (town meetings) held to discuss the preliminary draft of the constitution made it clear that there was a potential base of support for feminist demands.

The Second National AMNLAE Assembly marked another turning point in the Nicaraguan Revolution with respect to feminism. Clara Murguialday Martinez, a Spanish feminist who had been involved in Nicaraguan women's struggles from the beginning, observed that

> from that moment on, women dared to talk for themselves, breaking with centuries of silence in order to convert their isolated laments into collective shouts, their individual dreams into collective conquests. They began to interpret anew their domestic

conflicts and the impact of the war and the crisis on their daily lives, feeling strong, united, and legitimate in addressing their issues without feelings of guilt, without accusations of "diversionism" with respect to the urgent topics of the revolution.[21]

Despite this ideological earthquake, AMNLAE became increasingly paralyzed internally because of the tension among those who continued to feel they had to choose between women and the priorities of the revolution, those who feared disapproval by the FSLN, and those who were afraid they might be unleashing a war between the sexes. As a result, AMNLAE lost its monopoly over the leadership of the women's movement and other groups, institutions, and individuals, including the women's secretariats in some of the unions (particularly ATC and CONAPRO, the Confederation of Professional Organizations, Confederación Nacional de Organizaciones de Profesionales), and Sandinista feminists took the initiative. This change led to a more feminist public discourse but limited the feminists' capacity to organize grassroots women and bring the full weight of the revolution behind them. Without the support of AMNLAE, the feminists could not be an effective voice in shaping the strategy of the FSLN. When it became clear that the FSLN would not allow an alternative organization to compete with or replace AMNLAE, feminists decided once again to do their best to transform it from within.[22]

Meanwhile, a two-year debate within the FSLN on the "woman question" was beginning to come to a head. At one point the National Directorate appeared to rally around the argument that the weakness of AMNLAE was evidence that gender-specific organizing was a mistake and that AMNLAE should be the FSLN's detachment within sectoral and class organizations to facilitate the *integration* of women into them. Feminists countered that AMNLAE should be a social movement, not a branch of one political party, and that as long as serious obstacles to women's incorporation on an equal basis into all sectors of the revolution continued to exist, AMNLAE had a critical role to play.

The first indication that a feminist position had won out occurred in an official statement of the FSLN read November 8, 1986, at its twenty-fifth anniversary celebration, in which it promised to "guarantee the rights women have gained and struggle with determination against remnants of machismo left over from the past." The extent of the victory became clear on March 8, 1987, when the "Proclama," or the official FSLN proclamation, was read to 3,000 women gathered at the Third National AMNLAE Assembly. The statement reviewed the historical commitment of the FSLN to combat discrimination against women; the gains that women, and the revolution in general, had made since 1979, particularly in the unprecedented levels of women's participation in government and political organizations; and the difficulties that had been encountered, because of the anti-Contra war, in implementing plans and programs that would have benefited women. The proclamation also stated that despite the gains, the levels of women's participation were still inadequate. Organizations and individuals were called upon to help create conditions—*including fighting sexism and cultivating women's leadership*—that would make women equal participants in decisionmaking in the revolution.[23]

There was no reference in the Proclama to birth control, sex education, and abortion, but it did include the concept that the family is the basic unit of society and guaranteed not only biological and social but cultural reproduction, a view associated with the Catholic Church and conservative social theorists. An explicit reference to the struggle against machismo and the lack of statements counter to a more explicitly feminist position, however, was widely interpreted by feminists as an important ideological and political victory. The statement constituted an implicit critique of verticalism (top-down leadership) in past women's organizing, offered a greater degree of support for women's self-organization, and accepted the view that a more explicitly feminist perspective was important even during a national emergency.[24]

For the next four months, AMNLAE concentrated on making sure that the Proclama was studied by all Sandinista militants. As before, however, AMNLAE leaders lacked a clear strategy for putting the precepts of the Proclama into practice and for strengthening its identity as leader of the women's movement. Furthermore, in a public debate on the decriminalization of abortion, organized as part of the celebration of AMNLAE's tenth anniversary, President Daniel Ortega shared his personal view that, since men were the ones fighting in the front lines of the war, promoting a policy of abortion or sterilization would be equivalent to "depleting our youth" and that a woman who "aspire[s] to be liberated by not bearing children negates her own continuity and the continuity of the human species."[25] This served as a rude reminder that significant differences still existed among the Sandinista leadership.

In the days following the forum, as though in response to Ortega, AMNLAE leaders announced their most concrete program of feminist goals to date and their intentions to promote the program in other popular organizations. By June 1988, however, AMNLAE's leadership acknowledged that its work was paralyzed, in part because the unions' women's secretariats did not want organizers from outside telling them what to do and in part because of AMNLAE's bureaucratic structure of 130 activists whose responsibilities were not clearly defined. Even more important, however, in the opinion of one feminist activist, was the mechanical acceptance of the idea of working with women in the different social sectors without being clear as to why and how.

Although the fundamental theoretical and political questions did not get resolved, other important changes did occur. AMNLAE leaders agreed that sectoral leaders should lead the women's movement, with coordination and support supplied by AMNLAE.[26] A democratic process to elect a new national assembly and executive committee of AMNLAE was begun. Hundreds of women were elected from farms, factories, neighborhoods, and cooperatives. Simultaneously, AMNLAE began to decentralize its administrative apparatus and to convert its offices to neighborhood women's centers *(casas de mujeres)*. By March 1989, 34 centers had been established offering legal assistance, sex education, and settings for discussions and exchanges among groups. The office of AMNLAE became the Casa Nacional de la Mujer, where training, research, information gathering, and project planning took place. Two autonomous centers offering gynecological attention, sex education, and family planning were established in Managua and Masaya.[27]

During the same year, other gains were made in expanding the institutional and power base of the women's movement. The Governmental Office on Women (Oficina Gubernamental de la Mujer) achieved greater autonomy from the state and became the Nicaraguan Women's Institute (Instituto Nicaraguense de la Mujer), focusing on research and documentation, interinstitutional coordination, and channeling of funds for economic projects. A chair in Women, Family, and Society was created in the Department of Sociology at the National University. After Hurricane Juana, women on the Atlantic coast were successful in forming their own women's association. By March 1989, statistics presented at the First Annual Encounter of Nicaraguan Women from (Sandinista-affiliated) Mass Organizations, held under the slogan "Consultation without conciliation, in the nation and in the home," seemed to show significant gains in women's popular movement leadership. Women were said to constitute 40 percent of the affiliates and 35 percent of the leadership of the ATC, 37 percent of the affiliates and 40 percent of the base leaders of the Sandinista Workers' Central (Central Sandinista de Trabajadores, or CST), 70 percent and 30 percent of the Asociación de Educadores (ANDEN) and 80–90 percent of the Health Workers' Federation (Federación Nacional de Trabajadores de la Salud, or FETSALUD) and 40 percent of CONAPRO. The National Farmers' and Ranchers' Union (Unión Nacional de Agricultores, or UNAG) had 918 women as base leaders.[28]

Furthermore, the lobbying activities of a small nucleus of Sandinista feminists who occupied positions of leadership in government, party, and popular organizations—the same ones who had been pushing for reform from within AMNLAE from early on—began to make clear what an alternative theoretical and organizational approach would look like. They emphasized the need to make demands on the (mostly male) leadership of the mass organizations, to create the conditions for greater representation of women in leadership as well (as winning the support of male leaders), and to understand more clearly the underlying causes of women's subordination. Much of the dynamic activity achieved in this period can be linked to the activities of these women, who in 1987 loosely organized themselves into a network humorously named the Party of the Erotic Left (Partido de la Izquierda Erotica, or PIE).

Coup d'État for a More Democratic Women's Movement

In May 1989, only six months before the scheduled installation of AMNLAE's first democratically elected assembly that was empowered to make independent decisions (and elections widely conceded to have favored openly identified feminists and women sympathetic to feminism), the FSLN gave what one activist has described as a coup d'état to AMNLAE's new direction.[29] As a result of the peace accords signed with the Contras of February 14, 1989, and of U.S. pressure associated with the Central American peace process, the FSLN decided to move up the timetable for national elections to February 25, 1990. During the electoral period, the agendas and activities of all Sandinista-affiliated organizations were to be subordinated to the National Directorate of the FSLN. In order to put a lid on the internal debate in AMNLAE, FSLN ordered the internal electoral process frozen and substituted Doris Tijerino (ex-chief of police), Monica Baltadano, and three other trusted FSLN militants for AMNLAE's existing national executive committee. With new leadership in place, AMNLAE was assigned the task of delivering the women's vote for FSLN.

Out of respect for the political legacy of Doris Tijerino, one of the women pioneers of the FSLN, and a desire to contribute to unity in the preelectoral period, women activists resisted the FSLN's reassertion of control more passively than openly. AMNLAE returned to trying to influence its traditional base of housewives, slum dwellers *(pobladores)*, and urban vendors. The horizontal communication and coordination ties that had been forged across different sectors were not maintained. The more feminist Sandinista women activists were caught between their sense of loyalty to the FSLN's progressive project for change and the requirement that they support a sexist set of campaign symbols and styles.[30]

Feminism, Antifeminism, and the Government of Doña Violeta

The Sandinista revolutionary party's surprising electoral loss to a heterogeneous, mostly right-wing coalition dramatically changed the framework for feminist and women's struggles in Nicaragua. No longer was it a struggle for respect for greater organizational autonomy in relation to the ruling political party and for a more explicit feminist perspective within party and state policies. Now the struggle had become multidimensional, against ideological policies that attempted to restore more traditional women's roles and structural adjustment policies and for the right to autonomy and the acceptance of feminist ideas within the revolutionary movement. But it took time to absorb the shock of the electoral loss before new strategies for the women's movement could be articulated and debated.

The election itself has been interpreted by some as evidence that Latin American women are politically conservative because some sectors of women, particularly housewives, voted disproportionately for the winning opposition presidential candidate, Violeta Chamorro. But as Sandinista feminists have pointed out, both the FSLN and the opposition projected traditional images of women. Doña Violeta, the opposition (UNO) candidate, was a mother and the widow of a martyr; she was portrayed as the good mother, pure, as a not very politicized middle-aged woman dressed in white and dedicated to peace and tranquility at home and the reconciliation of her "children" (who encompass the political spectrum of Nicaragua). Daniel Ortega, for the FSLN, was portrayed as the "fighting cock" *(el gallo enavajado)*, young, strong man of the household, hardworking breadwinner, defender against external attack.[31]

On both sides, the campaign was played out using symbols and codes that bore little relation to the reality of most Nicaraguan women's lives. There was little emphasis on program or on the specific needs of different sectors. Women overall voted for the FSLN in roughly the same proportions as men, with working and urban women's greater support making up for lower support among housewives and rural women. Despite the FSLN's image of actively defending women's rights and the relatively large number of women candidates on its ticket, many women interpreted the FSLN's message as little more than a call for continued sacrifice.

During the campaign, neither Chamorro nor her coalition members took an explicit position on women. But their call for "social healing" suggested classic right-wing codes for an antifeminist stance. UNO's social program called for "greater respect for parents on the part of children" and "the recuperation of the moral and social function of the Nicaraguan family." Programs were to be directed to women to "strengthen their sense of dignity and [their] integration into family, economic, social, and political functions."[32]

Once in power, the fundamentally conservative and antifeminist character of the Chamorro government became more visible and concrete. UNO blamed the FSLN for the destruction of the family, loose sexuality, the high divorce rate, and the increase in women working outside the home. They advocated traditional family gender roles, the rhythm method as the only acceptable form of contraception, and procreation as the fundamental purpose of sex. Economic policies that cut health, education, and other social services and reduced state-sponsored employment and training resulted in extra hardships for female-headed families, 81.4 percent of which were in poverty and 37.5 percent in extreme poverty. Fees for previously free public education were especially damaging to the education of young women, particularly in rural areas.[33]

On June 11, the Nicaraguan National Assembly passed (by a bare majority) the most repressive antihomosexuality law in the hemisphere. The introduction of the bill took Sandinista legislators and their allies by surprise. Its constitutionality was contested, although it was signed by President Chamorro. The fact that legislation this repressive managed to pass the Assembly after 10 years of relative official tolerance of homosexuality is an ominous indicator. The message to feminists, poor women, and progressive women in general seemed clear: "The Frente lost and so did you."[34]

The FSLN in Opposition: New Tensions and Opportunities for Women's Organizing

The loss of the elections relieved the FSLN of the often contradictory role of wanting to mobilize from below but having to govern from above. It also lessened pressures on Sandinista feminists to withhold public criticism. For the first time in over a decade, the FSLN could reflect in depth and critically on the relationship between popular organizations and a revolutionary party, between democracy and social transformation, and between gender and democracy.

Prior to the First Party Congress, July 19–21, 1991, FSLN leaders seemed to be encouraging debate and self-criticism within the party, in FSLN-backed popular organizations and nongovernmental organizations (NGOs), and in the sympathetic press. At the FSLN congress, a number of weaknesses and errors were acknowledged, among them the authoritarian and bureaucratic tendencies resulting from wartime pressures, top-down leadership, the arrogance of leaders, the unresponsiveness of leaders to complaints from below (including complaints of corruption), insufficient openness and democracy, and an agrarian policy that alienated the rural population and helped build the Contras' social base. Although no explicit critique was made regarding sexist images in the campaign or previous approaches to women's organizing, the focus on issues related to leadership style and democratic procedures were enthusiastically welcomed by feminists.

That enthusiasm was short-lived, however, when the National Directorate resisted efforts to replace its unpopular or ineffective members or to make the directorate more representative of women, youth, and the unions. Rank-and-file efforts to draft Dora María Tellez to become the first woman on the National Directorate failed. Elections were held, but the deck was stacked against change by the fact that candidates were voted publicly as a single slate and by the vigorous pre-congress lobbying efforts of the National Directorate. A number of candidates representing new blood were voted into the Sandinista Assembly, but only 18 out of the 98 delegates were women.

Although the reformers were pleased with the expanded space they had created for open debate and criticism, many of them were also frustrated by what they felt was a victory of "back-room politics ... over internal democracy."[35] Although they were promised that members of the National Directorate would be elected individually by secret ballot at the next congress, many were deeply disappointed that the FSLN leadership did not take advantage of the electoral loss to make the organization more internally democratic.

After a period of what one Nicaraguan feminist called a "prolonged popular depression" (an allusion to the antidictatorship strategy of "prolonged popular war"), the remaining AMNLAE leadership (weakened by resignations), some Sandinista militants, some independent feminists, and later the women's secretariats of the unions agreed to begin a process of reactivation of the women's movement, starting with a series of eight workshops that would ask women what kind of women's movement and what type of platform, coordination, and relationship with the government, the FSLN, and other political parties they wanted.

Criticisms of the past leadership made clear AMNLAE's reluctance to adopt a more democratic style of leadership or to change its relation to the FSLN.

AMNLAE's goal seemed to be simply to pick up where it left off before the elections. It planned to hold its national assembly meeting on March 8 and 9, 1991, inviting Sandinista-affiliated mass organizations but excluding women's centers, women's collectives, independent *casas de muljere*, feminist or gender-focused NGOs, and independent feminists on the grounds that they did not represent a mass base. The narrowness of AMNLAE's vision alienated many women, however, and four of the key labor union women's secretariats—the ATC, Sandinista Workers' Central (Central Sandinista de Trabajadores, or CST), State Employees Union (Unión Nacional de Empleados, or UNE), and FETSALUD—refused to attend the assembly in protest over what they called AMNLAE's "hegemonistic leadership style."[36]

Some 40 groups and a large number of individuals not attending AMNLAE's national assembly celebrated March 8 with a three-day Festival of the 52 Percent—with workshops, exhibits, videos, art, music, poetry, and theater—open to all women without regard to political, religious, or ideological stance. The festival's underlying philosophy and its obvious popularity—an estimated 3,000 people attended despite a boycott by the Sandinista press—signaled another turning point in the Nicaraguan women's movement.

But it was not without its costs. Sandinista-affiliated women's union secretariats were under strong pressures from the FSLN not to disagree with other Sandinista women in public. AMNLAE remained intransigent in its rejection of political autonomy for popular organizations and acted aggressively against its opponents. Many women in mixed Sandinista organizations felt caught as one or another side questioned their loyalty. An earlier indication of these conflicting loyalties had been the opposition of ATC and CST, along with AMNLAE, to the candidacy of Dora María Tellez for the National Directorate of the FSLN during its first congress in July 1991 because of what they perceived to be her antiunion stance while a member of the Sandinista administration.[37]

By August 1991, some 30 groups had begun preparations for a National Nicaraguan Women's Encounter to be held in preparation for the First Central American Women's Encounter in March 1992 in Montelimar, Nicaragua. By most criteria, including that of a broad spectrum of national press, the encounter was a great success.[38] Eight hundred women, more than three times the number expected by organizers, came together in what was probably the most diverse gathering of Nicaraguan women ever: organized and independent women, and women from different parts of the country and representing different political tendencies. In her opening speech, well-known Sandinista feminist Sofia Montenegro called for a new political culture and a new ethic among women, one that would "transcend those styles of work we have inherited from the patriarchy: abuse of power, utilization of people, inability to dialogue, the cult of hierarchy, competition and sectarianism."[39]

In spite of this success, two divergent positions on a strategy for the women's movement became clear by the end of the gathering. One group felt that the success of the encounter was adequate evidence that a women's movement with its own identity, agenda, and leadership could and should now be established. The other felt that conditions were still not sufficiently developed and that the distrust left over from past mistakes was more likely to be overcome by a step-by-step process of working in loosely coordinated networks with specific foci: sexuality, health, education, economy and environment, violence, women in communications, and women's participation in mixed organizations. To the disappointment of some of the *encuentro* organizers (but with the approval of others), the latter position prevailed, reflecting not only lingering problems from organizing strategies but differences about how "pure" and explicitly feminist the Nicaraguan women's movement should be.

These events generated an intense discussion within Nicaragua and within the Central American women's movement (the latter encouraged by Nicaraguan feminists) about the meaning and importance of autonomy for feminism. Although it may be true, as Norma Vasquez and Clara Murguialday argue,[40] that feminism and autonomy—with the latter defined as the capacity for self-determination and independence and the absence of subordination—are inseparable, it is also true that autonomy is a complex, multifaceted process that can occur in various ways and at different levels: organizational, political, ideological, individual, and collective. Thus, women activists may achieve organizational autonomy but not personal autonomy in relationship to their families, spouses, or boyfriends or vice versa. A women's group may not be organically dependent on a political party, religious institutions, or the state—that is, it may have carved out its own space and have the right to choose its own leadership and agenda. But it may still base its strategy, style, activities, and evaluation of successes and failures on a theory or philosophy that it shares with other groups (e.g., Marxism, Sandinismo, etc.). A feminist group may have a considerable degree of ideological autonomy—that is, clear and independent visions and social practices—but maintain organizational links with political parties or religious organizations.[41]

Finally, women's groups may achieve autonomy on all these levels but have little importance or influence in societal institutions or broad-based movements for social change. Some women activists fear that autonomous women's groups will be ghettoized, have little influence, and lack access to women who might already be organized by political parties, unions, the state, or religious institutions. Such concerns have motivated some Nicaraguan feminists to want to play a mediating role between those whom they see as the feminist radicals—some of whom still maintain membership in FSLN but many of whom are now independent feminists—and the distinctly nonautonomous leadership of AMNLAE. They would prefer that the lines between openly identified feminists in autonomous organizations and other women activists who recognize and defend the importance of gender-specific demands not be so clearly drawn in order to defuse attempts to isolate feminist groups or force women in nonautonomous popular organizations to choose sides. Ana Criquillón points out that women's secretariats within the labor unions are in a weak position to push their demands and take positions radically autonomous from the FSLN because of the desperate economic situation of their membership, which declines as women are pushed into the informal economy.[42]

Nicaraguan feminists who still sympathize with the goal of politically and socially transforming Nicaragua in the direction of less exploitation and greater equality believe that women will continue to wear down their creative energies and their capacity to offer alternative visions and political projects if they do not make the vital break with organizational, political, and ideological subordination. Whether women are within political parties or mixed (male-female) popular organizations or outside them, these feminists believe women activists should cease being obedient militants and openly declare their commitment to feminism. Otherwise,

> many feminists remain in a state of permanent dependence, ... unable to think as individuals or autonomous groups capable of elaborating alternative political projects. In practice, this translates into many hours dedicated to persuading the men, in one's personal as well as political-organizational circles. How many hours are spent convincing them one by one that could be spent constructing a women's force that would permit a more "head to head" confrontation in the mixed organizations.[43]

In the current context, however, feminists such as Criquillón feel it is a mistake to push women in Sandinista-affiliated organizations to choose between their divided loyalties. The unions with traditionally the strongest, most advanced women's secretariats—CST and ATC—are struggling to respond to their new condition of no official support, declining membership because of unemployment, and desperate cries for help from members who are faced with an economy that threatens their survival. The women's secretariats have lost strength within their organizations and are in a weak position to take positions radically autonomous of the FSLN.

At the same time, the unions' request that the entire women's movement mobilize to support them and their economic priorities led to charges that they were trying to reestablish hegemony over neighborhood women's groups such as women's centers, women's houses, and feminist collectives, all of which tend to emphasize issues related to the services they provide—educating about violence against women, skills training, and counseling on sexuality and health.

Thus, the current schism in the Nicaraguan women's movement is not only over autonomy but also over how to respond to the desperate situation the majority of Nicaraguans face in the post-Sandinista economy. Increasingly, so-called popular demands seem to be counterposed to so-called feminist demands, renewing a tension that seemed to have been overcome during the Sandinista period of women's organizing. This tension has led to a distancing of some unions such as ATC and CST from the more feminist wing of the movement. Others, such as the government workers' UNE and CONAPRO, remain active participants.

Although the Nicaraguan women's movement is divided over strategy and lacks a strong infrastructure or a single coordinating center, it is more diverse than ever before. In addition to AMNLAE and the women's secretariats of the CST and ATC, there are research and service centers; neighborhood groups and women's houses; feminist collectives such as La Malinche and the Women's Radio Collective of Matagalpa; gay and lesbian groups; a university women's studies program; newspapers such as *La Gente;* foundations such as Xochiquetzal, which works for a more holistic understanding of sexuality and against sexually repressive laws; and NGOs such as Cenzontle, which focuses on youth with an explicit gender commitment.

Even the UNO government, under pressure from external funders, has developed some projects and campaigns that promote better conditions for women and lead to limited alliances with feminists in their execution. Additionally, the government has elevated the National Institute on Women to the level of a ministry and established a National Commission Against Violence Against Women, under the sponsorship of the president.

Feminism, Revolution, and Democracy in Nicaragua

The importance of the Nicaraguan experience in deepening our understanding of the interrelationship of democracy, feminism, and revolution cannot be underestimated. Prior to the revolution, democracy was virtually nonexistent in Nicaragua. Feminism, likewise, had little historical importance in Nicaragua prior to the Sandinista revolution, which has served as its incubator, catalyst, and framework.

The Sandinista revolutionary experience, combined with the Central American context of underdevelopment, backwardness, and a high degree of external intervention and influence, has marked the Nicaraguan feminist experience. In the revolution, women gained a heightened consciousness, and a capacity for organization and analysis, that they could not have gained by any other means. In the struggle against the dictatorship, they had their first experience with grassroots democracy and empowerment.

At the same time, the political movement that served as the framework for Nicaraguan women's political coming of age was heavily influenced by the tradition of clandestine armed struggle, which emphasized military hierarchy and discipline, centralization of leadership, compartmentalization of information, the subordination of individual needs to the collective, and the public (productive) sphere as the force behind all change. It was also influenced by the Catholic Christian tradition of self-sacrifice and self-denial. To both traditions, the basic feminist tenets of politicizing the private sphere, analyzing the forms of oppression that occur in daily life, and using personal experiences as the starting point for theoretical understanding represented a serious challenge.

Given this context, it is perhaps not surprising that, of all the Sandinista-affiliated mass organizations, AMNLAE appears to have had the most difficulty asserting its own agenda and choosing its own leadership. Most of the other organizations gained greater autonomy as the revolution progressed, but with the
exception of brief moments, AMNLAE probably had greater autonomy in the first
period of the revolution than at any time since.

Radical feminists might point to this simply as one more example of the threat
that feminism poses to all progressive movements, and as evidence of the use of
threats to keep women in line. Yet there is also evidence that AMNLAE's experience can be traced to its own passivity and timidity, which was linked in turn to
the personal and political challenge that feminism represented to the culture
women activists had inherited, their superficial understanding of gender inequality, and their underestimation of the importance of expanding democratic relations within the movement as a condition for creativity and growth.

AMNLAE leaders' initial view that women would gain greater equality through
integration into the general tasks of the revolution derived not only from a fear of
being seen as divisionist but from a genuine belief that women's liberation
progresses in stages from participation to equality without passing through gender-specific demands and direct reclamation of power. When their integrationist
strategy did not seem to work, AMNLAE leaders were left without a theoretical or
political model to fall back on. But even when an alternative model emerged—
based on attempts to organize women in the ATC and the Sandinista Workers'
Central by more aggressively challenging sexism, raising women's self-esteem,
and promoting women's leadership—AMNLAE leaders were reluctant to join
other Sandinista feminists in waging a battle for its acceptance because they
feared confrontations with some of the Sandinista leadership.

In contrast, the experiences of feminist researchers and activists within the ATC
and CST demonstrated the potential for linking strategic and practical gender interests, as outlined by Maxine Molyneux.[44] Necessary conditions included support from the political leadership (in this case, the all-male leadership of the
union) and the activism of feminists who were convinced of the need to increase
women's power (not just their participation) and attack sexism directly, constructing alliances with sympathetic men and other organized forces along the
way.

Pragmatism and flexibility, two characteristics commonly cited as important
contributions of the Sandinista revolution, represented advantages as well as dis-
advantages for arriving at an effective strategy for women's organizing. There is
no doubt that the Sandinista movement's pragmatic and flexible approach helped
to expand the practice of democracy in Nicaragua far beyond what the history of
Central America and the more traditional Latin American Left would have predicted. For the implementation of the FSLN's ideology of gender equality, however, the effects were mixed. Pragmatism allowed the Sandinistas to avoid the
dogmatic view that the woman question is subsumed under class conflict. But

their theoretically and empirically weak understanding of the dynamics of gender difference and inequality in Nicaraguan society encouraged the "pragmatic" view that feminism was something of a luxury that only the most conscious women, mostly urban and educated, saw as a priority. Efforts to get high-ranking leaders to reexamine this conception were undermined by war, the struggle for economic survival, and pragmatism itself. Murguialday Martinez concludes that

> Nicaraguan feminism has its own profile, somewhat different from other feminisms on the Latin American continent. Two characteristics mark this profile: the particular version of "autonomy" which the women's movement seeks with respect to the mass organizations, the state and the Sandinista Front, on the one hand, and, on the other, the vision of feminism as an "integrative" project which does not make women the only ones interested in ending their oppression but which also places this responsibility on society as a whole.[45]

Although some Nicaraguan feminists would now put more emphasis on accumulating power directly for feminist projects and ideas and less reliance on their adoption by society or the revolution as a whole, the goal of building a feminist movement that has a mass base is still a shared one. The question, however, is how to accomplish this in a period when economic conditions for the majority of people are deteriorating at an alarming rate, the state is weak and not particularly friendly, and the FSLN remains the strongest organized political force. That feminism and women's organizing have great potential is clear from the number of experiments taking place and the amount of organizing that is occurring in a general context of demobilization. The strength of the Nicaraguan experience is evident, as well, in the strong leading role Nicaraguan women have taken in the rapidly growing Central American women's movement. Out of this vast reservoir of unique experiences, there is reason to believe that the Nicaraguan women's movement will continue to contribute to our understanding of the relationship between feminism and democracy in the future.

Notes

1. Carole Pateman, *The Problem of Political Obligation* (Berkeley: University of California Press, 1985).

2. Richard Harris and Carlos M. Villas, *A Revolution Under Siege* (New Jersey: Zed Books, 1985). See also José Luis Corragio, *Nicaragua: Revolution and Democracy* (Winchester, Mass.: Allen and Unwin, 1985); and Gary Ruchwarger, *People in Power: Forging a Grassroots Democracy in Nicaragua* (South Hadley, Mass.: Bergin and Garvey, 1987).

3. Latin American Studies Association, *The Electoral Process in Nicaragua: Domestic and International Influences,* report of the Latin American Studies Association delegation to observe the Nicaraguan general election on November 4, 1984 (Pittsburgh: Latin American Studies Association, 1984).

4. Norma Stoltz Chinchilla, "Mobilizing Women: Revolution in the Revolution," *Latin American Perspectives* 4 (1977): 83–102; and "Women in Revolutionary Movements: The

Case of Nicaragua," in Stanford Central America Action Network, ed., *Revolution in Central America* (Boulder, Colo.: Westview Press, 1983). See also Jane Deighton, Rossano Horsley, Sarah Stewart, and Cathy Cain, *Sweet Ramparts: Women in Revolutionary Nicaragua* (Birmingham, England: War on Want/Nicaragua Solidarity Campaign, 1983); Margaret Randall, *Sandino's Daughters* (Vancouver, B.C.: New Star Books, 1981); and Susan E. Ramirez-Horton, "The Role of Women in the Nicaraguan Revolution," in Thomas W. Walker, ed., *Nicaragua in Revolution* (New York: Praeger, 1982).

5. Elizabeth Maier, *Nicaragua: La mujer en la revolución* (Managua: Ediciones de Cultura Popular, 1980); and *Las Sandinistas* (Managua: Ediciones de Cultura Popular, 1985).

6. Ana María Portugal, "On Being a Feminist in Latin America," in *Isis International* (Santiago, 1985).

7. Clara Murguialday Martinez, *Nicaragua, revolución y feminismo (1977–89)* (Madrid: Editorial Revolución, 1990); "Una brecha en el muro del machismo: Diez años de lucha de las mujeres nicaraguences," *Terra Nuova Forum* (June 13, 1988): 9–65; *Ser mujer en Nicaragua: Testimonios de mujeres haciendo revolución* (Montevideo: Imprenta Cunatai, 1987).

8. See Deighton, Horsley, Stewart, and Cain, *Sweet Ramparts*.

9. Maxine Molyneux, "Mobilizing Without Emancipation? Women's Interests, State and Revolution," in Richard R. Fagen, Carmen Deere, and José Luis Coaggio, eds., *Transition and Development: Problems of Third World Socialism* (New York: Monthly Review Press and Center for the Study of the Americas, 1986). See also Norma Stoltz Chinchilla, "Women in the Nicaraguan Revolution," *Nicaraguan Perspectives* 11 (Winter 1985–1986): 370–396.

10. See Murguialday Martinez, *Ser mujer en Nicaragua.*

11. AMNLAE, unpublished balance sheet presented at Fourth Anniversary Meeting (September 1981) and documents from the First National Assembly (December 1982). See also Harry Fried, "Nicaraguan Women Demand Rights: Battling Sexism Remains a Key Task," *Guardian*, December 21, 1981.

12. See Norma Stoltz Chinchilla, "Marxism, Feminism, and the Struggle for Democracy in Latin America," *Gender and Society* 5, 3 (September 1991): 291–310; and "Women in the Nicaraguan Revolution," *Nicaragua Perspective* 11 (Winter 1985–1986).

13. Ana Criquillón, *The Nicaraguan Women's Movement: Reflections from Within the Movement* (Washington, D.C.: EPICA, 1993). See also Murguialday Martinez, *Nicaragua, revolución y feminismo;* and Chinchilla, "Women in the Nicaraguan Revolution."

14. See Norma Stoltz Chinchilla, "Revolutionary Popular Feminism in Nicaragua: Articulating Class, Gender, and National Sovereignty," *Gender and Society* 4, 3 (September 1990): 370–396.

15. See Criquillón, *The Nicaraguan Women's Movement;* and Murguialday Martinez, "Una brecha en el muro del machismo."

16. See Criquillón, *The Nicaraguan Women's Movement.*

17. Rosario Murillo, *Ventana* (San José), (September 1985).

18. See Murguialday Martinez, *Nicaragua, revolución y feminismo.*

19. See Murguialday Martinez, "Una brecha en el muro del machismo," 63.

20. See Criquillón, *The Nicaraguan Women's Movement.*

21. Murguialday Martinez, *Nicaragua, revolución y feminismo,* 196.

22. Ibid.

23. "Emancipation for Everyone," *Barricada Internacional,* March 26, 1987. See also FSLN, "El FSLN y la mujer en la revolución popular Sandinista" (Managua, Vanguardia, March 8, 1987), pamphlet. Excerpts in English in the *Militant,* May 22, 1987.

24. Desireé Pallais, "Para la plena paridad se necesitará mas tiempo," *Terra Nuova Forum* 13 (June 1988): 66–68. See also Ana Criquillón, "Acabamos on el mito sexo débil," *Terra Nuova Forum* 13 (June 1988): 31–35; and Chinchilla, "Marxism, Feminism, and the Struggle for Democracy in Latin America."

25. Cindy Jaquith and Roberto Kopec, "Advances, Challenges for Women in the New Nicaragua," *Militant,* November 20, 1987. See also Lois Wessel, "Reproductive Rights in Nicaragua: From the Sandinistas to the Government of Violeta Chamorro," *Feminist Studies* 17 (Fall 1991): 537–549.

26. See Murguialday Martinez, *Nicaragua, revolución y feminismo;* and also Criquillón, *The Nicaraguan Women's Movement.*

27. Malena de Montis, "Una perspectiva de poder para las mujeres: El movimiento de mujeres de Nicaragua," unpublished paper, February 25, 1992.

28. Murguialday Martinez, *Nicaragua, revolución y feminismo.* See also Cenzontle, *Subordinación de genero en las organizaciones populares Nicaraguences,* notebook no. 2, Managua, Nicaragua, 1991.

29. See Criquillón, *The Nicaraguan Women's Movement.*

30. See Murguialday Martinez, *Nicaragua, revolución y feminismo;* and also Criquillón, *The Nicaraguan Women's Movement.*

31. Karen Kampwirth, "The Mother of the Nicaraguans: Dona Violeta and the UNO's Gender Agenda," paper presented at the Congress of the Latin American Studies Association, Los Angeles, September 24–27, 1992. See also Criquillón, *The Nicaraguan Women's Movement.*

32. Chinchilla, "Marxism, Feminism, and the Struggle for Democracy in Latin America,"*Gender and Society* 5, 3.

33. See Kampwirth, "The Mother of the Nicaraguans"; Wessel, "Reproductive Rights in Nicaragua"; and Midge Quandt and Barbara Seitz, "Report on a Trip to Nicaragua: Women Under Chamorro's Regime," *Against the Current* (1992).

34. Midge Quandt, *Guardian,* September 26, 1990.

35. Criquillón, *The Nicaraguan Women's Movement.*

36. Julie Light, "Sandinistas Play with Stacked Deck," *Guardian,* August 14, 1991.

37. See Julie Light, "Women's Confab Turnout Elates Managua Feminists," *Guardian,* February 5, 1992.

38. See Puntos de Encuentro, *La Boletina* (Managua) 4 (February-March, 1992).

39. Norma Vasquez and Clara Murguialday, "Sobre la decision vital de algunas feministas Centroamericanas," unpublished paper, July 1992.

40. Ibid.

41. See Criquillón, *The Nicaraguan Women's Movement.*

42. Ibid.

43. See Norma Vasquez and Clara Murguialday, "Sobre la decision vital de algunas feministas Centroamericanas," unpublished document, 1993.

44. Molyneux, "Mobilization Without Emancipation?"

45. In Murguialday Martinez, *Nicaragua, revolución y feminismo,* 275.

EIGHT

Women's Movements, Feminism, and Mexican Politics

CARMEN RAMOS ESCANDÓN

To date, very little has been published on the political participation of women in Mexico. Even the extensive studies of Mexican women's participation in the economy, their strategies for survival and changes in household composition, have paid little attention to how the changes in economic status and conditions have affected the activity and attitudes of women in the public and private spheres.[1] Women's response to recent liberal economic policy and modernization in Mexican politics remains largely unexplored. Although Mexican women have been active in community organizations and village protests since colonial times, a feminist movement as such emerged only in this century; the movement has become increasingly visible since the 1970s.[2]

In this chapter I examine the political participation of women in Mexico between 1970 and the early 1990s, paying particular attention to the organizational forms and demands that emerged after the 1982 crisis. I also gauge how feminist ideas have impinged on the Mexican political process. To this end, the chapter is divided into three sections: a historical overview of women's political participation in Mexico after 1916, when the first feminist congress in Mexico took place; two case studies of women's political participation during the 1980s (the women's movement in defense of the vote in Chihuahua [1982–1986] and women's participation in the popular urban movements in Mexico City); the principal elements of the feminist agenda in Mexico in the early 1990s and its impact on Mexican politics.

A Neglected Heritage

The Mexican postrevolutionary political culture was slow to incorporate women into political life. For much of the first half of the twentieth century the political efforts of women in Mexico were aimed at obtaining the basic political rights required for fuller participation; chief among them was suffrage.

In a country in which politics had traditionally been the domain of a small male elite, political rights for women were ignored until the late nineteenth century, when they began to be espoused by Porfirio Díaz's opponents, particularly the Magonistas. It took the Mexican Revolution, however, to produce the first small breach in the wall of indifference. The participation of women in this struggle has been well documented.[3] Their combat-related activities represented a profound change in their usual confined roles. In the heat of armed struggle women served as couriers, arms runners, spies, nurses, and in other roles that would have been unthinkable in peacetime.[4]

The fact that women participated in the revolution and the acknowledgment of their contributions are important because the revolution became the founding myth of the Mexican political state.[5] The legitimacy of the current Mexican state rests on its official interpretation of the revolution of 1910, which in turn has largely determined the organization of the state apparatus and the political relationships between social sectors during much of the twentieth century. Because they participated in the struggle, women could at least invoke their moral right to be heard when they pressed their social, legal, and political demands.

The revolutionary period produced some modest reforms in the legal status of women but no change in their political status. By a decree dated December 29, 1914, the Carranza government authorized divorce and remarriage.[6] The Law of Family Relations, approved in 1917, extended to women the right to receive alimony, to manage and own property, to take part in legal suits, and to have the same rights as men in the custody of their children, changes that implied a reorganization of the social relations between the sexes.[7]

This period also produced the first of many congresses devoted to women's issues. The First Feminist Congress in Mexico was held in Mérida in January 1916 and considered issues ranging from the function of schools, the importance of secular education, and the need for sex education to the political participation of women. The participants, mostly middle-class women, were divided on the latter issue. The feminists argued that women were the moral and intellectual equals of men and should participate as full citizens. The antifeminists contended that women were different from men and should never participate in public life, and the moderates suggested that women were still not psychologically ready to participate politically and that political rights should be reserved for men until women could be adequately prepared to exercise these rights.[8]

At this point, the demand for the enfranchisement of women came mainly from a small number of radical feminists. In 1917, Hermíla Galindo, a Venustiano Carranza supporter and editor of *La Mujer Moderna,* and several other women presented their demands for women's suffrage to the all-male constitutional convention meeting in Querétaro. In her arguments Galindo invoked the liberal concept of equality of individual rights before the law. She contended that as active members of society and as taxpayers, women should have full political rights, especially suffrage. For her the equal rights of citizens were a matter of "strict justice."[9] Despite the strength of these arguments, the subject was debated only briefly and the majority sentiment was against it. As Ward Morton suggests, most of the delegates to the convention probably feared the conservative influence of the Church on women voters precisely at a time when social reforms required limiting the Church's power.[10]

The 1917 constitution as approved retained intact Articles 34 and 35 of the 1857 constitution, which qualified as citizens all married residents of the republic over 18 years of age and all single residents over 21. Citizenship conferred the right to vote, to run for office in popular elections, and to participate in political activities. The provisions of these articles did not textually deny women's suffrage, but the 1918 National Election Law explicitly limited the vote to registered males 18 years or over if married and 21 if not. Candidates for national office were required to be "qualified electors."[11]

This setback limited but did not quash women's participation. During the next decade Mexican women attained greater visibility in the political, economic, and cultural life of the nation. Significant signs of change were the increasing numbers of women in the labor force, in the newly created government agencies, in education, and in women's organizations fighting for political rights. As expected, women were present in greater numbers in government agencies concerned with social welfare and education, functions traditionally considered female tasks.[12]

Several Mexican states granted suffrage to women in the 1920s, affording them the first limited opportunity to participate in electoral activities. Yucatán and San Luis Potosí allowed women to vote in state and local elections in 1923, although these rights were soon rescinded. In 1925, Chiapas became the first state to enact complete equality of political rights for women in local and state elections, extending to them the same political rights as men, including the right to vote and stand for all offices. Its example, however, was not followed by other states until much later.[13]

The 1920s also saw the emergence of women's associations and leagues organized specifically to fight for women's rights.[14] In time this push became more persistent and better-organized. The deaths in 1924 of Salvador Alvarado and Felípe Carrillo Puerto, the two radical Yucatán governors who had championed women's rights, shifted the focus of feminist activity to Mexico City. As in other countries, feminist organizations drew support primarily from urban women of above-average education, professionals, office workers, and schoolteachers.[15] Working-class and peasant women also formed organizations concerned mostly with labor and economic issues and tended to be affiliated with labor unions or the Communist Party.[16] The Mexican Feminist Council (Consejo Feminista Mexicano), a broad-based organization that sought to lead the women's movement toward socialism,[17] and the Mexican Section of the Pan American League of

Women included leading feminists such as Elena Tórres, Refugio (Cuca) García, and Margarita Robles de Mendoza.[18]

Also about this time the first Congress of the Pan American League for the Elevation of Women, held in Mexico City in 1923, sent a petition to the Mexican Congress demanding equal political rights for men and women.[19] However, other events hindered the advancement of this cause. Many women participated actively in the religiously motivated Cristero war against the government,[20] and when President-Elect Alvaro Obregón was assassinated by a religious fanatic who allegedly had been encouraged by a nun, many in power again feared that women voters would be manipulated by the Church.[21] Although the decade of the 1920s was an important period in terms of women's political participation, the early years of the women's movement were difficult and marked by women's generally unsuccessful efforts to participate politically as individuals or as a group.

The organized presence of women gained force during the following decade, in part because political parties began to sense that women's rights could be a useful political issue. The 1929 platform of the newly created Partido Nacional Revolucionario (PNR, or National Revolutionary Party), the government party, recognized, for instance, the need to stimulate Mexican women's involvement in civic activities. For its part, the opposition Partido Nacional Antireeleccionista (Antireelectionist National Party), which ran José Vasconcelos for president in 1929, included women's suffrage in its political platform and a large number of women in its ranks.[22] Although they agreed on the importance of increasing women's political participation, women party activists differed on what form this participation should take. Communist women opposed an autonomous feminist movement and attacked the women of the PNR, accusing them of mounting a bourgeois struggle and putting feminist interests before class interests. For their part, PNR members concentrated on obtaining political gains within the ranks of their own party.

These differences were openly expressed at the National Congresses of Women Workers and Peasants held in 1931, 1933, and 1934, where the communist women demanded changes for women workers and peasants and the PNR women presented papers on women's suffrage and on the need for a unified women's organization. The debate about whether women should pursue an autonomous agenda or subsume the gender struggle to the class struggle was bitterly divisive, but in spite of their internal differences, these periodic national congresses produced some positive results. Delegates agreed on the need for an eight-hour workday and minimum wages, paid leaves of absence for women before and after childbirth, support for single mothers, punishment for husbands who abused their wives, easier divorce proceedings, and, especially, the creation of jobs for women in general and for prostitutes in particular. They also suggested that women of all ideological persuasions were prepared to rally around the issue of women's suffrage. The ideological rivalries were finally bridged at the fourth congress in Chihuahua in 1935, which incorporated women from both camps and began a tactical alliance among women activists. The resulting organizational structure was used to advantage by the ensuing Frente Unico pro Derechos de la Mujer (Sole Front for Women's Rights).[23]

Women's Organizations
Gain Strength in the 1930s

The emergence of the Frente Unico pro Derechos de la Mujer was the most important development for the organized women's movement during the mid-1930s. Structured as a broad-based organization combining several smaller groups, the Frente Unico included at one point over 50,000 members distributed among some 800 women's organizations throughout the country. The Frente Unico fought openly for recognition of women's political rights, particularly the vote, pinning its hopes on the reformist presidency of Lázaro Cárdenas.

Organized officially in October 1935, the Frente Unico succeeded where earlier efforts to create a unified feminist organization had failed. This first effective mass feminist organization in Mexico united feminists from the Left and Right, liberals, communists, Catholics, and the various factions from the women's sector of the PNR. Its greatest success was in coalescing its diverse supporters around the issue of women's suffrage.

Despite class, regional, and ideological differences, the Frente Unico succeeded in large measure due to the leadership of lower-class women in grassroots organizations. Adelína Zendéjas, a militant of the period, recalled,

> The activities centered on born leaders (some 150) who had begun the struggle and had become leaders by the respect and recognition of their reason and logic. There were many rural schoolteachers of peasant extraction who were the leaders or agrarian leagues in the states. The centers of these leagues were at the municipal and ejido seats, but they radiated out, and mobilization meant that the league reached not only the women who were members, but to all those in the region.[24]

The Frente Unico's agenda concentrated on practical measures to improve the daily life of women and on political demands. It advocated employment centers, the creation of a children's bureau, and reform of the labor law and civil code.[25] Politically it sought the liberation of Mexico from foreign oppression, social and political equality for peasants and indigenous populations, opposition to fascism and war, and, most important, women's suffrage.[26] The only exclusively feminist demand was for women's right to vote, but it was this demand that gave the organization its cohesion and political character.

Although maintaining its independence from the government and the PNR, the Frente Unico banked heavily on president Lázaro Cárdenas to aid the cause of women's suffrage. Cárdenas, in turn, saw the opportunity to garner the support of a large number of women for his far-reaching reforms. In the context of Cárdenas's effort to consolidate the support of mass segments of workers, peasants, the military, and the bureaucracy within the structure of his governing party, organized groups, including women, attracted his attention. Women were encouraged to vote in the 1936 PNR primaries as members of the party sections to which they were affiliated (labor unions, peasant organizations, women's groups), and they convinced the leadership that women voters associated with the party were not a threat.[27]

Despite an effective, unified mass organization of women willing to demonstrate, strike, and picket and the official support from an influential president, success was not forthcoming when Cárdenas proposed to amend Article 34 of the constitution to make women eligible for all the rights of citizenship. On November 23, 1937, however, the Senate and Chamber of Deputies both approved the amendment.[28] The amendment was submitted to the states for ratification in 1938, when 16 of the 28 states had already given women the vote, and was ratified by all states by May 1939.[29]

One step remained, the formal declaration by Congress that the amendment had been ratified and was in force. Despite mass demonstrations by the Frente Unico and other organizations during 1939 and 1940 and the pleas of President Cárdenas, nothing was done. The usual explanation is that the legislators feared a backlash by masses of enfranchised women voters against the government's reforms. They also feared that women would support the conservative opposition candidate in the 1940 presidential election.[30]

The election of Manuel Ávila Camacho marked a turning point in 1940, moderating the thrust of the Mexican Revolution and reducing the tension between church and state. The bitter defeat of the suffrage issue turned the attention of women's organizations to other goals such as child care centers, cooperatives for indigenous women, and legislation to protect domestic servants. Feminist activity in Mexico in the first half of the twentieth century reached its peak of enthusiasm and participation in the 1930s, but the disappointing defeat of its unifying issue proved too much to overcome.

The 1940s and 1950s:
Some Women, No Movement

The gradual weakening of Mexican feminism lasted over two decades. Ironically, it coincided with the gradual accession of women to full political rights. Massive foreign investment in the mid-1940s led to industrialization and urbanization and opened new opportunities for women's economic participation. Women were granted the right to vote and hold office in municipal elections. President Miguel Alemán (1946–1952) appointed women to highly visible positions and reorganized the official party. The newly founded Partido Revolucionario Institucional (PRI,

Party of the Institutionalized Revolution) included the first woman, Margarita García Flores, on its national executive committee.

Alemán's successor, Adolfo Ruíz Cortines, had promised a new women's group, the Mexican Women's Alliance (Alianza de Mujeres Mexicanas), that he would support women's suffrage if elected. When the alliance's president, Amália Castillo Ledón, presented a petition with half a million signatures, President Ruíz Cortines succeeded where Cárdenas had failed. The constitution and the electoral law were changed in 1953, finally giving Mexican women equal rights with men to participate in politics, almost four decades after Hermíla Galindo demanded it as an act of "strict justice."[31] Four women were elected to the national Congress in 1955, and women's voting patterns proved to be not too different from men's.[32] In the 1958 presidential election, the first to include women voters, the total number of voters nearly doubled, but the electoral practices and political controls used by the PRI were unaltered.[33]

The fact that equal political rights were not achieved until 1953, and then only when the ruling party (PRI) was confident of political control, underscores the persistent weaknesses of the women's movement to that point. Its lack of effectiveness stemmed from its somewhat elitist character, narrow urban base, and fragmentation over class issues. Efforts to counter the ingrained sexual stereotyping made little headway and were repeatedly frustrated at critical times by the activism of Catholic and conservative groups.

In its early years the movement was much too disorganized to parlay women's contributions to the revolution into political gains. At full strength, as the Frente Unico in the 1930s, the movement lacked the political clout to carry its agenda. When the government finally acceded to the political demands of women in the 1950s, it did so on its own terms and at a period when the women's movement had been progressively weakened and its issues were dismissed as politically irrelevant. By the late 1960s the movement was practically nonexistent as an autonomous movement. Economic growth meant less activism in the women's movement and, in fact, most women's organizations in the 1960s were government-sponsored or sympathetic to the official party.[34] Within what was effectively a one-party political system, the PRI absorbed many politically active women and channeled them into positions within the bureaucracy.

According to longtime militant Adelína Zendéjas, women themselves were to blame for favoring personal interests over the collective interests of the women's movement: "They gave us the vote, and then everything went downhill, because women would not fight for women's causes but for their own personal interests, to become a director or a deputy—and they forgot everything."[35] Inevitably, this co-optation reflected the class bias of the Mexican political system. Many of the powerful women obtained their positions through family or through affective or political links to powerful men.[36]

The Second Wave

A new wave of feminism emerged in the 1970s, mostly among young profession-als, students, and middle-class women.[37] This new brand of feminism was more intellectual. It questioned women's role in society and was particularly concerned with exposing the inequality between men and women in everyday life—in the daily relationship between men and women at home and in the workplace. The political opening of the Echeverría regime, from 1970 to 1976, permitted the regis-tration of new opposition parties, gave greater latitude to labor unions, and al-lowed the emergence of new social movements.[38] Women's groups voiced their criticism of the political system and expressed their grievances as an organized group. In doing so feminists were forced to confront the problems arising from the deep race and class differences among women in Mexico.

The middle-class university women who constituted the core of this new wave of activist Mexican feminism were eager to build alliances with lower-class women because they perceived that feminism had the potential for radical social change at all levels. Over a dozen feminist groups, each stressing different issues, emerged during the mid-1970s. They all agreed, however, on the need to define feminism in Mexican terms and emphasized consciousness-raising groups. A need was felt to make women at all social levels aware of their double exploitation as women and as workers and to realize the link between their daily life and op-pression in the private sphere and their social situation.[39] In 1972, the women's group Mujeres en Acción Solidaria (MAS, Women for Solidarity Action) became involved with striking women textile workers in an effort to build a cross-class al-liance based on the new feminist ideas. This initial proselytizing effort was not very successful because most of the women workers were more concerned with union issues than with organizing as women. In general terms, this exemplified the initial difficulties in establishing cross-class alliances.

The new feminist groups were more successful in attracting urban middle-class women. MAS members, for example, caught the public eye by staging a countercelebration on Mother's Day 1971, criticizing consumerism and the ma-nipulation of women. Since city authorities thought women were celebrating motherhood, they allowed the meeting to take place, and the feminists even got national television coverage.[40] Publications, workshops, and discussion groups flourished, giving the feminist movement wide visibility. The new adepts were militant and eager to participate in feminist groups, but the difficulty of incorpo-rating other social groups remained a major weakness. Lack of leadership and fragmentation was also a problem for the women's movement.[41] This fragmenta-tion was evident in the reaction to the celebration of the UN-sponsored Interna-tional Women's Year in Mexico City in 1975. Although some groups were enthusi-astic in their support, others criticized the celebration as demagogic.

As in the past, differences emerged within the middle-class groups. A "bour-geois" group, the Movimiento Nacional de Mujeres (National Women's Movement), emphasized the need for women to ally on the basis of gender without questioning the existing social order. The socialist feminists, in contrast, expressed the belief that women's subordination is caused by social, political, economic, and sexual oppression and thus that changing women's role in society required changing the social and economic conditions. Groups such as the Movimiento de Liberación de la Mujer (Women's Liberation Movement) (1974), Colectivo la Revuelta (the Revolt Collective) (1975), and the Colectivo de Mujeres (Women's Collective) were part of this political orientation and tried to combine gender and class analysis. Applying the feminist insight that "personal is political" led these women to question their social role and the class structure of Mexican society.

Although reminiscent of the class-gender split of the 1930s, the political context had changed. In the 1970s, groups on both sides organized to enable women to participate politically outside the traditional context of male party politics, but in the cases where women chose to participate in party politics, the concept of double militancy, as women and as party members, was created.[42] The women's movement was keenly aware of its need for autonomy from the traditional corporatist structure of the Mexican state. Official organizations and political parties, in turn, felt the need to incorporate feminist concerns into their programs. Feminist groups appeared both in the PRI and the Mexican Communist Party, and most independent labor unions also had women's commissions. Even the more conservative women of the Partido Acción Nacional (PAN, National Action Party), who do not consider themselves feminists, began to claim their right to autonomy as women.[43]

Both independent and party-controlled feminist groups included the issues of decriminalization of abortion, stronger punishment for rapists, and assistance for battered women in their agenda.[44] Of these, the decriminalization of abortion provoked the greatest interest and consensus among women's groups. Debates and discussions in public forums and in the media, conferences, and demonstrations led the Grupo Parlamentario de Izquierda (Leftist Parliamentary Group), an alliance of opposition members of Congress, to introduce an abortion bill in the Chamber of Deputies in 1979.[45] Although the bill was rejected, abortion remains a central issue for feminists and other sectors of Mexican civil society.[46]

Overcoming its initial difficulties, the women's movement gradually succeeded in building links with other broad social movements during the late 1970s.[47] This alliance between the new wave of feminists and the urban movements was instrumental in shaping a new mode of political participation for Mexican women that expanded in the 1980s.[48]

Women's Mobilization in the Popular Movements of the 1980s and Political Change: Two Cases

Ernest Laclau (1985) and Alain Touraine (1987), among others, have pointed out that Latin American social movements are defined not by the interests they represent but by the demands they make.[49] This distinction is crucial because it implies a continuously shifting relationship between political demands and the groups expressing them. The experience in most Latin American countries is that the demands of social movements emerge in the process of organizing the groups. Besides requesting benefits from the state, popular movements insist on basic rights.[50] According to Manuel Castells, popular social movements are enormously important because they push for an alternative social organization, an alternative use of space, and an alternative kind of city.[51] Elizabeth Jelín argues that "what is at stake is not a new politics, but a new kind of society."[52]

In Mexico popular movements increased substantially from 1976 to 1982, when "the crisis" became an everyday fact of life. A depressed economy incapable of sustaining economic growth and a reduction of resources increased the economic and political needs and demands of disadvantaged sectors of society.[53] Popular movements during this period demanded housing, education, health, and a variety of other services, particularly in the poor urban areas. The success of these movements has depended on their ability to solve problems and meet demands in an effective, immediate way.[54] Participants in these social movements in Mexico are not defined by class interest but rather by their specific demands and by their relations with the state.

The proliferation of popular movements was one of the most significant political developments in Mexico during 1970–1990.[55] For the Mexican political system, with its enormous reliance on a state bureaucracy and co-optation, autonomous self-organized urban movements present a strong challenge to the traditional system of *cacique* control and party machine politics. Women have been the most numerous and consistent participants in urban social movements, and their specific demands as women have been a key feature in shaping the new strategies and the modalities of political participation. In effect, women's participation in social movements is changing the way of doing politics in Mexico, both at the grassroots level and in electoral politics.[56]

The Mexican case offers additional evidence that women's participation in urban popular social movements is a key factor in the long-term process of democratization in Latin America. Women in contemporary Mexican politics wield sufficient power to be taken into account as serious political actors and have even led demands for proportional representation of women in the Chamber of Deputies and the Senate.[57] The usual definitions of political legitimacy and the forms by which political power has been exercised are being challenged by blurring the differences between politics and private life. By bringing personal concerns to the public arena and demanding them as rights, women have given a new dimension to what is considered political. The legitimacy of their involvement in the public political arena draws on their traditional domestic roles as mothers and providers.[58] The election of women does not necessarily imply a change in the mechanisms of the political system, as Beatriz Paredes, the 1986–1992 PRI governor of the state of Tlaxcala and member of the national executive committee of that party, has noted, but even she acknowledges that women's movements are relevant in Mexican society today.[59]

In today's Mexico a significant number of women have moved away from party and electoral politics to a more immediate, decisive way of doing politics. Two relevant cases illustrate these processes of change: the lower-class urban movements in Mexico City and the civil disobedience campaign in Chihuahua in 1986. In both cases women played a key role, and their participation made a difference in the traditional male political arena.

Campamentos and Political Activism

Rural migration and high birthrates since 1940 have increased demographic pressures on Mexico City and have forced urban marginal families to establish squatter settlements known since the 1970s as *campamentos,* from which popular urban organizations have emerged. In the mid-1970s, encouraged by the social ideology of the Echeverría regime, these urban movements challenged private property by occupying empty areas on the outskirts of the city.[60] In 1979, an umbrella organization known as the Coordinadora Nacional del Movimiento Urbano Popular (CONAMUP, National Coordinating Committee of Urban Popular Movements) was established to provide national coordination for the numerous local organizations.[61] Most of the participants in these movements were women, in many cases recent migrants to the city. They became active in the struggle for the recognition of property rights and for property legalization and basic household services (water, sewage, schools, health centers). By 1983, a women's organization, the Woman's Regional Council, was formed within CONAMUP.[62] The Consejo Regional de Mujeres (CRM, Woman's Regional Council) sought to provide women with a forum to voice women's demands and obtain basic services for the community and organized collective kitchens, self-help workshops for women, and government-subsidized meal distribution for children. The CRM provided a space for women's issues and recognized women's need for a specific space in which to voice their grievances, express their concerns, and increase their political power within CONAMUP.

As an umbrella organization, CONAMUP gave women leeway to push for their specific issues within the broad objectives of the movement. Feminist concerns received increased attention at CONAMUP meetings. At Monterrey in August 1985, CONAMUP women stated that the family, school, and Church were perpetuating patterns of women's submission and passiveness. They proposed sexual education workshops for the whole family, help for rape victims, harsher punishment for rapists, self-defense courses, and workshops to analyze the effects of the economic crisis on women. To cope with the economic crisis, they proposed the formation of cooperatives for buying, cooking, and producing food staples, as well as workshops to increase awareness about healthier eating habits and to fight against price increases.[63] In September 1986, they organized meetings against price increases in domestic gas and school tuition and supplies. They also marched in support of World Day Against Hunger and joined forces with the "19 de septiembre" seamstresses' union to demonstrate against violence against women and denounce sexual aggression toward women in the home, workplace, streets, and health institutions. In December of that year they demanded increased services in health and day care centers, government subsidies for staples and tortillas, increases in the free-breakfast program for children and free food *(despensas)* on major holidays such as Christmas, Mother's Day, and Children's Day.[64] These demands for basic products reflected the rising concern of women attempting to cope with a rapid decline in their purchasing power.[65]

The economic crisis of the 1980s increased the harsh conditions faced by the urban poor. Women, in particular, bore the brunt of inflation, lack of services, and deteriorating living conditions. They became the overwhelming majority participating in urban popular movements, largely in response to increasing poverty.[66] For some women the crisis led to depression and escapism.[67] However, for others participation had the effect of increasing their personal self-esteem and making them aware of their political power. As a militant woman put it in 1988, "Since I've been here I've felt a very important change. Before I had only my home and my work and went from one to the other. Now it's not only my home and my work, it's the group. I think that women are useful not only at home, and that's one of the main things I've learned in this organization."[68]

Women frequently faced opposition to their organizational activities from their husbands and sometimes they experienced domestic violence, but in many instances women gradually convinced their husbands and families that women's demands were beneficial to their families and communities. The frequent meetings, marches, and long waits to be heard by public officials often took a toll on women's domestic activities. Women made up for this by collectivizing their domestic tasks and relying on other women to share the burden. On the whole women seem to be increasingly aware of their political bargaining strength and find satisfaction with their new roles as organizers.[69]

By the mid-1980s the demands of women in the popular movement included clear feminist issues. Responses to the economic crisis focused on strategies for survival that affected the whole family as more housewives were forced to enter the labor force;[70] feminist issues such as violence against women also became part of their agenda.[71]

Rebels Who Rose from the Rubble

On September 19, 1985, at 7:15 A.M., a major earthquake hit the central and western portion of Mexico. The effects of this natural disaster on the Mexican political system could not have been anticipated.[72] Specifically, for the women's movement the increased political participation in spontaneously organized groups meant a new alliance among women of different classes.[73] The Mexican garment workers union "19 de septiembre" exemplifies this new alliance well. The union was formed by seamstresses who lost their jobs after the earthquake practically destroyed the garment district in Mexico City. About 40,000 women were left unemployed. Women were outraged by the fact that factory owners were more concerned with saving what was left of the machinery than with trying to find their missing coworkers. This initial rage served as motivation for an unprecedented event in Mexico, a rapidly organized autonomous union led by women. The "19 de septiembre" is "the first industry wide union in the history of the Mexican garment industry, the first independent national union to be registered in the last 13 years in Mexico and the only trade union that is led entirely by women."[74]

By electing a female leader (Evangelína Corona) who emerged from their own rank and file, the women in this union overturned a long-standing pattern by which men led organizations consisting predominantly of women. The "19 de septiembre" union members also used traditional women's skills to raise money for their organization. They sold handmade dolls based on designs made by famous artists specifically for the seamstresses. Continuing the effort to build cross-class alliances, the feminist magazine *FEM* organized an auction of jewelry donated by upper middle-class women, the proceeds from which went to the seamstresses' union.

The novelty of the "19 de septiembre" union went far beyond its fund-raising procedures. By organizing an autonomous union that refused to recognize the official PRI-sponsored Confederación de Trabajadores Mexicanos (CTM, Confederation of Mexican Workers), they took an independent political stance in a strongly controlled labor movement. From a feminist perspective the most interesting feature of the "19 de septiembre" union is the fact that it is a collective effort with mostly women participants. Middle-class feminist organizations offered legal advice and participated with the seamstresses in staging demonstrations, performing organizational tasks, and informing the public about the union. This network across class barriers facilitated the integration of feminist demands into the union's program. Teresa Carrillo notes that the role of the advisers has not been sufficiently explored,[75] but it is already clear that even in this rather traditional role of advisers, middle-class urban women joined forces with urban proletarian women in confronting the factory owners and male-controlled labor movement in Mexico. So far the union has succeeded in staying outside of the corporatist state and "is breaking new ground for popular female leadership and collective action."[76]

New Women, Same Old Politics

The 1986 governor's race in the northern border state of Chihuahua drew considerable interest. PAN candidate Francísco Bárrio, a successful and popular mayor of Ciudad Juárez since 1983, faced the PRI candidate, Fernando Baéza, who also had distinguished professional credentials and the support of the PRI party machine.

Both candidates attempted to attract the women's vote by praising both homemakers and women workers, an appeal calculated to win votes in a city where women constitute a majority of the labor force in export-processing industries and also work in the professional services and informal sectors.[77] Women played a leading role in the political campaigns of their candidates. Female participation in this campaign ran the gamut from the enhanced role played by the spouses of both candidates to the innovative civic campaigns led by women against electoral fraud and corrupt politics. Women saw it as a feminine task to put an end to these practices. PAN women argued that part of their responsibility as mothers who must provide for their children and take care of their future is the responsibility of leaving them a more democratic political environment. These women denied that they had an individual stake in politics, justifying their political participation in the name of their children.[78]

The race also featured two female candidates contending for the position of national deputy. Clara Tórres (PAN) and Iséla Tórres (PRI) presented contrasting personal and political styles. Iséla was a candidate of working-class origin who ran a campaign based on her ability to represent the workers, especially the *maquiladora* (foreign-components assembly plant) workers; Clara came from a professional background that appealed to the more conservative PAN constituency. Both emphasized that being a woman would make a difference in their politics.[79]

Women participated actively in the unusually strong political confrontations that preceded the election, especially in the civil disobedience campaigns staged by PAN to protest electoral fraud. Women also took part in watching the polls and encouraging people to vote. Yet although women participated actively in the 1986 election at a time when the political arena was becoming very polarized between PRI and PAN, the parties still failed to offer women specific programs to address gender inequalities.[80] The role of women in this campaign has been discussed by some of the women who participated in it. Most of them agreed on the need for even greater women's participation and acknowledged the changes in their personal lives that resulted from being politically active.[81]

Although women's activism in Chihuahua did not profoundly change the political agenda and women were not able to prevent an allegedly tainted PRI victory, women themselves saw a significant change in the self-conceptualization of their gender roles. One 42-year-old participant named Vicky stated: "I think that before women did not express their feelings so completely. ... We, the women of Mexico, were used to accepting everything that was said to us, but all that changed, now we scream and fight for our rights."[82]

As examples of women's political participation, the elections in Chihuahua and the popular movements in Mexico City reveal very different objectives. Women in Chihuahua participated within the framework of an electoral movement, the novelty being the extent to which they engaged in the electoral campaign and their rationale for participating, their responsibilities as women and as mothers. As women and as mothers they expressed the need to "clean up politics" by defending the vote. In this defense women engaged in nonconfrontational, peaceful resistance and moral persuasion. One participant declared: "I agree with peaceful resistance. I think it's perfect because it's a way to show our rejection of the system, to make our disagreement with injustices felt. I think it's the best way to show the system our point of view, by resisting it peacefully."[83]

Women in popular movements, in contrast, concentrated on a less traditional area of political participation. These movements coalesced around immediate needs (for housing, water, schools). Demands were not presented through political candidates but directly to the state by those concerned, mostly women.

In each instance, it is clear that women have become less hesitant to politicize their concerns, within or outside the context of electoral politics. These movements clearly show a new form of relationship between civil society and government, and one of the features of this new relationship is the increased participation of women.

A New Feminist Awareness

The previously mentioned cases reflect a feature common to women's movements: Although women's participation may not bring immediate changes in the political agenda of traditional parties, changes do take place in the increasing awareness women have of the importance of women's issues and of their political power as an organized group. Feminism is certainly not new in Mexico, but a new female-feminist consciousness is emerging. Unlike 1970s middle-class feminism, which was primarily concerned with personal issues and did little to modify the course of traditional politics, the women's movement in the 1980s proved to be innovative in its demands and forms of organization as well as in constructing links with lower-class urban movements.

This intermingling of lower-class urban movements and the women's movement continues to occur. A popular type of feminism has emerged where women express their class demands with a feminist perspective.[84] The distinction between female participation, women's movements, and feminism is becoming increasingly irrelevant as women incorporate their specific demands as women into a broader political agenda. This agenda formulates traditional private demands as political issues. The increasingly effective presentation of women's demands is beginning to command attention in traditional political circles. President Salínas de Gortári declared women a priority for his government.[85] In the 1991 national election for congressional deputies, for instance, all three major parties (PRI, PAN, and PRD [Partído de la Revolución Democrática, Democratic Revolution Party]) included women's issues in their political platforms, although they still ran a disproportionately small number of female candidates.[86]

Although the relationship between organized women's groups and political parties is still a difficult one, women's concerns have become politically visible and relevant.[87] Traditional women's issues such as abortion, violence against women, and increased penalties for rapists are now part of the platforms of the major parties and government organizations. Abortion rights has been one of the issues consistently brought forward to public debate and has engaged large segments of Mexican society.[88] As elsewhere, women in Mexico continue to be divided on this issue.

The effects of this increased concern with women's issues have also been important for women as individuals. Political participation has meant a reeducation for women, and increased self-esteem often leads to greater achievement, as Alejandra Massolo's studies of the urban movement have proved.[89]

Women have also discovered that by voicing their gender-specific concerns as a group they are more likely to gain concessions from the state. Motherhood and its social practices are central to the symbols that women have used to assert themselves and legitimize their movement. Family and community concerns have been politicized. As the case of the PAN women in Chihuahua clearly shows, the formerly private responsibilities assumed by many mothers for feeding their families, allocating resources, and educating their children have been transformed into political issues for which women fight. The well-being of their families was the practical goal; their struggle to achieve this goal has been a powerful force in forming women's organizations. Women's shifting "practical gender interests"[90] have enabled women to have a dual access to power as organizers in their own communities and as organized groups vis-à-vis the state. This new attitude among women runs counter to the stereotype of the passive Mexican woman.

The feminists of the 1930s realized the importance of women's political participation, but the main difference between contemporary feminism and that of its *precursoras* is that women today do not see party politics as the only space for women's issues. Feminist concerns are no longer marginal. Women's presence is felt in high official appointments; in spring 1993, for the first time, both houses of Congress were led by women.[91] In Mexican politics the organized women of the lower-class urban movements have become actors to contend with in the political arena.

Organized groups of middle-class women such as the Mujeres por la Democracia (Women for Democracy), the Convención Nacional de Mujeres (National Convention of Women), and the Mujeres para el Diálogo (Women for Dialogue) have been able to discuss the issues that are specifically relevant to women and to party platforms. A new breed of Mexican feminist scholar-activists analyzes and provides intellectual content for women's issues in magazines such as *FEM* and *Debate Feminista* and in monthly newspaper sections such as *La Doble Jornada*. The "woman question" is no longer a separate issue. By placing women's concerns center stage women in Mexico have made real progress toward erasing the idea that politics is the exclusive domain of men.

In terms of organization, Mexican women have used traditional female forms of communication such as networking and inviting family, friends, and neighbors as coparticipants. Most movements do not handle substantial amounts of money, but when they have needed income they have raised it using traditional skills, such as preparing food or making handicrafts for sale, as was the case with the "19 de septiembre" seamstresses.

The relationship between activism and motherhood is a complex and increasingly complementary one. Unlike in the past, when women's position in the family limited their political activity,[92] now being a mother legitimizes political activism, and activism is increasingly becoming a mother's activity. Children of both sexes frequently attend women's gatherings and protest meetings.

Women's participation in not a new feature in Mexican politics, but, unlike some of their predecessors in the 1930s and 1940s, the 1980s women organizers have not used their political prominence to advance their personal ambitions. This is particularly noteworthy in the context of Mexican politics, where political cohesiveness has been achieved by means of personal loyalties to leaders (*caciquism*). Women's movements are organized in relation to immediate issues rather than in terms of personal ties to their leaders.

Organizational methods have also been innovative and integrate practical and strategic gender interests. In general, communal self-help and group decisions have prevailed over party-line politics and *acarreo* (forced attendance).[93] Nongovernmental organizations (NGOs) have created a new form of political organization outside the parties. NGOs may not yet offer a real challenge to the powerful Mexican state, but their influence has been felt in traditional government circles. Their community-centered activities provided a pattern for one of the most successful government organizations of the 1990s, the Programa Nacional de Solidaridad (PRONASOL, National Solidarity Program), which assists with community development.[94]

In the Mexican contemporary political arena the presence of women and their demands cannot be ignored. "Feminism" is no longer a dirty word in Mexican politics. Rather, in Salinas's current discourse about modernization in Mexican society, women's issues are frequently included. Furthermore, women-led inclusive groups such as *Ganando Espacios* (Gaining Spaces) are pushing for the increased participation of civil society by urging citizens to organize politically and have also asked for support for a new society, one that changes the power relations in the country. They also claim the right to introduce legislation outside of parties and the right of both female and male citizens to organize politically. Along the same lines, the 1993 National Feminist Encounter put forward a political platform that includes a "positive action" policy aimed at the subversion of the traditionally unequal relationship between men and women.[95] Such demands are a real challenge to the Mexican political system. In the end, Mexican traditional political groups may yet come to grips with the fact that "democracia" is feminine.

Notes

1. On the subject of economic participation and survival strategies, see Liliana Acero, *Mujer y trabajo en América Latina* (Montevideo: Gremcu, 1986); L. Beneria and M. Roldán, *The Crossroads of Class and Gender: Industrial Homework, Subcontracting and Household Dynamics in Mexico City* (Chicago: University of Chicago Press, 1987); Jennifer Cooper, Teresita de Barbieri, Teresa Rendón, Estela Suárez, Esperanza Tuñón, comps., *Fuerza de trabajo femenina urbana en México,* 2 vols. (Mexico: Porrúa, 1989); Sylvia Chant, *Women and Survival in Mexican Cities: Perspectives on Gender, Labour Markets and Low Income Households* (Manchester, England: University of Manchester Press, 1991); Mercedes González de la Rocha, *Social Responses to Mexico's Economic Crisis* (San Diego: Center for U.S.-Mexican Studies: University of California at San Diego, 1991), 195–221, and *Los recursos de la pobreza* (Guadalajara: El Colegio de Jalisco, 1986); Elizabeth Jelín, *Family, Household and Gender Relations in Latin America* (London: UNESCO/Kegan Paul, 1991), and *Memoria Pronam, Programa Nacional de Integración de la Mujer al Desarrollo* (Mexico City: Secretaría de Gobernación/Consejo Nacional de Población, 1982); Orlandina de Oliveira, "Empleo femenino en tiempos de recesión económica: Tendencias recientes," in Jennifer Cooper et al., eds., *Fuerza de trabajo femenina urbana en México* (Mexico City: Miguel Angel Porrúa, 1989); Katie Willis, "Women's Work and Social Network Use in Oaxaca City, Mexico," *Bulletin of Latin American Research* 12, 1 (January 1993): 65–83; Fiona Wilson, *De la casa al taller: Mujeres, trabajo y clase social en la industria textil y del vestido* (Zamora: El Colegio de Michoacán, 1990).

2. Alan Knight, "Historical Continuities in Social Movements," in Joe Foweraker and Ann Craig, eds., *Popular Movements and Political Change in Mexico* (Boulder, Colo.: Lynne Rienner, 1990), 90.

3. See Carmen Ramos and Ana Lau, *Mujeres y revolución: 1907–1917* (Mexico City: INEHRM, 1993); Elizabeth Salas, *Soldaderas in the Mexican Military* (Austin: University of Texas Press, 1990); Sherlene Soto, *Emergence of the Modern Mexican Woman* (Denver: Arden Press, 1990); Anna Macías, *Against All Odds: The Feminist Movement in Mexico to 1940* (London: Westview Press, 1982); Angeles Mendieta Alatorre, *La mujer en la revolución mexicana* (Mexico City: INEHRM, 1963).

4. Frederick Turner, "Los efectos de la participación femenina en la revolución de 1910," *Historia Mexicana* 64, 4 (April-June 1967): 603–620.

5. On the Mexican Revolution as a social movement and its use to legitimize the Mexican state, see Alan Knight, "La revolución mexicana: Burguesa, nacionalista o simplemente una gran rebelión," *Cuadernos Políticos* 48 (October-December 1986): 5–32; also Hector Aguilar Camín, *Saldos de revolución* (Mexico City: Siglo XXI, 1988).

6. Divorce was authorized in Mexico for the first time on January 2, 1915. *Codificación de decretos del C. Venustiano Carranza, primer jefe del ejército encargado del poder ejecutivo de la unión* (Mexico City: Imprenta de la Secretaría de Gobernación, 1915), 150.

7. C. Venustiano Carranza, "Ley sobre relaciones familiares" in *Diario Oficial,* April 14, 1917, 3–71.

8. *Congreso feminista de Yucatán. Anales de esa memorable asamblea* (Mérida, Yucatán: 1916). See also Anna Macías, *Against All Odds,* 70–80; and Carmen Ramos Escandón, "Mujeres mexicanas, historia e imágen," *FEM* (November 1989): 25–31.

9. Gabriela Cano, "Es de estricta justicia: Un projecto feminista en las filas del constitiucionalismo," in *Congreso Internacional sobre la revolución mexicana* (Mexico City: INEHRM, 1992).

10. Ward M. Morton, *Woman Suffrage in Mexico* (Gainsville: University of Florida Press, 1962), 8.

11. *Ley electoral de poderes federales,* June 1, 1918, reprinted Mexico City: Imprenta de la Camara de Diputados, 1932, 16–17.

12. Outstanding women of the period were Antonieta Rivas Mercado, Frida Kahlo, Guadalupe Zuñiga, Alúra Díaz, and Josefina Vicens. See Fabienne Bradú, *Antonieta* (Mexico City: FCE, 1990); Herrera, Hayden, *Frida: A Biography* (New York: Harper & Row, 1983). For an oral history of the last three see Gabriela Cano and Verena Radku, *Ganando espacios* (Mexico City: UAM Iztapalapa, 1989).

13. Morton, *Woman Suffrage in Mexico,* 11–12.

14. Anna Macías, "Antecedentes del feminismo en México en los años veinte," *FEM* 11 (November-December 1979): 5–32.

15. Macías, *Against All Odds,* 106.

16. The presence of Alejandra Kollontai as USSR ambassador to Mexico was influential for leftist women's organizations in the 1920s. See Esperanza Tuñón Pablos, *Mujeres que se organizan* (Mexico City: Porrúa, 1992), 22.

17. Ibid., 26.

18. Julia Nava de Ruiz Sánchez. *Informe que rinde la secretaría de la delegación feminista al Congreso de Baltimore ante el Centro Feminista Mexicano sobre la comisión que le confirmo la Liga Nacional de Mujeres Votantes* (Mexico City: National Library, 1922).

19. "Resoluciones tomadas por el Primer Congreso Feminista convocado por la Sección Mexicana de la Liga Panamericana del 20 al 30 de mayo de 1923," *Debate Feminista* 1, 1 (May 1990): 309.

20. Ana Lau Jaivén, *Nueva ola del feminismo en Mexico* (Mexico City: Planeta, 1987), 38. Barbara Miller, "The Role of Women in the Mexican Cristero Rebellion: Las Señoras y las Religiosas," *The Americas* 40, 3 (January 1984): 303–323.

21. Morton, *Woman Suffrage in Mexico,* 13.

22. John Skirius, *José Vasconcelos y la cruzada de 1929* (Mexico City: F.C.E., 1978), 124.

23. Macías, *Against All Odds,* 134–137. Maria Rios Cárdenas, *La mujer mexicana es ciudadana* (Mexico City: Editiorial Cultura, 1940).

24. Interview with Adelina Zendejas cited in Tuñon Pablos, *Mujeres que se organizan,* 72. See also Adelina Zendéjas, "El movimiento femenil en Mexico," *El Dia,* June 21, 1975.

25. Macías, *Against All Odds,* 142.

26. *El Machete,* October 19, 1935.

27. Macías, *Against All Odds,* 141.

28. Morton, *Woman Suffrage in Mexico,* 30–31.

29. Ibid., 37.

30. Macías, *Against All Odds,* 144–145.

31. Morton, *Woman Suffrage in Mexico,* 83–84.

32. In April 1954, the state of Baja California Norte held the first election in Mexican history in which women participated equally with men in the election of a governor, the state legislature, and members of Congress. Aurora Jiménez Palacios was the first woman to be elected a deputy to the federal Congress. In the 1955 election, the four contending parties

nominated 14 women among the 355 candidates for deputy. Four women were elected, all PRI candidates. In 1958 women voted for the first time in the presidential election. Ibid., 86–87. Based on a 1958 survey of the political attitudes of men and women in Mexico, William Blough concluded that both had essentially similar attitudes about the political system, but women were less prepared politically and had more negative feelings toward the political system and that the more participatory women were, the more they favored the regime. See William Blough, "Political Attitudes of Mexican Women, *Journal of Interamerican and World Affairs* 14, 2 (1972): 201–224.

33. Morton, *Woman Suffrage in Mexico,* 112.

34. See ANFER, *Participación política de la mujer en México* (Mexico City: ANFER, 1984).

35. Margarita García Flores, "Adelina Zendéjas: La lucha de las mujeres mexicanas," *FEM* 1, 20 (October-December 1976): 76.

36. Luz de Lourdes de Silva, "Las mujeres en la elite política de México, 1954–1984," in Orlandina de Oliveira, ed., *Trabajo, poder y sexualidad* (Mexico City: El Colegio de Mexico, 1989).

37. Lau Jaivén, *Nueva ola del feminismo.*

38. On the Echeverría government, see Julio Labastida, "Proceso político y dependencia en México," *Revista Mexicana de Sociologia* 39, 1 (1977): 20.

39. Esperanza Tuñon Pablos, "Women's Struggles for Empowerment in Mexico," in Jill M. Bystydzienski, ed., *Women Transforming Politics* (Bloomington: Indiana University Press, 1992), 98.

40. Marta Acevedo, interview, August 1981. Lau Jaivén, *Nueva ola del feminismo,* 83.

41. Tuñon Pablos, "Women's Struggle for Empowerment," 99.

42. Ibid.

43. Carlos Monsivais, "De resistencias y últimos recursos: Notas para una crónica del feminismo en México," *Casa del Tiempo* 8, 71 (May-June 1987): 17.

44. Norma Mongovejo, "El movimiento feminista en busca de hegemonía," *FEM* 97 (January 1991): 4.

45. Marta Lamas, "Le nouveau feminism au Mexique," *Cahiers des Ameriques Latines* 26 (July-December 1982): 79.

46. María Luisa Tarrés, "El movimiento de mujeres y el sistema político mexicano: Analisis de la lucha por la liberalización del aborto," paper presented at the Seventeenth LASA International Congress, Los Angeles, September 24–27, 1992, 22.

47. Marta Lamas reconstructs the issues and organizational alliances in "Feminismo y organizaciones políticas de izquierda en México," *FEM* (February-March 1981): 35.

48. Although not explicitly feminist, another social movement led by a woman was the *"desaparecidos"* campaign headed by Rosario Ibarra after the 1975 disappearance of her son. See Rosario Ibarra, "La voz del silencio: Las madres muertas," *La Casa del Tiempo* 8, 71 (May-June 1987): 19.

49. Ernest Laclau, "New Social Movements and the Plurality of the Social," in David Slater, ed., *New Social Movements and the State in Latin America* (Amsterdam: CEDLA, 1985); Alain Touraine, "Los movimientos sociales," in A. Touraine and J. Habermas, eds., *Ensayos de teoría social* (Mexico City: UAP, UAM-Azcapotzalco, 1986); Joe Foweraker and Ann Craig, eds., *Popular Movements and Political Change in Mexico* (London, Boulder: Lynne Rienner, 1990); Lyn Stephen, "Women in Mexico's Popular Movements: Survival

Strategies Against Ecological and Economic Impoverishment," *Latin American Perspectives* (Winter 1992): 73, 96.

50. Foweraker and Craig, *Popular Movements and Political Change*, 8.

51. Manuel Castells, *The City and the Grassroots: A Cross Cultural Theory of Urban Social Movements* (Berkeley: University of California Press, 1983). Manuel Castells, *Crisis urbana y cambio social*, 2nd ed. (Mexcio City: Siglo XXI, 1981).

52. Elizabeth Jelín, *Los movimientos sociales en la Argentina contemporánea: Una introducción a su estudio* (Buenos Aires: CEDES, 1985); Elizabeth Jelín, comp., *Ciudadanía e identidad* (Ginebra: UNRIDS, 1987), 7.

53. See Carlos Tello et al., *Mexico 82: A mitad del tunel* (Mexico City: Oceano/Nexos, 1983), 80.

54. Manuel Castells, *La cuestión urbana* (Mexico City: Siglo XXI, 1976); Castells, *Crisis urbana cambio social*, 2nd. ed. (Mexico City: Siglo XXI, 1981); Castells, *The City and the Grassroots*.

55. Foweraker and Craig, *Popular Movements and Political Change*, 3.

56. Nikki Craske, "Women's Political Participation in Colonias Populares in Guadalajara, Mexico," in Sarah A. Radcliffe and Sallie Westwood, eds., *Viva: Women and Popular Protest in Latin America* (London: Routledge, 1993), 113.

57. José Woldemberg, "Cuotas para las mujeres," *La Jornada*, May 27, 1993.

58. Joann Martin, "Motherhood and Power: The Production of a Women's Culture of Politics in a Mexican Community," *American Ethnologist* 17, 3 (August 1990): 470.

59. Beatriz Paredes, "Algunas consideraciones sobre el ejercicio del poder y la condición femenina," in *Seminario sobre la participación de la mujer en la vida nacional* (Mexico City: UNAM, 1989); Carlos Monsivais et al., "De quién es la política?" *Debate Feminista* 2, 4 (September 1991): 36.

60. Alejandra Massolo, *Por amor y por coraje: Mujeres en movimientos urbanos de la ciudad de Mexico* (Mexico City: El Colegio de Mexico, 1992), 152.

61. Ricardo Hernández, *La Coordinadora Nacional del Movimiento Urbano Popular, su historia: 1980–1986* (Mexico City: CONAMUP, 1987).

62. Stephen, "Women in Mexico's Popular Movements," 73–96; Oscar Nuñez, *Innovaciones democrático-culturales del movimiento urbano popular* (Mexico City: UNAM, 1990), 363.

63. *La Jornada*, July 22, 1986; Alejandra Massolo, "La mujer callada jamás será escuchada," *FEM* 58 (October 1987): 53–55.

64. Ricardo Hernández, *La Coordinadora Nacional*, 100.

65. Patricia Muñoz Rios, "La deuda que nos cayó encima," *FEM* 56 (August 1987): 33–35.

66. Stephen, "Women in Mexico's Popular Movements"; Norman Walbeck, "The Women's Movement in Mexico: Potential Links Among Grassroots Popular Movements, the Feminist Movement and the Political Left," paper presented at the Annual Meeting of International Studies Association, Acapulco, Mexico, March 1993; Jane Jaquette, ed., *The Women's Movement in Latin America* (Boulder, Colo.: Westview Press, 1991).

67. Mercedes Charles, "Navegando por el mar de historias," *FEM* 56 (August 1987): 38–39.

68. Amparo Sevilla, "La participación de las mujeres en el Movimiento Urbano Popular MUP," *FEM* 107 (November 1991): 38; Hernández, *La Coordinadora Nacional*, 90.

69. For specific case studies of women's participation in urban movements after the 1985 earthquake, see Alejandra Massolo and Martha Schteingart, *Participación social,*

reconstrucción y mujer: El sismo de 1985 (Mexico City: UNICEF/Colegio de Mexico, 1987).

70. Orlandina de Oliveira, "Empleo femenino en Mexico en tiempos de recesión económica: Tenencias recientes," in Neuma Aguiar, ed., *Mujer y crisis: Respuestas ante la recesión* (Mexico City: Editorial Nueva Sociedad/Mujeres por un Desarrollo Alternativo, 1990), 50.

71. *Las mujeres en las colonias en el movimiento urbano popular* (Mexico City: CONAMUP, n.d.); *Opresión, explotación y organización de las mujeres* (Mexico City: Mujeres para el Diálogo, 1988); Ricardo Hernández, *La Coordinadora Nacional*, 98.

72. For the experiences of individual participants, see Elena Poniatowska, *Nunca, nada, nadie* (Mexico City: ERA, 1990); also Massolo and Schteingart, *Participación social*.

73. A large number of spontaneously organized groups in which women had an active role emerged immediately after the earthquake. For detailed accounts of specific groups, see ibid.

74. Teresa Carrillo, *Working Women and the "19 of September" Mexican Garment Workers Union: The Significance of Gender,* Michigan State University Working Paper no. 179, 1979, 2; and Teresa Carrillo, "Women and Independent Unionism in the Garment Industry," in Foweraker and Craig, *Popular Movements and Political Change*, 231.

75. Carrillo, "Women and Independent Unionism," 229.

76. Ibid., 232.

77. Kathleen Staudt and Carlota Aguilar, "Political Parties, Women's Activists Agendas and Household Relations: Elections on Mexico's Northern Frontier," *Mexican Studies* 8, 1 (Winter 1992): 93.

78. Ibid., 94.

79. Ibid.

80. Ibid., 105.

81. Dalia Barrera Bassols and Lidia Venegas Aguilera, *Testimonios de participación popular femenina en la defensa del voto, Ciudad Juarez, Chihuahua, 1982–1986* (Mexico City: INAH/CNCA, 1992), 92, 100.

82. Ibid., 101.

83. Ibid., 98.

84. Esperanza Tuñon Pablos, "Women's Struggle in Mexico 1970–1990," in *Women Transforming Politics: World Wide Strategies for Empowerment* (Bloomington: Indiana University Press, 1992), 102.

85. Carlos Salinas de Gortari, *Ideas y compromisos* (Mexico City: PRI, 1988), 107.

86. The PRI had 32 candidates for the Senate and 300 for national deputies. Only two candidates to the Senate and 21 for the Chamber of Deputies were women. No data are available for other parties. Monsivais et al., "De quién es la política?" 12.

87. Monsivais et al., "De quién es la política?" 24. Hector Aguilar Camín, "Mujeres en Marcha," in *Despues del milagro* (Mexico City: Cal y Arena, 1991); Kathleen Logan, "Women's Participation in Urban Protest," in Foweraker and Craig, *Popular Movements and Political Change,* 156.

88. María Luisa Tarrés, "El movimiento de mujeres y el sistema político mexicana," paper presented at the Seventeenth LASA International Congress, Los Angeles, California, September 1992, 33.

89. Massolo and Schteingart, *Participación social,* 109.

90. Maxine Molyneux, "Mobilization Without Emancipation? Women's Interests, State and Revolution in Nicaragua," in David Slater, ed. (Amsterdam, Netherlands: CEDCA, 1985).

91. For the first time in Mexican history, two women presided over the two houses of Congress, Laura Alicia Garza Galindo and Silvia Hernández, *La Jornada,* April 6, 1993, 6.

92. Soledad Loaeza, "Las formas de participación política de la mujer en Mexico," *Encuentro* 2, 1 (October-December 1984): 136.

93. *Acarreo* is the PRI practice of forcing people to attend meetings by discounting a day's salary if they don't attend or by providing them with meals and small gifts if they do.

94. For a study of the political uses of PRONASOL, see Denise Dresser, *Neopopulist Solutions to Neoliberal Problems* (San Diego: Center for U.S.-Mexican Studies, 1991).

95. "Campaña ganando espacios," *FEM* 17, 122 (April 1993): 38; "Feminismo, vida cotidiana y politica: Una propuesta de accion positiva," *FEM* 17, 123 (May 1993): 32.

NINE

Conclusion: Women's Political Participation and the Prospects for Democracy

JANE S. JAQUETTE

The chapters in this volume show that women's political participation is regionwide and extensive and that it is addressed to issues ranging from human rights and the environment to consumer movements and violence against women. Women's participation in national movements such as the revolution in Nicaragua or the oppositions to military rule in the Southern Cone and Peru has allowed women's groups to claim political space in the governments that they helped bring to power. The continued capacity of women to mobilize for specific issues and to create sustained movement organizations has made women visible political actors and has expanded the political agenda.

This chapter addresses two areas of interest to both feminist theory and democratic practice. The first issue is the implications for feminist theory of the successful pattern of women's mobilization *as mothers*, both in human rights groups and in urban neighborhoods. Latin America's experience is highly relevant to ongoing debates about the potential of maternal and "difference" feminisms to go beyond what many have criticized as the male model of citizenship. Does women's participation in Latin American politics create a "collective citizenry of political motherhood," as Jennifer Schirmer has argued? What are the political consequences of having "Family and Justice ... collapsed into one moral domain"?[1]

The second issue is central not only to democratic theory but to the prospects for democratic consolidation in Latin America and in other regions such as the former Soviet Union and Eastern and Central Europe. In all of these regions, civil society is no longer in an oppositional relation to the state, but new ties of representation and accountability must be built among civil associations, political parties, and the executive in order for democracy—however flexibly interpreted—to work. The "creation, nurture and spread of more egalitarian social relations and norms of leadership and authority," which Daniel Levine finds essential to "democratization,"[2] are important themes in these chapters. But what links "group life … to the big structures of national politics"?[3]

In the political practice of women's organizations in Latin America, this issue has been debated by and large in terms of how much *autonomy* women's groups should maintain vis-à-vis other groups, political parties, and the state itself. This chapter addresses this issue and its implications for the future of democratic politics.

Militant Motherhood

The image of mothers in politics has been given heroic form by the Madres of the Plaza de Mayo. The idea that political action is a legitimate part of a mother's duties has changed the understanding that many women have of their political capabilities. As Gloria Bonder writes, the politicization of motherhood breaks down the rigid boundary between public and private, which has kept women in the home and denied them their place as political subjects:

> The identification of politics with public life and with power emanating from the state excludes a whole set of social practices which are labeled private and therefore non-political. … Social functions traditionally attributed to women, namely reproduction, domestic tasks, socialization of children within the family, sexuality, etc., … are regarded as private and also as "natural." Because they are not identified as political, they lose the character of social practices and are relegated to the sphere of nature.[4]

Feijoó and Perelli ask in their chapters whether political practices that moralize politics and break down the barriers between public and private are always good for women and for politics. Feijoó's discussion focuses specifically on the Madres, asking whether their political stance "above politics" and "for life," so effective against the corruption and amorality of a repressive military regime, is not ultimately antipolitical, less suited to the politics of participation than the politics of opposition. In Feijoó's judgment, the Madres add a new secular argument to positions long associated with the conservative Church: that women have a moral role and that their place is in the home.

Studies of the evolution of women's human rights groups by Feijoó, Jo Fisher,[5] and others show that these groups have maintained their role as a moral voice. Although their demands that all those responsible for the torture and deaths of the "disappeared" be punished and that their children be returned alive have not been met, they act as a political conscience, resisting the tendencies to reconstruct the periods of military rule as times of stability or economic growth, in contrast to the volatile politics and straitened economic circumstances that have coincided with the return to democracy in many of these countries.

Perelli's interpretation of the politics of motherhood in Uruguay contests the widely held feminist belief that a politics based on the demands of mothers can fulfill the feminist ideal of a moral politics of care. Instead of enhancing the communitarian and compassionate dimensions of politics, as many feminists would claim, Perelli argues that women's use of the rhetoric of motherhood to seek a "private" good (the welfare of their families) can reduce politics to moral posturing. Portraying one's demands as moral (and thus nonnegotiable) because they are made in the name of the family "debases political discourse," she argues, and she denies the value of political negotiation among what are, after all, competing interests. In the process, any notion of the public good is lost.[6]

Perelli and Feijoó provide a much-needed brake on the feminist tendency to romanticize popular women's movements in Latin America.[7] But the reality is complex. Unlike the Madres, the women who participate in the urban movements do not claim to be above politics. They represent concrete interests and make claims on scarce resources in competition with others,[8] political behavior by any measure. In the context of women's participation, the Madres have had an impact on how women see themselves. Interviews show that women throughout the region know the story of the Madres and use the Madres' example to justify their own political activism. Acting as mothers, women achieve new identities and roles. From perceiving politics as alien (men's business), women come to see the public sphere as a positive arena in which their experiences *as women* take on larger meaning.[9]

There is also evidence that women do not join movements simply to obtain material benefits. Feijoó, in a study of women's self-help organizations in Buenos Aires, found that women were satisfied with very modest returns and that the programs succeeded in part because many women were rewarded by the respect they received from their neighbors.[10] Women in movements often speak of how their participation has changed their lives, expanded their awareness of the unjust structures of society, and given them new self-esteem—even when their involvement brings them into conflict with husbands, children, and other family members.[11]

However, the argument can still be made that when women participate as mothers, not as citizens in their own right, they reinforce traditional gender roles in societies where male-female distinctions are already well-entrenched.[12] If interests define citizens,[13] can women be citizens if they always act in the interests of *others*? Does this kind of participation guarantee that feeding the family and keeping it healthy will remain a woman's job—in the public as well as the private sphere? Do "practical" gender claims ensure "welfarist" responses, thus reinforcing the traditional patterns of patronage and clientelism that have long been employed by political parties and the state?

In the 1980s, the question was asked under what circumstances, if any, the pursuit of practical gender interests can promote feminist (strategic) outcomes, and today there are those who say that the attempt to measure the success of women's movements by their commitment to strategic gender awareness is nothing more than the imposition of a false standard, alien to the day-to-day experiences of movement women. Yet there is a growing body of data to show that practical and strategic gender interests are positively linked to one another.

When women join organizations, they are radicalized in at least two important ways: They begin to see the connections between their immediate concerns and broader political issues, and they are forced to confront directly the sex role biases that have long barred women from entering the public sphere. Women who participate in the movements must deal with the conflicts that arise when they leave the house to attend meetings or participate in demonstrations, and when they no longer have the time to do all the domestic tasks that have traditionally been assigned to them.

Experience in the movements—coordinating an organization, keeping accounts, mobilizing other women, speaking up in neighborhood meetings, and dealing with other organizations, the government, and international NGOs—is empowering. Though often rejecting feminism as a middle-class ideology,[14] movement women merge practical and strategic perspectives in their understanding of what they are doing and in their political demands.[15] Women find a voice inside and outside the home. Cross-class cooperation to confront violence against women, which has become an issue in every country in the region, is a powerful example of this process.

Families are also a site of change. Women increasingly ask men to share in domestic responsibilities. Even when men do not recognize their obligation to help with household tasks, the gender division of labor is altered. As a carpenter interviewed by Caroline Moser reports, "I earn the money, and my wife looks after the children and attends the meetings."[16] Of course, these new roles for women are not without costs. Women are increasingly expected to assume a triple burden of housework, income generation, and community organizing, and they may also pay the price of male resentment and even domestic abuse.

Despite these conflicts, and the new identities that women develop in confronting them, women do not conclude that men are the enemy. This viewpoint, expressed by a leader of the communal kitchens movement in Lima, is typical: "In the neighborhood organization I am learning how to seek input and propose ideas, and how to fight for space; the men need to learn how to listen. We don't have anything against men, our fight is not against the masculine gender, but against the way in which society is structured, against a system which is deeply rooted." She added that to change, men would have to do what women do, to be in solidarity with them: "The men who have become aware of the value of women need to say if they are seeking women's equality only in words or also in deeds. If we are all looking for equality in housework or in work in general, this means having solidarity, not just coming [to the communal kitchens] and asking for a plate of food."[17] In this same discussion, another woman observed that "*ma-*

chismo" is a strong force that "cannot be torn out by the roots, but if we work together, it will eventually diminish."[18]

These women are maintaining a delicate balance between their demands for a real voice in local decisionmaking and their desire to act as a community, not just as women. Practical and strategic gender interests come together, but not in a feminist way. These women have brought their most domestic role—cooking family meals—into the public sphere, making an effective response to the economic crisis. This gives them an opening to argue that men should also take responsibility for these "female" obligations. Solidarity means coming to help in the kitchens, not just coming by for a plate of food.

Researchers are interested in the effects of women's different values on their ways of "doing politics." Successful strategies, such as those of the Madres or of the women who use the media and "symbolic-cultural" politics to get environmental issues on the national agenda in Venezuela, result from the fact that women have different political motivations, different ways of interacting with others, and different ways of framing their demands.[19]

Women's movements are based on face-to-face and primary group relations, which makes groups less structured but arguably more resilient. Women's groups resist bureaucratization and hierarchy, and there is evidence that women's interactions are less competitive and less instrumental than men's. Some argue that women's mobilization as mothers is a natural and positive extension of the values of the home into the public sphere, and they contrast women's altruistic approaches to politics with the male model of calculated self-interest. And although hierarchy and competition for power can be found in women's groups as in all organizations, the normative expectations among women are different. There is a sense of the importance of individual dignity, of the need for everyone to have a voice, and an explicit concern with what is "correct." "We are fighting to make a new kind of politics," one woman leader in Lima says. "We should not have the attitude of trying to 'liquidate' or to be the most severe critics of the other women in our organization."[20]

Yet the motives and strategies of the women in these movements are as consistent with rational actor and "resource mobilization" models of social movements as they are with any theory that begins with women's natural or socialized differences from men. In the absence of strong parties that can deliver on their promises, and with states in perennial fiscal crises and unable to provide social services, the self-help, relatively autonomous organizational strategies that characterize the *movimientos de mujeres* are practical and effective responses to survival needs.[21] Being face-to-face and self-help organizations does not prevent them from making demands on the state or from seeking additional resources from the Church and international agencies.

It makes sense for women to organize as mothers and to emphasize communitarian values within political cultures where motherhood is sacred, where men's and women's roles are sharply distinguished and considered both natural and normatively appropriate, and where the political culture rests on a Catholic concept of community rather than on an individualistic social contract.[22] The rhetoric of political motherhood is thus rational and powerful for women, a "collective action frame"[23] that avoids the costs of a frontal attack on traditional values while leaving considerable room to maneuver in the public sphere. Many intellectuals and leftists, who used to rely solely on class conflict to achieve progressive change, are now looking to marginalized peoples and "submerged discourses" as their hope for the future. Thus they are prepared to accept and legitimize gender-based identities and political demands, although they do not nurture them as intensely as they supported the identity and demands of the working class in the past.

The growing acceptance of a sex-differentiated definition of citizenship on the left (it was never in doubt on the right) has reinforced motherhood as the role through which women become active citizens. For all these reasons, women's politics in Latin America is taking different forms from the patterns found in the advanced industrialized countries. The success of mothers in politics further underlines the need to look at how women's political practices will be affected by, and will help determine, broader political trends in the region.

Autonomy

The relationship between women's movements and the political system has been seen in women's groups primarily as an issue of autonomy, of *independence* from political parties, from the state, and from other groups in civil society. In the late 1970s and early 1980s, autonomy was heatedly debated between the *feministas* and the *militantes*. The feminists, critical of conventional politics and of machismo in the political parties, championed autonomous organizations for women. The party women learned to practice "double militancy," which meant bringing party issues into feminist meetings and taking feminist issues into party decisionmaking. One result of the relative autonomy of the feminists was that during the transitions, women's groups could facilitate the coordination of a political opposition to dictatorship while the men often remained divided along party lines. In Chile, for example, women helped bridge the bitter rift between the Christian Democrats and the other leftist parties, which was essential to building the opposition coalition against Pinochet.

Autonomy also made feminist organizations impatient with the popular women's movements. As Maruja Barrig observes, in the 1980s the feminists viewed "popular organizations ... with mistrust because they do not raise the purely feminist flag."[24] Barrig points out, however, that autonomy was a losing strategy when translated into electoral politics. The feminist candidates isolated themselves from potential supporters and, by distancing themselves from their party, lost political leverage there as well.

Autonomy has also become an issue for the Madres in Argentina, who have split into two groups over the question of whether to broaden their definition of human rights to include women's rights and economic issues or stay identified with their original demands. As this debate has unfolded within Argentina, some have accused the Madres of undermining the prospects for democracy by refusing to work within the party system.

As the 1980s progressed, autonomy also became an issue for the *movimientos de mujeres*.[25] The return to electoral politics combined with the cutback in central government expenditures as a result of the economic crisis increased the competition for local government offices. Grassroots movements were more intensely politicized.[26] This created problems as well as opportunities for the women's movements. How should they relate to the neighborhood organizations, which had male and female members but which were often led by men? Could they take support from outside sources—the Church, NGOs, even feminist groups—without losing their independence?

In 1990, Yunta, a nongovernmental organization that has published a newspaper in Lima's shantytowns since 1981, organized a series of roundtable discussions that drew together a number of women leaders from independent and state-sponsored groups, local, elected female officials (including María Elena Moyano, who was killed in 1992 by Sendero Luminoso), and male leaders from the neighborhood organizations. Their discussions provide an unusual window into the politics of women's organizations and provide insights on how the issue of autonomy has evolved as women's groups attempt to maintain their unity and effectiveness under rapidly changing conditions.

The male leaders were respectful of the accomplishments of the women's groups, which had responded effectively in the economic crisis by organizing communal kitchens and the Vaso de Leche program for children. But they were critical of the women's demands for autonomy. As one *dirigente* (male leader) put it,

> I have seen conflict between neighborhood organizations and women's organizations ... since the beginning of the 1980s.[27] One thing that bothers me is this business of autonomy. ... It's been taken up so strongly that it has become autonomy against the whole world. In my view ... we need to distinguish who we need to be autonomous against, who we need to coordinate with, and how we gain hegemony. They are two distinct things: the autonomy we want is autonomy against the state. ... But between the organizations in the popular sector, we need coordination.[28]

For their part, the women leaders saw coordination as an excuse for the neighborhood organizations to intervene in the management of their organizations. "The neighborhood organizations should not feel that they are better than we are; they should not confuse their role with that of a superior."[29] They pointed out that the men were slow to recognize that the economic crisis made food and health priority issues for the neighborhoods. The *dirigentes'* failure to change their agendas left a vacuum that the women had filled, but now the men were unwilling to share power.

The women leaders also criticized the men for not running their neighborhood organizations democratically: "There's another problem and it is that, for many years the *companeros* in the leadership are *caudillos* [strongmen] who will not give up their power, they believe they own the positions they hold, and besides, there is *machismo* everywhere. The women's organizations are different. In the Glass of Milk program in my district, for example, we rotate our leaders from the lowest levels to the highest."[30] Another added that, unlike the men, "We can't stay in our jobs, our time is too valuable and we have too much to do."

One of the male leaders agreed that the neighborhood organizations were not democratic enough. But, he said, the idealization of the women's organizations does not reflect reality, either. He had seen cases of state-funded *comedores* (kitchens) that seemed to be "the private property of certain *comedor* presidents." When his neighborhood organization tried to complain, it was told that it could not intervene because that would undermine the principle of autonomy.[31]

At the end of this contentious session, a male sociologist tried to convince the *dirigentes* that the women's organizations felt they had to protect their autonomy against the neighborhood organizations for the same reasons that the neighborhood organizations wanted autonomy from the state—each feared that the other would make use of its resources but not give up any decisionmaking power in return.[32]

Divisions between women's and men's neighborhood organizations have undermined the legitimacy of some of the women's and men's groups. As one of the Lima roundtable organizers described it, the men, "feeling their lack of direct access to information, began to ask questions and plant doubts about the efficiency of the women's organizations."[33] This contributed to the distance between leaders and members that has weakened the communal-kitchens movement, making it more vulnerable to Senderista tactics.

Political parties pose serious problems of autonomy for the women's movements, especially when the parties control state resources. In Chile, as Chuchryk points out in her chapter, the Pinochet regime promoted mothers' clubs under the sponsorship of the dictator's wife to train women in domestic skills and reinforce traditional norms, explicitly attempting to depoliticize lower-class women who were a potentially powerful source of support for the redistributional politics of the Left.

In Mexico, the women organized by Mexico's dominant party, the PRI, understood their participation as an exchange of political support for government services and individual benefits, according to a study by Nikki Craske. By contrast, the women who belonged to an independent group saw themselves as engaged in action for the community; they criticized the clientelist practices of the PRI and were more willing to take risks.[34] In Brazil, the close alliance between feminists and the opposition produced early successes for the state and national *conselhos* but later made it difficult for them to weather changes of government and loss of presidential support. The challenge, which was not successfully met, was to create bases of popular support in order to prevent the government from reneging on its original commitment.

Movement women often express concern that party politics will divide their organizations. The views of the women at the Lima roundtable were typical. As one leader said, "One thing is doing politics, as we do every day when we set policy for our organization in accordance with our objectives, and for this it is important to practice democracy. Party politics is something else."[35] And another added, "We always support the emergence of a woman political leader—because we know that politics runs through everything. But I want to distinguish party politics which divides organizations for its own political advantage. By contrast, when we women who are organized work to obtain an adequate food policy, we are being political, but in favor of the people, without sectarianism or proselytizing."[36]

If parties divide, the danger is that the state will co-opt them. The history of gender-state relations[37] is complicated by the corporatist tradition in Latin America. Corporatism conditions the political options available to all groups, including women's organizations. Under corporatism, major groups are recognized by the state, have institutionalized access to policymaking, and are directly or indirectly state-supported.

In its ideal form, corporatism regularizes bargaining relationships and can create a sense of solidarity, with the state managing group relations in the collective interest. It can be contrasted both with the Marxist view of class conflict and with the pluralist model in which a large number of relatively independent groups compete with one another to determine policy, with the state acting as an umpire.

Although it is theoretically more communitarian, corporatism in practice has reinforced the hierarchical, personalist, and repressive practices of the ruling elites. Such practices perpetuate race, class, and gender barriers, creating subjects[38] rather than citizens. There are signs that the state has tried to incorporate women's groups in a variety of ways. In some cases, governments have used women's organizations as delivery mechanisms for emergency aid, which is ostensibly available to all but in fact is provided in exchange for political support. The PRONASOL program in Mexico[39] and the Program of Social Emergency (Programa de Emergencia Social, PES) in Peru are good examples of this kind of corporatist pattern.

Women may also *seek* state protection and support both because the establishment of independent pressure groups is difficult and costly under the best of circumstances and because corporatist practices discourage independence. Parties that are out of power seek support from independent groups, which in turn will be in a favored position should the party win an election. The "independent" women's group that Craske studied in Mexico, for example, was in fact sympathetic to an opposition party and would have benefited directly had that party won an election.

These cases provide concrete examples of a structural problem for democracies not only in Latin America but elsewhere in the world: how to build a civil society that is independent yet not disarticulated from parties and from the state.

Corporatist traditions also affect other initiatives that women have taken to ensure that their issues will be taken seriously. Feminists have pushed for women's offices and ministries, what the United Nations calls "national machineries." But these too can reinforce corporatism by concentrating access at a single point in the system and by treating women as a single sector whose demands must be channeled through that point. Because the women's ministry or office is often funded by the president, he or his party may limit the kinds of issues that it can raise without risking all its other initiatives, as has happened with the *conselhos* in Brazil and SERNAM (the National Women's Service) in Chile.

A similar set of issues arises with electoral quotas. U.S. feminists are astounded at the ease with which some Latin American (and European) parties have committed themselves to nominating a certain percentage of women on their lists of candidates, an idea that has yet to receive serious discussion in the United States. Quotas can be defended on the grounds that they will assure women that they will have a critical mass in legislative bodies, will expand the recruitment process, will give women more political experience, and will overcome skepticism about whether women are competent to hold political office.

However, in the Latin American context, quotas will make it easier for men to treat women as a special sector and to enforce a gender division of political labor. Women will be expected to take care of women's issues, leaving the rest to men. And the men can deny any responsibility for women's issues on the grounds that they have already met their obligations by giving women guaranteed representation.[40]

What some have described as the totalizing nature of social movements   their nonnegotiable, utopian goals and their promotion of solidarity rather than interests—may mean that such movements will adapt more successfully to corporatist forms of democracy than to interest-group pluralism. Corporatism favors a close relationship between the state and a few key groups; it puts pressure on women's organizations to form federations in order to become effective interlocutors of the state and to demonstrate a credible capacity to deliver support. Under corporatism, the state can decide which groups will receive legal standing as civil associations and which will be forced to operate outside the formal system.

The process of centralization and the importance of state recognition can discourage the formation of new organizations and may marginalize many that now exist, reducing them to self-help groups with virtually no access to state-managed resources. That women's groups and grassroots leaders are so firmly committed to autonomy is a sign that they are wary of traditional corporatist and clientelist political relationships. But autonomy alone is a weak strategy and is likely to result in women's organizations' being denied the resources they need. Autonomy may conflict with the needs of democracy, which requires a party system strong enough to ensure that policies are formulated on the basis of popular representation and that governments are accountable. Historically, social movements have opposed the state, but the state must be strong enough to meet the demands made on it by mobilized electorates, including the ability to tax in order to redistribute wealth and to provide essential public goods. There is very little in the theory of social movements or the practice of women's organizations that recognizes the need for a strong state or gives groups a role to play in establishing political accountability.

Social Movements, Feminist Values, and Democratic Politics

Women's movements have shown that they are durable and innovative and that they can change women's domestic and public lives, creating new confidence that women have "inserted themselves too decisively into the public sphere to retreat."[41] Women's organizations operate at the crucial border between civil society and the state and create new hope that citizenship can be expanded and that a political consensus for greater social justice can be negotiated.

Social movements are seen by many as the cure for contemporary political ills through their creation of new values and new forms of social interaction. For those who are disheartened by the decline of Marxism, social movements are seen as finding new ways to curb the excesses of capitalism and new forms of resistance to the state. Women's movements in Latin America have drawn international interest because they appear to be fulfilling many of these expectations. They "focus on grass-roots politics," creating "horizontal, directly democratic associations" that "target the social domain of civil society, rather than the economy or the state." They "are self-limiting in terms of their own demands" (although not, as we have seen, in Perelli's view), and the self-limitation practiced by women's groups may be a function of their political weakness rather than of the maturity of their political self-analysis. Women's movements are clearly "reintroducing the normative dimension of social action into political life"[42] and are "reflexive," that is, self-aware, about "existing societal norms and the structures involved in their maintenance."[43]

The problem, as Alain Touraine has warned, is that social movements are the perfect screen onto which researchers can project their own values and ideologies.[44] Because women's groups provide identity and solidarity, it is easy to assume that they are already-existing communities and thus should be valued in themselves, regardless of their relationship to other groups or to the state. Yet this assessment is misleading. It ignores the fact that the state is exploiting women's autonomy by letting women's self-help voluntarism replace the state's obligations. And although women may be transformed by the experience of participation, few activists view their organizations as ends in themselves or as permanent alternatives to structural poverty or to the elites' monopoly of power. As one of the women leaders in Lima put it, "How much longer are we going to keep cooking in communal kitchens? How much longer are we going to go on receiving donations of milk? How much longer are we going to stay a culture of poverty? How much longer are we going to continue to cook for 100 or 200 people when what is just and what we want is to cook in our own houses, as it should be?"[45]

The women stay in the kitchens because they feel they have no choice. "Are we going to wait for revolution to change the economic structures?"[46] asks one leader. She believes that the solution for women lies in the market, that the state should provide not just food for day-to-day survival but capital so that women can start small businesses. To those dependent on the state for survival, the market economy offers hope of escape. Women in the Vaso de Leche program recognized that they represent a large, guaranteed market for milk; they want to contact Peruvian farmers to supply the program rather than continue to rely on surplus milk from the United States.

The relationship between social movements and democratic politics has not received sufficient attention in the transitions literature. Effective parties and an efficient, accountable state are essential to the healthy functioning of representative democracy. Yet both feminist theory and the studies of new social movements are hostile to the state, and women's political practices are antiparty and at times antipolitical. Existing connections between women's groups and the state may be more conducive to corporatist outcomes than to representation and accountability.

Women still equate "doing politics" with having a voice and making proposals; having been excluded for so long, they fear institutionalization and are likely to blame individual politicians for policy failures and for the corruption that has undermined the legitimacy of most of the democratic governments in the region. They do not see the relationship between their organizations and the political parties or the state as part of a larger political equation that will determine the long-term viability of democratic politics.

The "self-coup" of President Alberto Fujimori in April 1992 is an example of how a lack of articulation between popular movements and the state led to a breakdown of democracy in Peru. Fujimori—a last-minute candidate—was elected because the political party system was fragmented and because Fujimori captured the "none of the above" vote. Because he did not campaign as the candidate of a national party, Fujimori did not have allies in the legislature to carry his programs or to develop a political base for his policies. Instead, he gained popular support by attacking the parties that were divided and contentious, and perceived by many as corrupt. Owing nothing to the parties or to the party system, he closed the legislature when it obstructed his plans, and he proceeded to rule by decree with the support of the army.

Maxwell Cameron attributes this undemocratic outcome to the growth of the "informal sector" of the economy, which "undermined partisan loyalties, broke the tenuous linkages between parties and civil society, interrupted channels of communication between elites and masses, weakened the class cleavage, and contributed to the formation of a huge 'floating' ... electorate which was not represented by the programs, appeals, and symbols of traditional, class-based parties."[47] Because we know that women are a substantial part, a majority perhaps, of the informal sector, and that the informal sector *is* organized in neighborhood-based movements, it is clear that despite their positive qualities, urban social movements may not reinforce democratic institutions and practices. Fujimori has a high approval rating among the urban poor despite—or perhaps because of—the coup and despite his implementation of the "fujishock," an economic austerity program widely considered the most severe in Latin America. Fujimori has survived, but democracy has been compromised.

Giorgio Alberti has observed that the current enthusiasm for social movements has not been critically examined: "From a theoretical point of view, politics based on movements has some interesting consequences: if successful, it tends to be associated with unanimity and plebiscitarian tendencies; if unsuccessful, it tends to generate fragmentation. Either way it is an impediment to the consolidation of an organized pattern of interaction between differentiated interests and groups." He finds that political parties are under attack almost everywhere, "no matter what their ideological bent," and the "space between the state and society is almost a *tabula rasa*."[48]

The late twentieth-century conditions under which feminism matured and women's movements flourished have led to integrated class and feminist issues and have given poor women organizational experiences that enabled them to survive high levels of unemployment and sharp cutbacks in state spending. Women's votes have determined the outcome of elections and women's demonstrations have forced political leaders to change course.

Yet few who study Latin American politics have thought about the growing impact of women's political participation, and few who study women's movements have cared about political parties or the state. Democracy, and women, deserve better.

Notes

1. Jennifer Schirmer, "The Seeking of Truth and the Gendering of Consciousness: The Comadres of El Salvador and the Conavigua Widows of Guatemala," in Sarah A. Radcliffe and Sally Westwood, eds., *Viva: Women and Popular Protest in Latin America* (London: Routledge, 1993), 61.

2. Daniel H. Levine, "Paradigm Lost: Dependence to Democracy," *World Politics* 40 (April 1988): 389.

3. Ibid., 383.

4. Gloria Bonder, "The Study of Politics from the Standpoint of Women," *International Social Science Journal* 35 (1983): 570.

5. Jo Fisher, "Where Are Our Children?" in Fisher, *Out of the Shadows: Women, Resistance and Politics in Latin America* (London: Latin America Bureau, 1993); Feijoó, in this volume.

6. Perelli, this volume.

7. An example of the genre for social movements in general is Tilman Evers, "Identity: The Hidden Side of New Social Movements in Latin America," in David Slater, ed., *New Social Movements and the State in Latin America* (Amsterdam: CEDLA, 1985).

8. See Alessandro Pizzorno, "On the Individualistic Theory of Social Order," in Pierre Bourdieu and James Coleman, eds., *Social Theory for a Changing Society* (Boulder, Colo.: Westview Press, 1991), on the relationship between interests and citizenship; and Perelli, this volume.

9. Kathleen Logan, in "Women's Participation in Urban Protest," argues that "by accepting [their gender] roles and their attendant responsibilities, activist women claim the rights that their obligations entail." In Joe Foweraker and Ann L. Craig, eds., *Popular Movements and Political Change in Mexico* (Boulder, Colo.: Lynne Rienner, 1990), 153.

10. María del Carmen Feijoó, *Alquimistas en la crisis: Experiencias de mujeres en el Gran Buenos Aires* (Buenos Aires: UNICEF, 1991), 86.

11. The Cuban movie about women's activism portrays not only the husband but the mother as a significant barrier to Teresa's activism outside the home. But accounts of resistance by both husbands and children are common in the growing testimonial literature on women's mobilization.

12. Helen Safa observes that the attachment to the family explains why the distinction between the public and private spheres is stronger in Latin America than in the United States but does not add that this difference means that the distinction is more available to be politicized. See "Women's Movements in Latin America," *Gender and Society* 4, 3 (September 1990): 366.

13. This is an important tenet of liberalism but one that has been contested by feminist theorists and by social movement theorists as well. For a defense of the sociality of interests, see Pizzorno, "On the Individualistic Theory," and for a feminist discussion, see Kathleen Jones and Anna Jonasdottir, *The Political Interests of Gender* (London: Sage, 1988). Caroline Moser has changed Molyneux's distinction between strategic and practical gender interests to strategic and practical gender *needs*. Cited in Helen I. Safa and Cornelia Butler Flora, "Production, Reproduction and the Polity," in Alfred Stepan, ed., *Americas: New Interpretive Essays* (New York: Oxford University Press, 1992), 132.

14. On the relation between class and feminism, see Yvonne Corcoran-Nantes, "Female Consciousness or Feminist Consciousness: Women's Consciousness Raising in Community-based Struggles in Brazil," in Radcliffe and Westwood, *Viva*.

15. See Schirmer, "The Seeking of Truth"; Carmen Barroso and Cristina Bruschini, "Building Politics from Personal Lives: Discussions on Sexuality Among Poor Women in Brazil," in Chandra Talpade Mohanty, Ann Russo, and Lourdes Torres, eds., *Third World Women and the Politics of Feminism* (Indianapolis: Indiana University Press, 1991); Marysa Navarro-Aranguren, "The Construction of a Latin American Feminist Identity," in Stepan, *Americas;* Chinchilla, this volume.

16. Caroline Moser, "Adjustment from Below: Low Income Women, Time and the Triple Role in Guayaquil, Ecuador," in Radcliffe and Westwood, *Viva*.

17. Patricia Cordova, ed., *Mujer y liderazgo: Entre la familia y la política* (Lima: Yunta, 1992), 126. Leaders who participated in the roundtable discussions included Victoriana Calquisto, Donatilda Gamarra, Emma Hilario, María Elena Moyano, Esther Moreno, Nelly

Rumrrill, Luz Salgado, Carmen Takayama, Elvira Torres, Oscar Ugarte, Samuel Yanez, Zenaida Zuniga.

18. Ibid., 80.

19. María-Pilar García Guadilla, "*Ecologia:* Women, Environment and Politics in Venezuela," in Radcliffe and Westwood, *Viva;* and Catherine M. Boyle, "Touching the Air: The Cultural Force of Women in Chile," in Radcliffe and Westwood, *Viva.* These essays coincide with Alain Touraine's view that the new social movements are about the control of cultural values. See his "On the Individualistic Theory of Social Order," in Pierre Bourdieu and James Coleman, eds., *Social Theory for a Changing Society* (Boulder, Colo.: Westview Press, 1991). For a criticism that argues that women need to move from symbolic politics to political outcomes, see Annie G. Dandavati, "The Women's Movement and the Transition to Democracy in Chile," Ph.D. dissertation, University of Denver, 1992, chap. 8.

20. Cordova, *Mujer y liderazgo,* 110. But see Kathleen Logan, "Women's Participation in Urban Protest": "Perceived personal affronts and mistrust, especially about money, seem particularly problematic for women within their interwoven social communities of family and neighborhood." In Foweraker and Craig, *Viva,* 153.

21. Jean L. Cohen writes, "We are in an intellectual situation in which revolutionary ideology has moved from Marxism, with its rational theoretical core, to eschatologies that have no discernible relation to the potentials or limits of the social structures to which they are addressed. ... The new identity within contemporary social movements ... is in fact the *only rational* identity that is compatible with the organizational forms and conflict scenario of movements today." In "Strategy or Identity: New Theoretical Paradigms and Contemporary Social Movements," *Social Research* 52, 4 (Winter 1985): 667.

22. Norbert Lechner, *Los patios interiores de la democracia* (Santiago: Fondo de Cultura Económica, 1988), 131.

23. Sidney Tarrow, "Mentalities, Political Cultures and Collective Action Frames; Constructing Meanings Through Action," in Aldon D. Morris and Carol McClurg Mueller, eds., *Frontiers in Social Movement Theory* (New Haven, Conn.: Yale University Press, 1992).

24. Barrig, this volume.

25. See, for example, essays by Cecilia Blondet and Teresa Caldeira in Elizabeth Jelín, ed., *Ciudania e identidad: Las mujeres en los movimientos sociales latinoamericanos* (Geneva: UNRISD, 1987); and Fisher, *Out of the Shadows.*

26. María-Pilar Guadilla, *Ecologia;* and Barrig, this volume.

27. Cordova, *Mujer y liderazgo,* 145.

28. Ibid., 166–167.

29. Ibid., 126.

30. Ibid., 161.

31. Ibid., 173.

32. Gustavo Riofrio, in ibid., 178–180.

33. Ibid., 141.

34. Nikki Craske, "Women's Political Participation in *Colonias Populares* in Guadalajara, Mexico," in Radcliffe and Westwood, *Viva.*

35. Cordova, *Mujer y liderazgo,* 77.

36. Ibid., 65.

37. For a comparative approach, see Sue Ellen M. Charlton, Jana Everett, and Kathleen Staudt, *Women, the State and Development* (Albany: State University of New York Press, 1989), especially chap. 1.

38. "Subjects" in the sense of oppressed nonparticipants, as used by Gabriel Almond and Sydney Verba in *The Civic Culture* (Princeton, N.J.: Princeton University Press, 1963), and not in the sense of "women as subjects of their own history."

39. Denise Dresser, "Neopopulist Solutions to Neoliberal Problems," La Jolla: Center for U.S.-Mexican Studies of the University of California, Current Issue Brief no. 3 (San Diego, 1991).

40. I wish to thank Fernando Bustamante and others at FLACSO, Sede Ecuador, for reminding me of the importance of these criticisms of electoral quotas.

41. Safa and Flora, "Production, Reproduction and the Polity," in Stepan, *Americas*, 129.

42. Taken from Cohen, "Strategy or Identity," 667, 670–671.

43. Ibid., 694.

44. Touraine, "On the Individualistic Theory of Social Order," 749.

45. Cordova, *Mujer y liderazgo*, 153.

46. Ibid., 154.

47. Maxwell Cameron, "The Breakdown of Democracy in Peru: The Impact of the Informal Economy on Political Parties," paper presented at the NECLAS meeting, Boston University, October 1992, 2.

48. Giorgio Alberti, personal communication, February 1993.

About the Book

For those interested in democratic transition and consolidation, social movements, and gender politics, this volume is the most comprehensive, up-to-date, and probing analysis available of how women's groups are helping to reshape Latin America. The contributors document and assess the remarkable wave of women's political participation in Latin America over the past two decades. The first five case studies, on Brazil, Argentina, Uruguay, Chile, and Peru, examine the origins, evolution, and goals of women's organizations as they worked together to end authoritarian rule and elaborate how women's groups have adapted in the 1990s to the day-to-day realities of democratic politics. In the 1990s, the challenge has shifted from mobilizing opposition to the very different task of working with parties and government bureaucracies in order to maintain and implement their agendas. The chapters on Nicaragua and Mexico broaden our understanding of political transitions.

Seven case studies vividly illustrate the variety of women's movements in the region, ranging from the communal-kitchens movements to human rights groups. Each author discusses the strategies and debates of the feminist movements in question and records their political successes and failures. Jaquette's introductory and concluding essays provide a comparative framework, highlighting the innovative ways in which Latin American women are making gender a political issue.

About the Editor and Contributors

Sonia E. Alvarez is associate professor of politics at the University of California at Santa Cruz. She has been involved in national and international feminist politics since the mid-1970s. She is the author of *Engendering Democracy in Brazil: Women's Movements in Transition Politics* (1990) and coeditor, with Arturo Escobar, of *The Making of Social Movements in Latin America: Identity, Strategy, and Democracy* (1992). Her writings on Latin American gender politics, social movements, and democratization have appeared in *Signs, Feminist Studies,* and several edited collections. She is currently researching the cultural and institutional dimensions of citizenship in Brazil and is serving as program officer in rights and social justice for the Ford Foundation in Rio de Janeriro.

Maruja Barrig studied journalism and literature and has worked as a freelance writer on political themes for various Peruvian newspapers and magazines. In 1979 she published *Cinturon de castidat* (Chastity belt), one of the first books on modern feminist themes to be published in Peru. Since the early 1980s she has published a number of studies on urban women and work. Today Barrig is an independent consultant for projects and training courses on gender and development. She is a member of the Women's Studies Committee of the Americas under the auspices of the Latin American Studies Association.

Norma Stoltz Chinchilla received her Ph.D. in sociology from the University of Wisconsin–Madison and is currently professor of sociology and women's studies at the California State University–Long Beach, where she is also director of the Program in Women's Studies. She has written extensively on political and economic change and women and social movements in Latin America and on Central American immigration to California. She is currently working on a book of life stories of several generations of women activists in Guatemala.

Patricia M. Chuchryk is associate professor and chair of the Department of Sociology at the University of Lethbridge, Lethbridge, Alberta, Canada. She has been conducting research in Chile and Latin America since 1982, and her current three-year project, *Social Change, Democratization and Women's Movements in Latin America,* is funded by the Social Science and Humanities Research Council of Canada. She is coeditor of the forthcoming collection, *First Nations Women of Canada,* and is presently completing a book on the women's movement and the transition to democracy in Chile.

Carmen Ramos Escandón is assistant professor of history at Occidental College. She has a background in literature as well as history and has written on the textile industry in Mexico and on women in Mexican political history. Her most recent book is *Mujeres y Revolucion,* a study of women's roles in the Mexican Revolution, with Ana Lau.

María del Carmen Feijoó has a degree in sociology from the University of Buenos Aires. She is a research scholar at CONICET (The National Council of Scientific and Technological Research) and in the office of the United Nations Children's Fund (UNICEF), Buenos Aires. She has written on the history of women's movements and, more recently, on poverty and grassroots organizations. She was undersecretary of education for Buenos Aires province in 1992–1993 and has been elected as a national delegate to the assembly that will reform the Constitution of Argentina.

Jane S. Jaquette is professor of politics and chair of the Diplomacy and World Affairs Department at Occidental College, Los Angeles. She has written extensively on the comparative political participation of women, on the politics of international feminism, and on the UN Decade for Women. She served for two years (1990–1991) as president of the Association for Women in Development and is currently president-elect of the Latin American Studies Association.

Marcela María Alejandra Nari graduated with a degree in history from the University of Buenos Aires, where she teaches social history and researches the lives of working mothers in the early twentieth century. She is also involved in a project to research women's political participation in Argentina from the 1950s to the 1990s.

Carina Perelli is a political scientist and a director of Peitho, Sociedad de Analysis Politico, in Montevideo, Uruguay. She has written several articles on civil-military relations, political parties, and elections. She has also published essays on the culture of fear and on historical memory.

Index